1 7 ⁹⁵

The
101
Best-Performing Companies in America

The
101
Best-Performing
Companies in
America

Ronald N. Paul
James W. Taylor

Probus Publishing Company
Chicago, Illinois

Library of Congress Cataloging-in-Publication Data

Paul, Ronald N.
  The 101 best performing companies in America.

  Includes index.
  1. Corporations--United States--Case studies.
2. Efficiency, Industrial--United States--Case studies.
3. Success in business--United States--Case studies.
4. Organizational effectiveness--Case studies.
I. Taylor, James Walter, 1933-   . II. Title.
III. Title: The one hundred one best performing companies
in America.
HD2785.P38   1986   338.7'4'0973   86-4947
ISBN: 0-917253-39-6

CIP Data Available

Printed in the United States of America

    2   3   4   5   6   7   8   9   0

PREFACE

This book is an attempt to deal with a paradox. It goes like this: On one hand we seem to be deluged with business books and articles that tell us how excellent companies produce their excellent results. On the other hand, many of these supposedly excellent companies actually produce far less than excellent results (good public relations, maybe, but inferior results). What are we supposed to make of companies that are touted as role models, but when examined closely seem to be a lot less than they appear to be.

Normally, this is the kind of question that would probably be confined to the arcane arguments of scholars. However, these are not normal times! Market after market that once belonged to American businesses is being lost to overseas competitors. Record trade deficits occur one on top of the next. Our very standard of living is threatened by a long term decline in the productivity of U.S. business. In fact, these are very threatening times.

In threatening times, leaders are needed to show how to turn back the threats. And that is why resolving the paradox is too important to be left to arcane argument. We need companies that are *leaders*—that can show us how to survive and emerge stronger than ever. How then should we define leaders so that we can recognize them when we need them? What, in fact, are the characteristics of our excellent companies? Of our leaders?

Dealing with the paradox became a two-part problem. First we had to find some objective ways to define excellent performance, and second, we had to apply that definition to American businesses to find out if any could really qualify. Chapter 1 describes how our definition of excellent performance was developed and why we think it is appropriate. Chapter 2 presents the overall results of applying this definition to U.S. businesses.

Chapter 3 presents brief profiles of each of America's 101 best performing companies. Chapter 4 describes a "new" development that is forcing U.S. managers to find new tools to succeed in a fundamentally changing world market.

It is the combination of resolving the paradox and adapting to a changing competitive environment that defines our interest in doing the work that this book represents. We believe that it is important for the people of the United States to address the question of what expectations they hold for business. Far too many of the yardsticks that we use to measure business performance are one dimension and verge on irrelevancy.

Our primary purpose here is to suggest some new ways to evaluate the performance of U.S. businesses, to show some examples of how the criteria for excellent performance work in real life, and to argue that it is important for all of us to address what we expect from U.S. business for the rest of this century. We hope to call attention to truly excellent performance by the very best of America's businesses and to outline how a national debate on the real meaning of "excellence" might take place. Hopefully, the ideas and facts presented here can remove this important issue from the level of glib anecdotes and put it into a context where serious people can consider serious implications.

A large number of people contributed to this project over the past two years, and we would like to thank some of them specifically. For example, to perform the analysis that underlies this book, we had to examine over one million different performance measures of American businesses. We could never have accomplished this task without the help of Dr. Richard Bednar, Computer Center, California State University/Fullerton. Dick Bednar devised endless and ingenious computer programs to explore the countless avenues that were necessary to follow in order to give structure to this project.

Richard G. Taylor showed us how to use ITT Dialcom's database to bring life to Dick Bednar's numbers. Marketing Professors Grady Bruce and Bob Jones contributed important ideas just when we needed them. The editors at Probus did what good editors should do; they made quality suggestions at the right times and worked around missed deadlines.

Ann Ekstein and Georgann Paul typed at the manuscript, and then retyped and then typed again, and never once complained (at least out loud).

Joanne Taylor, Sam Taylor and Sue Cooper did lots of proofreading, but any errors belong solely to the authors.

And so it all finally came together.

Ronald N. Paul
James W. Taylor

Laguna Beach, California

CONTENTS

1

INTRODUCING AMERICA'S MOST IMPORTANT COMPANIES

Sometime in the late 1960s, American business allowed our preeminent position in the world's economy to begin to erode. An April 1984 report by the Committee for Economic Development put the problem this way:

> The era of unquestioned U.S. dominance in the world economy is clearly over, and has been for some time. The combined forces of lagging U.S. productivity performance and the rising competitiveness of other countries leave us with no choice but to adopt policies to strengthen our competitive position if we wish to increase the real economic well being of the American people and maintain our position as a leading economic power in the world.[1]

The reason that this development is of such great significance to all Americans is that business accounts for the great majority of our standard of living. At the end of every year, economists count up the total value of all of the goods and services produced by the entire U.S. economy during that year. The economists call that total number the Gross National Product (GNP), and it very directly represents the total output of the country. The GNP can be thought of as a very big pie that we

[1] *Strategy for U.S. Industrial Competitiveness*, Subcommittee on Industrial Strategy and Trade, Committee for Economic Development, 477 Madison Avenue, New York, NY 10022, April 1984, p. 1.

divide up amongst ourselves. As the pie gets bigger, we have more to divide up, but if the pie gets smaller we have, in fact, less to divide up.

In 1983, the U.S. GNP amounted to $3,304.8 billion.[2] Of that amount, business contributed $2,790.8 billion, or about 85 percent. (The remaining 15 percent is primarily accounted for by government expenditures.) Quite simply, in America, business produces about 85 percent of our standard of living. If American business loses its ability to compete in the world, our standard of living will inevitably fall.

If you wish to examine the consequences of a declining standard of living, you would do well to look at the case of New Zealand. At the end of World War II, this charming little country tucked away in the vastness of the Pacific Ocean had the third highest standard of living in the world. From this position of great wealth, the New Zealanders made a series of well intentioned, but wrong-headed, decisions about the importance of being able to compete in the world market. It is now 30 years later, and New Zealand's standard of living has dropped to 20th, and a new government is desperately attempting to halt the slide before New Zealand drops from the ranks of developed nations.

If the case of New Zealand doesn't convince you of the importance, and of the reality, of a declining standard of living, turn your attention across the Atlantic Ocean to Great Britain. Same story, same outcome. Falling productivity, falling living standards.

WHAT IS PRODUCTIVITY?

Productivity is, fundamentally, the relationship between output and input; that is, the relationship between the amount of goods and services produced and the quantities of labor, capital, and resources required to produce that amount. When a larger output of goods and services can be achieved from a fixed amount of labor and capital, productivity increases, and that's good. When a constant amount of goods and services are produced from a smaller amount of labor and capital, that also means that productivity is increasing.

The problem arises when it takes increasing amounts of labor and capital to produce the same amounts of goods and services. When that happens, productivity is falling, and the economy is heading for trouble. And that is exactly what has been happening in the United States. Listen to what two of America's foremost economists have to say on that score:

[2] *Statistical Abstract of the United States 1985*, U.S. Department of Commerce, Washington, D.C., p. 43.

This country's productivity growth performance in recent years is extremely disquieting. But the troubling trend is only symptomatic of much more serious productivity problems. For more than one and a half decades before 1983, there was a pervasive and very substantial decline in productivity growth rates throughout most sectors of the U.S. economy. Moreover, for at least the same length of time, productivity grew far less rapidly in the United States than it did in the countries that are our main economic rivals.[3]

This decline in productivity growth is widespread. It is occurring in construction, transportation, trade, and manufacturing. Public utilities represent a particularly worrisome situation because productivity growth fell from + 5.5 percent annual rate in the period from 1948 to 1965 to a - 2.2 percent during the 1979 to 1981 period. Only the area of communications seems to be an exception. In communications, productivity growth rose from + 3.2 percent a year in the period 1965 to 1973 to an annual + 4.0 percent rate in 1979 to 1981.

The U.S. Bureau of Labor Statistics keeps records on productivity in 116 industries all across our economy. Their data shows this pattern of decline in 80 percent of all industries recorded.

BUT IS PRODUCTIVITY REALLY IMPORTANT?

Yes, the evidence is clear that productivity growth is slowing down in a serious way in U.S. business, and the slowdown is taking place across a broad front of U.S. business. But is that really important? Can't we count on total growth in the economy to keep things stable? Unfortunately, the answer is no. Even if total growth is sufficient to support an ever growing standard of living, we are now in a period of very modest growth in the U.S. GNP. No easy answers here.

Yes, productivity is important. The Committee for Economic Development entitled its 1983 report, *Productivity Policy: Key to the Nation's Economic Future,* and it opens with these observations:

Increased productivity is the key to economic progress. It allows the nation to raise its standard of living, to support such social goals as education and health care, and to contribute to other aspects of the general welfare; it is an essen-

[3] William J. Baumol and Kenneth McLennan, *Productivity Growth and U.S. Competitiveness* (New York: Oxford University Press, 1985), p. 3.

tial underpinning of the nation's security. Higher productivity allows these "noneconomic" objectives to be achieved without absolute reduction of workers' living standards. Moreover, productivity growth offers intangible rewards through its contribution to national morale. A nation whose productivity is declining is likely to be beset by doubts and a decline in self-confidence as well as in material well-being.[4]

Growing productivity undoubtedly provides for the increased well being of individuals, improved social services, improved national defense, *and* (perhaps) a sense of psychological satisfaction. That certainly is important!

IS A DECLINING STANDARD OF LIVING IN THE U.S. INEVITABLE?

No, a declining standard of living is not inevitable. There are a significant number of U.S. businesses that have accomplished outstanding results over a long period of time in direct contradiction to the overall trends described earlier. If we can identify such companies (the purpose of this book) and use them as role models, we will have a "blueprint" for stemming our slide in productivity.

Accordingly, we need clear, unambiguous criteria against which to measure the performances of individual businesses over long periods of time. That means that the search for a way to avoid a declining standard of living must begin with a search for definitions of outstanding performance. We believe that there are four specific dimensions to outstanding performance that can be defined in unambiguous terms and measured over long periods of time.

Companies that meet *all four criteria simultaneously* over a long period of time are our best defense against a declining standard of living.

FOUR CRITERIA FOR OUTSTANDING PERFORMANCE

Truly important companies in the fight against a declining standard of living should be able to:

[4] *Productivity Policy: Key to the Nation's Economic Future*, Committee for Economic Development, 477 Madison Avenue, New York, NY 10022, April 1983, p. 1.

4

- *Increase employee productivity.* There should be a record of greater output per employee over time.
- *Increase the productivity of business capital.* In the same way that units of labor input must produce greater outputs of goods and services, units of money used as inputs must produce greater outputs—capital, in other words, must be used productively.
- *Create jobs.* It would be a truly Pyrrhic Victory if we succeeded in driving up productivity only to find that in the process we had created a huge pool of unemployed workers.
- *Increase the wealth of the businesses' owners.* If a business is to continue to have access to capital in the American financial system, then that business must demonstrate that it can make its owners/investors realize greater wealth than alternate forms of investment.

There are a large number of companies that can do one or two of these things, even three, over an extended period of time, but only a very small group that can accomplish all four simultaneously. Yet the four criteria are so tightly interconnected, that accomplishing less than all four turns out to be something less than an outstanding performance.

For example, one way to improve the productivity of labor is to replace live workers with robots to do the same job. In this case, whether output remains the same or goes up, labor productivity goes up because fewer total workers are doing the same amount of work, or even more work than before. But when that happens, the displaced workers require increased social services, and these increased services must be paid for with even greater increases in productivity, and a vicious circle is created.

Another example involves creating jobs in order to expand in labor intensive areas. But labor intensive industries tend to earn relatively small profits, which makes them unattractive to investors—they don't create much wealth for their owners.

So it goes. To meet fewer than all four criteria is not much of a performance. On the other hand, meeting all four criteria at once, over a long period, is an extremely demanding task.

Increasing the Productivity of Labor. The fundamental reasons that the United States has enjoyed such a high standard of living in the past (and still does today) are that (1) U.S. businesses have had an incredible wealth of natural resources to work with and, (2) U.S. businesses have had a rapidly expanding population to develop those resources.

In the recent past, both of those conditions have begun to change. We are now facing the fact that many of our resources are truly in finite supply, and their changing prices reflect that fact. Second, the rate of population growth in the United States has slowed dramatically, and, at times, actually dropped below the replacement rate.

What these facts mean is that we have lost much of the "engine" that used to drive our standard of living steadily upward. The exact causes for this condition are not at all well understood, and as a result, they are the subject of much speculation. One of the most recent attempts to delineate the problem was undertaken by the well-regarded research organization, Data Resources, Inc. DRI begins its report by describing the problem in this way:

> For much of the last 120 years, manufacturing led the growth of the American economy. After the completion of the rail-road network and the electricity grid, much innovation and capital formation centered on the growth of a succession of manufacturing industries—steel, machinery, automobiles, appliances, chemicals, and computers, along with more modest but persistent growth in textiles, apparel, paper and food processing.
>
> Until 1966, manufacturing industries grew substantially more than the economy as a whole. After 1966, this relationship changed. The margin of manufacturing growth over general growth disappears; and, with the economy as a whole entering a period of exceptional instability, much of the forward movement of manufacturing was lost. Productivity begins to slow, imports loom larger, and soon OPEC creates a setback for all industrial nations.
>
> The broad figures hide disparities among industries, of course, but the change in the relationship is so substantial that it already hints at a fundamental change in economic structure.[5]

Thus, we are confronted with the evidence of a major restructuring of the economy, which individual firms *can* do little to influence, and slackening productivity, which individual firms can influence. Beyond a doubt, one criteria for outstanding performance is increasing labor productivity.

Measurement of changes in overall labor productivity in businesses

[5] Otto Eckstein, Christopher Caton, Roger Brinner, and Peter Dufrey, *The DRI Report on U.S. Manufacturing Industries* (New York: McGraw-Hill Book Company, Inc., 1984), pp. 6-7.

is relatively simple. We divide the company's total sales at the beginning of the period by the number of employees at that time to measure sales per employee. Then we perform the same calculation at the end of the period and compare the two numbers to create an index of productivity growth.

Since inflation alone can drive a company's total dollar sales figure upward, and thereby give the illusion of increasing productivity, we required that the sales per employee growth rate exceed the inflation rate over the entire period.

Measuring labor productivity is extremely frustrating for economists, because they must contrive some measurement of the value of the output of public service agencies that has no market driven value assessment. Since we are dealing only with businesses here, we have no such difficulty and can rely fully on market forces to establish the value of the output of any individual firm.

Increasing the Productivity of Capital. Every management has just two basic inputs to manage—labor and capital, or employees and money. We have just discussed the importance of increasing the productivity of labor. The relationship between producing more units of output for each hour worked and an increasing standard of living is easy to grasp because we encounter many examples of the concept in practice. The salesperson who upgrades his or her skills to the point of making twice as many sales as before will enjoy twice the amount of commissions and has the opportunity to improve his or her standard of living.

The farmer who learns just the right time to irrigate and fertilize crops can double the land's output and, presumably, double the farm income. Every farmer who learns how to improve productivity in this way can also improve his family's standard of living.

Examples like the salesperson and the farmer occur throughout our experience, so the idea that working smarter, or faster, leads to a higher standard of living is easy to understand. What may not be equally easy to grasp is that increasing the productivity of capital is the exact counterpart of increasing the productivity of labor. What is involved in increasing the productivity of capital is making money work smarter or faster. The fact that money can be made to work smarter or faster, may not be intuitively easy for everyone to grasp, so here is a simple example.

Imagine a company that regularly generates a lot more cash than the business requires for short periods of time. Eventually, all of this cash gets used in the regular conduct of the business, but for short periods of time, it is necessary to "park" this cash somewhere. Now imagine Manager A. This manager used to keep the extra cash locked up in the company safe where it earned nothing. Then Manager B came along and replaced Manager A. Manager B knew that he could park the cash in the company's regular bank and earn 5 percent interest every day the funds were on deposit and, because the bank was insured by the federal government, the funds were just as safe as if they were in the company safe.

Manager B did so well at increasing the productivity of the companies cash that he was promoted to vice president, and his old job was filled by Manager C. This new manager knew that the company's short-term cash surpluses could be invested in commercial paper and earn a return of 10 percent with just as much safety as if they were in the bank so she shifted the "parked" cash from the bank to commercial paper and further increased the amount of money earned by the company's cash surpluses.

What has happened in this example is that management has, over time, learned how to increase the productivity of the company's capital. In fact, most well-managed companies have specialists like Manager C whose job is to get the best return from temporarily idle cash.

While this is a perfectly good example of increasing the productivity of the capital entrusted to a management, it is also a very simple example. Real life is much more complicated. The great majority of most companies' capital is not held in cash, but is invested in plants, land, equipment, inventories, and other less liquid forms. Therefore, great care must be taken in the initial decisions about how to invest the firm's capital to provide increasing returns, as such decisions are frequently very difficult to change. Money invested in land, for instance, is not readily available to invest in inventories.

All of this means that companies that produce truly outstanding results will increase the productivity of their capital as well as increasing the productivity of their employees.

Measurement of changes in overall capital productivity is also relatively simple. We divided the company's Invested Capital at the beginning of the period by either Net Income (earnings after taxes) or Funds from Operations (basically earnings before taxes).[6] We then made the

[6] Federal income tax laws fall very differently on different industries and can severely distort what appears to be the earnings performance of a company. To offset this potential distortion, we used the measure of earnings that showed the performance in the best light.

As you study the Profiles of America's 101 Best Performing Companies, you may find it instructive to notice the widely differing impact of income taxes in different industries. For example, Airborne Freight Corporation earned $19,736,000 in 1984 and paid 45 percent of that amount as income taxes while the Farmer's Group earned $104,117,000 in the same year but paid only 11 percent of its earnings in income taxes.

same calculation at the end of the period and compared the two ratios. Those companies that showed a larger ratio at the end of the period have increased the productivity of their capital and met this criteria. Since inflation affects *both* measurements, Total Invested Capital and Net Income, or Funds from Operations, it is not necessary to adjust this measurement for inflation.

Creating Jobs. Increasing both the productivity of labor and capital is certainly a demanding task, but it really becomes difficult when we insist that companies with outstanding performance also create *new* jobs. The reason that creating jobs and increasing the productivity of labor at the same time is difficult, stems from the fact that one of the most widely used methods to increase labor productivity is to replace workers with machines. When a company replaces employees with machines, it can produce the same, or a greater, amount of goods or services with fewer employees, and the productivity of the remaining workers goes up. That is exactly the purpose of robots in automobile plants and automatic teller machines in banks: replace humans with machines to do the same job.

Since we are concerned with protecting our standard of living, substituting machines for people has a very serious flaw: it results in fewer jobs to go around, just at a time when the U.S. economy needs to provide *more,* not *fewer,* jobs!

Here are the numbers that support that conclusion. In 1995, the United States will have 124,583,000 men and women between the ages of 16 and 64 available to work. That is an *increase* of almost 20 *million* workers over the number available in 1979. These numbers are inexorable! Every single one of those new workers is alive today.[7]

The social costs of large numbers of unemployed workers have been demonstrated repeatedly. In the United Kingdom, the riots in Tottenham, Handsworth, and Brixton in 1985 are an illustration of the terrible price that a society pays when large numbers of able-bodied workers are denied jobs. It seems inescapable to us that business must create those new jobs if our standard of living is going to continue to increase. The only alternative is for the government to create the jobs. It would be hard to imagine anyone arguing seriously that creating a Depression era WPA work force would be a mark of an increasing standard of living.

Measurement of this criteria is simple. Did the company have more employees at the end of the period than it had at the beginning? More employees mean that new jobs were created and the criterion was met.

[7] *Current Population Reports*, U.S. Bureau of the Census, Washington, D.C., series P-25, no. 922.

Of course, a number of the 101 companies, like many other firms during the period under study, added employees through acquisition. Yet, the 101 companies increased the productivity of the additional workers they acquired, along with their existing workforces, at higher rates than the other firms, as well as turned in superior capital productivity rates and higher returns for shareholders.

Increasing Stockholder Wealth. Much of the capital that business uses in the United States is raised in the form of equity funding. That is what happens when individuals and institutions (such as pension funds) invest some part of their own savings in equities (usually stocks) issued by businesses. By doing this, these investors become part owners of the particular business whose stock issue they have purchased. Basically, American businesses raise capital by selling partial ownership on a broad basis.

This form of capital acquisition is not used universally. In Japan, for instance, most businesses raise capital funds by borrowing, primarily from banks.

The reason that people purchase stocks is to increase their own wealth. This increase in wealth for the stockholder is a reward for risking his or her savings. Therefore, a business with truly outstanding performance will increase the wealth of its stockholders. In addition, the more that the wealth of the stockholders is increased, the easier it becomes for the company to raise additional capital through issuing equities.

Also, the increases in stockholder wealth must be real. That is, they must be increases that grow faster than the rate of inflation. If wealth grows only as fast as inflation grows, there is no real growth at all. If wealth grows at a rate *less* than the rate of inflation, wealth is actually diminished.

When shareholder wealth grows from period to period, but at a rate lower than the existing rate of inflation, the management is producing only an *illusion* of wealth. That is why managing in inflationary times is such a demanding management task. It is so easy to sit back and let inflation induced-price increases provide the illusion of real gains. During the late 1970s, when inflation reached its most severe condition, many managements took the easy path and let inflation create the illusion of increasing wealth.

Measuring the creation of wealth is quite straightforward. We compared stockholders' equity at the beginning of the period with stockholders' equity at the end of the period. If the rate of growth in stockholders' equity was greater than the rate of growth of inflation over the same period of time, the company had succeeded in increasing its stockholders' wealth.

Obviously, we could apply this criteria only to companies that are *publicly* owned, because those companies are the only ones that make their financial results publicly available. There is no question that there are many fine *privately owned* companies that are increasing the wealth of their owners, but there is no practical way to identify them.

THE MEASUREMENT PERIOD

The period over which we expected companies to meet all four criteria had some criteria of its own. First, the period had to be long enough to eliminate simple good fortune. Second, the time period had to be recent enough to be relevant to investors, prospective employees, managers looking for management role models, and others with an interest in identifying America's most productive companies. Third, there had to be complete data available on a wide variety of measures on a large number of companies.

Criteria two and three tend to work against each other. A very large proportion of companies have fiscal years that end at different times than December 31. To obtain comparable data, it becomes necessary to wait well into the following year for companies to release their annual results.

We settled on the years from 1975 through 1983 as meeting these criteria. Nine years is probably long enough to remove luck as a major factor in meeting our criteria. Cabbage Patch dolls, personal computers, video games, real estate investment trusts (REITs)—none of those more notable "darling" businesses of the 1970s and 1980s were able to sustain anything approaching nine years of continually improving performance.

What is more, those particular nine years were, beyond a doubt, the most challenging times any management has had to face in the 20th century. The beginning of the period was characterized by explosive inflation, a condition that few, if any, U.S. managers had *any* experience dealing with. From 1960 through 1965, for example, consumer prices rose at an average annual rate of 1.3 percent. In 1975, they rose 9.1 percent; 1976, 5.8 percent; 1977, 6.5 percent; 1978, 7.7 percent; 1979, 11.3 percent; 1980, 13.5 percent; and they rose 10.4 percent in 1981. That meant that any average manager had to raise prices almost 10 percent every year just to stand still.[8]

The run-up inflation was followed in rapid succession by sharp disinflation and the deepest and longest recession since the Great Depres-

[8] *Statistical Abstract of the United States 1985*, U.S. Department of Commerce, Washington, D.C., p. 485.

sion in the 1930s. The U.S. economy, as well as much of the world's economy, came to a virtual standstill in the early 1980s.

It would be hard to imagine nine tougher years in which to simply be profitable, let alone turn out performance that could meet all four criteria simultaneously.

Inflation

Rampant inflation plays havoc with comparisons of dollar values over time. Therefore, some measure of inflation must be included in the analysis. There are a large number of measures of inflation. Some are industry specific, and some are even product specific.

The measure of inflation that most people are familiar with is the Consumer Price Index. To create this index, the Bureau of Labor Statistics measures the price of a "fixed basket" of goods and services that would be purchased by urban consumers. Measures such as the CPI are too narrow for the job of adjusting and comparing dollar values in businesses representing virtually every sector of our economy.

The point at which price changes throughout the economy come to a head is in the GNP. In order to be able to compare the *real* GNP from year to year, economists have developed a very broad measure of price changes that they call the *Gross National Product Deflator.* We believe that the GNP Deflator is the most appropriate index for our purposes.

During the period 1975 through 1983, the GNP Deflator increased 170 percent. Therefore, every inflation-affected measure of performance—sales per employee, for instance—had to increase *at least 70 percent* just to keep even with inflation.

The Search Process

We spent over a year examining the detailed performance records of almost 7,000 publicly owned companies. We constructed the performance indexes described earlier. We eliminated companies that had gone private, or had disappeared through merger, because their *future* performance is not likely to be available for assessment.[9]

[9] This is a very dynamic group of companies and situations change very rapidly. At press time, the chances were good that Revlon and Texas Oil & Gas will both disappear through acquisition. Perhaps other listed companies will, as well.

The search process and analysis finally identified 535 U.S. publicly held companies that have met *all four* criteria at the same time. This represents about 7 to 8 percent of all of the companies we reviewed. Appendix A gives a complete list of all the companies that increased the productivity of labor *and* increased the productivity of capital *and* created new jobs *and* increased the wealth of the owners, all over a turbulent and extremely demanding period of nine years.

However, as we came to face the task of displaying all the data on the performance of over 500 companies, it became clear that simply too much detail would be involved. We decided that it would be most useful to concentrate on a smaller subset of companies to illustrate the contribution that these companies are making to our standard of living. That, in turn, required selecting one of the four criteria as being "more equal than the other criteria."

This is a point of some importance, because the composition of the list of America's 101 Best Performing Companies would change depending upon which of the four criteria was selected as being "more equal." It would not, of course, change the composition of the group of companies that had met all four criteria.

After considerable discussion, we decided that if one criteria *had* to be singled out, it should be Increasing Stockholders' Equity. The reasoning that led to this conclusion is as follows: In order to make the investments to create new jobs and to increase productivity, an American company is likely to have to raise funds in the equity markets. To the extent that this is true, then job creation and productivity improvements rest on increased shareholder wealth that, in turn, determines the ease with which a publicly owned company can sell its stocks.

We then arranged all of the companies in terms of how much they increased stockholder wealth over the nine years and selected the top 101. This group of companies are, without a doubt, America's 101 Best Performing Companies.

2

HOW AMERICA'S 101 BEST PERFORMING COMPANIES PERFORMED AS A GROUP

Before we examine how America's 101 Best Performing Companies actually performed from 1975 through 1983, it may be useful to examine where this group of companies fits in the overall business environment in the United States. What percentage of all business do they represent? How much do they contribute to all business revenues? The answers to these questions are a good place to start.

Table 2–1. Business Income Tax Returns Filed—1980

Business Size in Terms of Annual Receipts	Returns (000)						
	Total Number	Proprietorships		Partnerships		Corporations	
		Number	Percent	Number	Percent	Number	Perce
Under $25,000	10,290	9,095	71.6	638	46.2	557	20.5
$25,000 to $49,999	1,811	1,421	11.2	182	13.2	208	7.7
$50,000 to $99,999	1,589	1,028	8.5	184	13.3	323	11.9
$100,000 to $499,999	2,202	986	7.8	291	21.1	925	34.1
$500,000 to $999,999	412	84	0.7	48	3.5	280	10.3
$1,000,000 or more	488	33	0.3	37	2.7	418	15.4
Total	16,793	12,702	100.0%	1,380	100.0%	2,711	100.0

Statistical Abstract of the United States 1985, U.S. Department of Commerce, Washington D.C., p. 532

14

There are many different ways to count the number of businesses in the United States, and they all produce different numbers. Probably the most comprehensive count of U.S. businesses is the one compiled by the U.S. Internal Revenue Service in its *Statistics of Income* series. Table 2-1 shows the number of business that filed income tax returns in 1980 (about midway through the period) classified by type of ownership and by receipts.

The table indicates that 16,793,000 business income tax returns were filed. Only 2,711,000 of those returns were filed by corporations. Of the corporations that filed returns, only 418,000 had receipts amounting to $1,000,000. Corporations with annual sales of $1,000,000 or more account for 92.4 percent of all corporate receipts (and 81 percent of all business receipts).

Since all of the 101 companies are corporations with sales in excess of $1,000,000 they are clearly in the most important segment of the business environment. 101 companies out of a total of 418,000 is a *very* small percentage. However, the total sales of the 101 companies ($78.3 billion) represent about 1.5 percent of the total sales of corporations in the annual $1 million or more category.

America's 101 Best Performing Companies represent only an infinitesimally small fraction of all U.S. businesses, and a still quite small fraction of the large corporations that produce the great majority of the

Receipts ($ billions)						
Total	Proprietorships		Partnerships		Corporations	
$ Amount	$ Amount	Percent	$ Amount	Percent	$ Amount	Percent
64.7	57.3	11.3	4.6	1.6	2.8	nm
63.6	50.8	10.1	6.6	2.3	6.2	0.1
110.6	76.4	15.0	13.2	4.6	21.0	0.4
473.6	193.0	38.3	64.3	22.5	215.4	3.8
282.2	56.9	11.3	33.2	11.6	192.1	3.4
5,528.6	70.5	13.8	164.0	57.4	5,294.1	92.4
$6,523.4	$505.9	100.0%	$286.0	100.0%	$5,731.6	100.0%

Gross National Product. The sales of the 101 represent a very much larger portion of the total than their number would suggest.

HOW BIG ARE THEY?

As Table 2–2 shows, 22 of the 101 companies have sales in excess of $1 billion, 38 of them have sales in excess of $500 million, and 79 have sales over $100 million. These are obviously substantial companies, 43 would qualify for the Fortune 500 largest industrial firms list.

Table 2–2.   America's 101 Best Performing Companies Ranked by 1984 Sales Volume

Company	Rank	1984 Sales
American Stores Company	1	$7,983,677,000
Hewlett-Packard Company	2	6,044,000,000
Digital Equipment Corporation	3	5,584,426,000
Hospital Corporation of America	4	3,498,644,000
SmithKline Beckman Corporation	5	2,949,200,000
Tandy Corporation	6	2,784,479,000
National Medical Enterprises	7	2,559,000,000
American Medical International	8	2,422,716,000
James River Corporation of Virgini	9	2,301,076,000
Wang Laboratories	10	2,184,700,000
Texas Oil & Gas Corporation	11	2,094,440,000
Humana, Inc.	12	1,961,189,000
Lear Siegler, Inc	13	1,941,665,000
MCORP	14	1,446,517,000
Johnson Controls, Inc.	15	1,425,271,000
Limited, Inc.	16	1,343,134,000
G. Heileman Brewing Company	17	1,341,549,000
Waste Management, Inc.	18	1,314,761,000
Piedmont Aviation, Inc.	19	1,159,018,000
Entex, Inc.	20	1,092,852,000
EG & G, Inc.	21	1,071,653,000
Allied Bancshares, Inc.	22	1,012,759,000
Washington Post Company	23	984,303,000
Farmer's Group, Inc.	24	893,828,000
Pulte Home Corporation	25	841,988,000
E-Systems, Inc.	26	819,353,000
National Convenience Stores, Inc.	27	818,988,000
M/A Com, Inc.	28	768,449,000
Cox Communications, Inc.	29	742,855,000
MEI Corporation	30	734,262,000
Nucor Corporation	31	660,259,000
Tyco Laboratories, Inc.	32	650,064,000
Prime Computer, Inc.	33	624,779,000

Company	Rank	1984 Sales
Advanced Micro Devices, Inc.	34	583,346,000
Cooper Tire & Rubber Company	35	555,387,000
Smithfield Foods, Inc.	36	541,641,000
PHH Group, Inc.	37	531,333,000
Carlisle Corporation	38	527,177,000
Charter Medical Corporation	39	493,273,000
Mayflower Corporation	40	480,723,000
Public Service Co. of New Mexico	41	445,328,000
SCI Systems, Inc.	42	439,744,000
Airbourne Freight Corporation	43	417,854,000
Kansas Gas & Electric Company	44	410,753,000
Herman Miller, Inc.	45	402,524,000
Holly Corporation	46	401,614,000
Pacific Telecom, Inc.	47	399,064,000
Lear Petroleum Corporation	48	398,747,000
Data Products Corporation	49	398,636,000
Teradyne, Inc.	50	389,278,000
Alaska Air Group, Inc.	51	361,642,000
Family Dollar Stores, Inc.	52	340,919,000
El Paso Electric Company	53	329,015,000
Telex Corporation	54	325,432,000
Multimedia, Inc.	55	304,361,000
Grow Group, Inc.	56	276,130,000
Loctite Corporation	57	241,744,000
Pic'n Save Corporation	58	235,147,000
John H. Harland Company	59	217,400,000
Barry Wright Corporation	60	204,814,000
Standard-Pacific Corporation	61	192,941,000
Community Psychiatric Centers, Inc	62	182,612,000
Apogee Enterprises, Inc.	63	181,095,000
Luby's Cafeterias, Inc.	64	174,852,000
Gerber Scientific, Inc.	65	173,593,000
Unitrode Corporation	66	159,570,000
Teleflex, Inc.	67	155,736,000
Dynatech Corporation	68	149,424,000
Dreyfuss Corporation	69	143,634,000
Analogic Corporation	70	141,311,000
Aydin Corporation	71	137,500,000
Stewart Information Services, Inc.	72	131,951,000
Logicon, Inc.	73	126,514,000
Camco, Inc.	74	119,937,000
Zero Corporation	75	117,172,000
California Microwave, Inc.	76	112,493,000
Adams Russell Company	77	109,663,000
Bowne & Co.	78	109,193,000

Company	Rank	1984 Sales
Transtechnology Corporation	79	108,586,000
Communications Industries, Inc.	80	98,181,000
Pacific Scientific Company	81	92,192,000
Electrospace Systems, Inc.	82	79,503,000
Chilton Corporation	83	68,459,000
Whitehall Corporation	84	64,363,000
Alpha Industries, Inc.	85	60,148,000
Vishay Intertechnology, Inc.	86	48,531,000
Gelman Sciences, Inc.	87	43,135,000
Gray Communications Systems	88	41,521,000
D O C Optics Corporation	89	39,174,000
Aeroflex Laboratories, Inc.	90	36,234,000
Plenum Publishing Corporation	91	36,049,000
VersaTechnologies, Inc.	92	30,070,000
Porta Systems Corporation	93	29,434,000
Dranetz Technologies, Inc.	94	26,891,000
Vari-Care, Inc.	95	26,699,000
Auxton Computer Enterprises	96	23,960,000
State o Maine, Inc.	97	20,120,000
Astronics Corporation	98	12,530,000
General Microwave Corporation	99	11,876,000
RAI Research Corporation	100	7,022,000
Research Industries Corporation	101	5,778,000

More importantly, they represent a very wide range of sales. The largest is American Stores Company, with almost $8 billion in 1984 sales, while the smallest, Research Industries Corporation, didn't quite reach $6 million. The point is that outstanding performance isn't just confined to large corporations with extensive resources, nor is it confined to small companies with a small base to grow from. Outstanding performance can be found at any size.

The following compares the sales growth of the 101 companies with the growth of the business sector of the Gross National Product from 1975 through 1983.

Sales in Billions of Dollars

	Business Sector of the GNP	America's 101 Best Performing Companies
1975	$1,301.7	$10.7
1983	2,790.8	78.3
Percentage Increase 1975/83	114%	629%

Between 1975 and 1983, America's 101 Best Performing Companies grew in output at a rate 5.5 times greater than all business. A truly impressive performance.

FEATURES OF THE BEST PERFORMING COMPANIES

Increased Labor Productivity

Seventy-four of the 101 companies increased their sales per employee 100 percent or more between 1975 and 1983. Of particular interest is the fact that a service company, PHH Group, Inc., led the list of increased labor productivity (+ 660 percent) despite the fact that increasing labor productivity has been notoriously difficult to achieve in the service sector of the economy. In fact, some economists have been so disheartened as to suggest that America's transition from a manufacturing economy to a service based economy would forever destroy our standard of living, simply because increasing labor productivity seemed to be so hard to achieve.

And it is not just PHH Group, Inc. that has made remarkable progress in increasing employee output in the service area. In health care, Humana, Inc. (+ 197 percent), Hospital Corporation of America (+ 191 percent), Charter Medical Corporation (+ 169 percent), American Medical International (+ 127 percent) and Community Psychiatric Centers (+ 102 percent) have demonstrated significant increases in labor productivity. Allied Bancshares, Inc. (+ 138 percent) and MCORP (+ 118 percent) have shown that it can be done in banking. American Stores Company (+ 149 percent), Pic'n Save Corporation (+ 135 percent), Family Dollar Stores (+ 133 percent), D O C Optics, Inc. (+ 111 percent), The Limited, Inc. (+ 167 percent) and National Convenience Stores (+ 101 percent) have demonstrated how to improve labor productivity in retailing.

Table 2–3 displays the entire 101 companies ranked by their records in improving labor productivity between 1975 and 1983.

Table 2–3. America's 101 Best Performing Companies Ranked by Increases in Labor Productivity

Company	Rank	Percentage Increase In Labor Productivity
PHH Group, Inc.	1	660%
Lear Petroleum Corporation	2	344
Farmer's Group, Inc.	3	282
Dranetz Technologies, Inc.	4	261
Tyco Laboratories, Inc.	5	237
Entex, Inc.	6	226
Vari-Care, Inc.	7	202
Humana, Inc.	8	197
Smithfield Foods, Inc.	9	192
Holly Corporation	10	191

Company	Rank	Percentage Increase In Labor Productivity
Hospital Corporation of America	11	191
Research Industries Corporation	12	187
Gray Communications Systems	13	179
California Microwave, Inc.	14	178
Nucor Corporation	15	178
Gerber Scientific, Inc.	16	176
Pacific Scientific Company	17	176
Waste Management, Inc.	18	174
Pacific Telecom, Inc.	19	171
Charter Medical Corporation	20	169
Limited, Inc.	21	167
G. Heileman Brewing Company	22	166
Texas Oil & Gas Corporation	23	161
Washington Post Company	24	152
Advanced Micro Devices, Inc.	25	150
Multimedia, Inc.	26	150
American Stores Company	27	149
Data Products Corporation	28	149
E-Systems, Inc.	29	147
Porta Systems Corporation	30	147
Pulte Home Corporation	31	146
Camco Incorporated	32	145
Communications Industries, Inc.	33	141
Teleflex, Inc.	34	139
Allied Bancshares, Inc.	35	138
Carlisle Corporation	36	138
State o Maine, Inc.	37	138
Adams Russell Corporation	38	136
Dreyfuss Corporation	39	136
MEI Corporation	40	136
Herman Miller, Inc.	41	135
Pic'n Save Corporation	42	135
Chilton Corporation	43	134
Family Dollar Stores	44	133
Mayflower Corporation	45	133
Alaska Air Group, Inc.	46	132
M/A Com, Inc.	47	132
SCI Systems, Inc.	48	130
American Medical International, Inc.	49	127
El Paso Electric Company	50	127
Vishay Intertechnology, Inc.	51	127
Cooper Tire & Rubber Company	52	126
Johnson Controls, Inc.	53	125
EG & G, Inc.	54	123
Electrospace Systems, Inc.	55	123

Company	Rank	Percentage Increase In Labor Productivity
Public Service Co. of New Mexico	56	123
Astronics Corporation	57	119
MCORP	58	118
Whitehall Corporation	59	118
Plenum Publishing Corporation	60	117
Apogee Enterprises, Inc.	61	113
D O C Optics Corporation	62	111
SmithKline Beckman Corporation	63	111
Aeroflex Laboratories, Inc.	64	108
Bowne & Co., Inc.	65	108
Digital Equipment Corporation	66	108
John H. Harland Company	67	108
Kansas Gas & Electric Company	68	108
Aydin Corporation	69	105
Community Psychiatric Centers	70	102
Stewart Information Services	71	102
Hewlett-Packard Company	72	101
National Convenience Stores	73	101
Analogic Corporation	74	100
Alpha Industries, Inc.	75	98
Luby's Cafeterias, Inc.	76	97
Lear Siegler, Inc.	77	95
Cox Communications, Inc.	78	94
National Medical Enterprises	79	94
Piedmont Aviation, Inc.	80	94
Wang Laboratories, Inc.	81	93
Zero Corporation	82	93
Gelman Sciences, Inc.	83	91
James River Corporation of Virginia	84	91
Loctite Corporation	85	91
Teradyne, Inc.	86	91
Logicon, Inc.	87	89
Transtechnology Corporation	88	88
Unitrode Corporation	89	88
Barry Wright Corporation	90	86
RAI Research Corporation	91	84
Prime Computer, Inc.	92	83
Standard-Pacific Corporation	93	81
Telex Corporation	94	76
General Microwave Corporation	95	75
Versa Technologies, Inc.	96	74
Dynatech Corporation	97	72
Grow Group, Inc.	98	72

Company	Rank	Percentage Increase In Labor Productivity
Grow Group, Inc.	98	72
Tandy Corporation	99	71
Airbourne Freight Corporation	100	71
Auxton Computer Enterprises	101	71

Increased Capital Productivity

The results in increasing capital productivity tend to be different than the results in improving labor productivity. First, the extremes of improving capital productivity are greater. Four companies in widely different industries recorded capital productivity increases in four digits: Gerber Scientific, Inc. (+ 8,347 percent)—geologic services; Pulte Home Corporation (+ 2,625 percent)—single family house construction; Piedmont Aviation, Inc. (+ 1,290 percent)—air passenger and freight transportation; and Dranetz Technologies, Inc. (+ 1,195 percent)— electronic instruments.

At the other extreme, 17 companies could only improve capital productivity at a single digit rate. In general, increasing capital productivity seems to have been harder for most of these companies than was the case with labor productivity. Only 27 companies increased capital productivity by 100 percent, or more, compared with 74 companies that accomplished that level of improvement with labor productivity.

There is absolutely no pattern to the kinds of companies that were able to increase capital productivity 100 percent or more. There are manufacturing companies and service companies. There are high-technology and low-technology companies. Some of the companies produce consumer products and services and some produce industrial goods and services.

In view of America's run-away health care costs, it is especially encouraging to see American Medical International (+ 299 percent), Humana, Inc. (+ 254 percent), Charter Medical Corporation (+ 196 percent) and Community Psychiatric Centers (+ 95 percent) produce exceptionally high scores in improving both capital and labor productivity.

The details of America's 101 Best Performing Companies' results with improving capital productivity can be found in Table 2–4.

Table 2–4. America's 101 Best Performing Companies Ranked by Increases in Capital Productivity

Company	Rank	Percentage Increase In Capital Productivity
Gerber Scientific, Inc.	1	8347%
Pulte Home Corporation	2	2625
Piedmont Aviation, Inc.	3	1290

Company	Rank	*Percentage Increase In Capital Productivity*
Dranetz Technologies, Inc.	4	1195
Teradyne, Inc.	5	558
Teleflex, Inc.	6	478
Research Industries Corporation	7	370
Adams Russell Company	8	306
American Medical International	9	299
Humana, Inc.	10	254
Carlisle Corporation	11	244
Plenum Publishing Corporation	12	243
Whitehall Corporation	13	218
Charter Medical Corporation	14	196
Chilton Corporation	15	189
Washington Post Company	16	161
Advanced Micro Devices, Inc.	17	156
State o Maine, Inc.	18	149
Stewart Information Services	19	140
Waste Management, Inc.	20	139
Pacific Telecom, Inc.	21	136
Tyco Laboratories, Inc.	22	125
Aeroflex Laboratories, Inc.	23	124
Alpha Industries, Inc.	24	122
Family Dollar Stores	25	113
Wang Laboratories, Inc.	26	111
Farmer's Group, Inc.	27	102
Community Psychiatric Centers	28	95
Pacific Scientific Company	29	92
Tandy Corporation	30	92
Smithfield Foods, Inc.	31	90
National Medical Enterprises	32	89
Cooper Tire & Rubber Company	33	86
E-Systems, Inc.	34	86
Camco, Inc.	35	85
EG & G, Inc.	36	81
G. Heileman Brewing Company	37	80
Unitrode Corporation	38	80
Limited, Inc.	39	77
Versa Technologies, Inc.	40	60
Telex Corporation	41	57
Aydin Corporation	42	56
Analogic Corporation	43	54
Hospital Corporation of America	44	53
Kansas Gas & Electric Company	45	52
Auxton Computer Enterprises	46	51
Zero Corporation	47	51
SmithKline Beckman Corporation	48	50
Lear Siegler, Inc.	49	49

Company	Rank	Percentage Increase In Capital Productivity
Johnson Controls, Inc.	50	48
Barry Wright Corporation	51	47
El Paso Electric Company	52	46
Texas Oil & Gas Corporation	53	44
Herman Miller, Inc.	54	41
Public Service Co. of New Mexico	55	41
Standard-Pacific Corporation	56	40
Loctite Corporation	57	39
National Convenience Stores	58	39
D O C Optics Corporation	59	37
Gray Communications Systems	60	37
Pic'n Save Corporation	61	33
James River Corporation of Virginia	62	30
Grow Group, Inc.	63	28
Vishay Intertechnology, Inc.	64	28
Holly Corporation	65	27
Nucor Corporation	66	26
Porta Systems Corporation	67	26
Vari-Care, Inc.	68	23
Airbourne Freight Corporation	69	20
Mayflower Corporation	70	20
Logicon, Inc.	71	18
Luby's Cafeterias, Inc.	72	18
RAI Research Corporation	73	18
John H. Harland Company	74	16
MEI Corporation	75	16
PHH Group, Inc.	76	16
Bowne & Co., Inc.	77	15
Electrospace Systems, Inc.	78	14
Gelman Sciences, Inc.	79	14
California Microwave, Inc.	80	13
General Microwave Corporation	81	13
MCORP	82	13
Dynatech Corporation	83	11
Astroncis Corporation	84	10
Alaska Air Group, Inc.	85	8
Prime Computer, Inc.	86	8
Data Products Corporation	87	7
Lear Petroleum Corporation	88	7
Transtechnology Corporation	89	7
Cox Communications, Inc.	90	6
Multimedia, Inc.	91	6
Communications Industries, Inc.	92	5
Dreyfuss Corporation	93	5
M/A Com, Inc.	94	5

Company	Rank	Percentage Increase In Capital Productivity
American Stores Company	95	4
Digital Equipment Corporation	96	4
Hewlett-Packard Company	97	4
Allied Bancshares, Inc.	98	3
Apogee Enterprises, Inc.	99	2
Entex, Inc.	100	2
SCI Systems, Inc.	101	1

Comparative Productivity Increases

The next question to address is how the increased productivity of the 101 companies compares with the productivity increases of all U.S. business over the same period. That tends to be a difficult question to deal with in a precise manner. Dr. Edward N. Wolff, Professor of Economics at New York University outlines the problem:

> Before discussing the causes of the productivity slowdown, it is necessary to show that such a slowdown has, in fact, occurred; and before doing that, it is necessary to define the concept of productivity. There is perhaps as much divergence of opinion about the proper measure of productivity as there is about the causes of its growth over time. Generally speaking, productivity is defined as a ratio of some measure of output to some measure of input. The disagreements are about what to include in (or exclude from) the numerator and denominator of the fraction. This is true for the measures of both overall or aggregate productivity and sectoral or industry productivity.[1]

We believe that the U.S. Bureau of Statistics Index of Productivity, which appears in the Bureau's publication *Employment and Earnings*, does a good job of subsuming both our index of labor productivity and our index of capital productivity. The following compares the performance of the 101 companies with total "U.S. Business Sector Output."

---

[1] Edward N. Wolff, "The Magnitude and Causes of the Recent Productivity Slowdown in the United States: A Survey of Recent Studies," in *Productivity Growth and U.S. Competitiveness*, William J. Baumol and Kenneth McLennan, eds. (New York: Oxford University Press, 1985), p. 30.

	Average Annual Change 1975 through 1985
Bureau of Labor Statistics, Index of Productivity, Business Sector Output	1.3%
America's 101 Best Performing Companies	
Labor Productivity	15.2%
Capital Productivity	22.8%

Dramatic as these figures are on productivity, they become even more impressive when they are placed in a global perspective. While productivity data is difficult to obtain domestically, it is even more difficult to gain access to reliable cross-national data. However, we believe that the following provides a reasonably accurate picture of the relative positions of the major players in the world market.

	Index of Labor Productivity Average Annual Rate of Change 1970–77
Japan	4.8%
Netherlands	3.9%
France	3.5%
Federal Republic of Germany	3.4%
Belgium	3.4%
Italy	2.4%
Denmark	2.3%
Canada	2.0%
United States of America	1.5%
United Kingdom	1.2%
Sweden	1.1%

Source: *Social Indicators III*, U.S. Department of Commerce, Washington, D.C., December, 1980, p. 497.

The preceding exhibit also brings us full circle. The United States is losing its competitive position in the world. A primary factor in this declining competitiveness can be traced to declining productivity. Declining competitiveness must inevitably lead to a declining standard of living in the United States. There is an alternative, however. Some very small fraction of all U.S. publicly owned businesses have turned in remarkable performances in improving labor and capital productivity. If we can learn from America's most important companies the lessons of improving productivity, the future can be just as bright as the past has been.

Creating Jobs

America's 101 Best Performing Companies represent a very wide spectrum of employment opportunities. At one end of the spectrum, Digital Equipment Corporation, Hewlett-Packard Company, and Hospital Corporation of America all employ in excess of 70,000 people. At the other end, Research Industries Corporation has just 40 employees. It is clear that number of employees is not a factor in determining outstanding performance. Details about the number of employees of each company in 1983 are displayed in Table 2–5.

The 101 companies employed a total of 862,985 people in 1983. That represented the creation of 603,797 jobs since 1975. In turn, that means that 70 percent of the jobs at the 101 companies are new jobs since 1975!

Table 2–5. America's 101 Best Performing Companies Ranked by Number of Employees in 1983

Company	Rank	Number of Employees
Digital Equipment Corporation	1	73,000
Hewlett-Packard Company	2	72,000
Hospital Corporation of America	3	71,000
American Stores Company	4	66,000
National Medical Enterprises	5	55,100
Humana, Inc.	6	42,000
American Medical Enterprises	7	32,000
Tandy Corporation	8	32,000
SmithKline Beckman Corporation	9	31,317
Wang Laboratories, Inc.	10	24,769
James River Corp. of Virginia	11	21,000
Johnson Controls, Inc.	12	20,700
Lear Siegler, Inc.	13	20,004
EG & G, Inc.	14	20,000
Limited, Inc.	15	15,300
Advanced Micro Devices, Inc.	16	13,067
Farmer's Group, Inc.	17	12,431
E-Systems, Inc.	18	11,941
Piedmont Aviation, Inc.	19	9,908
M/A Com, Inc.	20	9,508
Waste Management, Inc.	21	9,100
Charter Medical Corporation	22	8,400
Tyco Laboratories, Inc.	23	7,443
Cox Communications, Inc.	24	7,200
MCORP	25	6,933
G. Heileman Brewing Company	26	6,315
National Convenience Stores	27	6,250

Company	Rank	Number of Employees
Prime Computer, Inc.	28	5,927
Data Products Corporation	29	5,627
Washington Post Company	30	5,300
Entex, Inc.	31	5,000
Luby's Cafeterias, Inc.	32	5,000
MEI Corporation	33	4,903
Carlisle Corporation	34	4,863
Cooper Tire & Rubber Company	35	4,455
Family Dollar Stores	36	4,400
Telex Corporation	37	4,193
John H. Harland Company	38	4,190
Teradyne, Inc.	39	3,900
Herman Miller, Inc.	40	3,703
Allied Bancshares, Inc.	41	3,700
Nucor Corporation	42	3,700
Community Psychiatric Centers	43	3,478
Texas Oil & Gas Corporation	44	3,405
Airbourne Freight Corporation	45	3,304
SCI Systems, Inc.	46	3,220
Smithfield Foods, Inc.	47	3,150
Unitrode Corporation	48	3,094
Multimedia, Inc.	49	3,000
Pacific Telecom, Inc.	50	2,895
Public Service Co. of New Mexico	51	2,783
PHH Group, Inc.	52	2,491
Loctite Corporation	53	2,355
Camco, Inc.	54	2,300
Pic'n Save Corporation	55	2,300
Alaska Air Group, Inc.	56	2,245
Stewart Information Services	57	2,225
Barry Wright Corporation	58	2,198
Apogee Enterprises, Inc.	59	2,185
Pulte Home Corporation	60	2,100
Aydin Corporation	61	2,000
Teleflex, Inc.	62	1,940
Grow Group, Inc.	63	1,930
Kansas Gas & Electric Company	64	1,928
Analogic Corporation	65	1,900
Logicon, Inc.	66	1,812
Chilton Corporation	67	1,663
Gerber Scientific, Inc.	68	1,650
Zero Corporation	69	1,530
Transtechnology Corporation	70	1,487
Whitehall Corporation	71	1,392
Mayflower Corporation	72	1,378
Adams Russell Corporation	73	1,370

Company	Rank	Number of Employees
Vari-Care, Inc.	74	1,352
Alpha Industries, Inc.	75	1,263
Bowne & Co., Inc.	76	1,200
California Microwave, Inc.	77	1,193
Electrospace Systems, Inc.	78	1,148
El Paso Electric Company	79	1,107
Vishay Intertechnology, Inc.	80	1,000
Communications Industries, Inc.	81	979
Pacific Scientific Company	82	728
D O C Optics Corporation	83	722
Gelman Sciences, Inc.	84	657
Dynatech Corporation	85	650
Dreyfuss Corporation	86	649
Versa Technologies, Inc.	87	492
Gray Communications Systems	88	488
Aeroflex Laboratories, Inc.	89	485
Standard-Pacific Corporation	90	397
Lear Petroleum Corporation	91	386
Porta Systems Corporation	92	366
Holly Corporation	93	362
Auxton Computer Enterprises	94	320
Plenum Publishing Company	95	310
State o Maine, Inc.	96	302
Dranetz Technologies, Inc.	97	234
General Microwave Corporation	98	212
Astronics Corporation	99	206
RAI Research Corporation	100	107
Research Industries Corporation	101	40

The U.S. Bureau of Labor Statistics indicates that there were 69,936,000 jobs in private industry in 1975. In 1983, that figure had increased to 82,663,000, an absolute increase of 12,727,000. Therefore, the 101 companies created almost 5 percent of *all of the new jobs* created by business from 1975 through 1983, even though the 101 companies represent only the smallest fraction of all businesses.

Here is how the 101 companies performed in relation to all U.S. business.

	Total Increase in Jobs 1975–83
Increase in civilian employment, persons 16 years old and over, in private industry	+ 18%
Increase in employees in *America's 101 Best Performing Companies*	+ 223%

It is quite clear that the 101 companies do an outstanding job of creating new jobs.

Increasing Stockholders' Wealth

Even the fact that the 101 companies were selected from the larger group of five hundred plus companies based on increased stockholder equity doesn't disguise the fact that America's 101 Best Performing Companies have racked up spectacular results in increasing the wealth of their owners.

Twenty-seven of the companies increased their stockholders' wealth more than 1,000 percent between 1975 and 1984. Fifty-nine increased stockholders' equity over 500 percent, and every one of them increased it over 300 percent. The details are in Table 2–6.

Table 2–6.   America's 101 Best Performing Companies Ranked by Growth in Stockholder's Equity

Company	Rank	Percentage Growth In Stockholder' Equity 1983/1975
Chilton Corporation	1	131,606%
Prime Computer, Inc.	2	9,603
Analogic Corporation	3	5,910
James River Corp. of Virginia	4	4,147
Limited, Inc.	5	2,881
Lear Petroleum Corporation	6	2,772
Wang Laboratories, Inc.	7	2,436
Advanced Micro Devices, Inc.	8	2,293
Dranetz Technologies, Inc.	9	2,060
Aeroflex Laboratories, Inc.	10	1,959
Alpha Industries, Inc.	11	1,869
Telex Corporation	12	1,586
National Medical Enterprises, Inc.	13	1,542
Dynatech Corporation	14	1,487
Electrospace Systems, Inc.	15	1,474
SCI Systems, Inc.	16	1,400
Porta Systems Corporation	17	1,382
Piedmont Aviation, Inc.	18	1,309
Aydin Corporation	19	1,300
M/A Com, Inc.	20	1.296
Transtechnology Corporation	21	1,262
Plenum Publishing Corporation	22	1,230
Community Psychriatic Centers	23	1,209
Adams Russell Co., Inc.	24	1,199
Gerber Scientific, Inc.	25	1,187

Company	Rank	*Percentage Growth In Stockholder' Equity* *1983/1975*
Auxton Computer Enterprises, Inc.	26	1,083
Pic'n Save Corporation	27	1,008
Pacific Telecom, Inc.	28	969
Cox Communications, Inc.	29	923
Humana, Inc.	30	920
Smithfield Foods, Inc.	31	916
Waste Management, Inc.	32	909
Alaska Air Group, Inc.	33	849
Hospital Corp. of America, Inc.	34	847
Pulte Home Corporation	35	834
Luby's Cafeterias, Inc.	36	816
California Microwave, Inc.	37	814
Digital Equipment Corporation	38	798
Herman Miller, Inc.	39	742
Public Service Co. of New Mexico	40	702
MCORP	41	663
Teradyne, Inc.	42	646
Communications Industries, Inc.	43	644
State o Maine, Inc.	44	642
RAI Research Corporation	45	636
SmithKline Beckman Corporation	46	633
G. Heileman Brewing Company	47	619
D O C Optics Corporation	48	616
Data Products Corporation	49	606
Allied Bancshares, Inc.	50	593
Washington Post Company	51	587
Tyco Laboratories, Inc.	52	581
El Paso Electric Company	53	581
Pacific Scientific Company	54	568
Texas Oil & Gas Corporation	55	566
Standard-Pacific Corporation	56	525
Teleflex, Inc.	57	522
American Medical International, Inc	58	520
Logicon, Inc.	59	506
Apogee Enterprises, Inc.	60	490
Tandy Corporation	61	489
Gray Communications Systems, Inc.	62	481
Nucor Corporation	63	479
E-Systems, Inc.	64	463
American Stores Company	65	462
Whitehall Corporation	66	461
Charter Medical Corporation	67	452
Multimedia, Inc.	68	450
Dreyfuss Corporation	69	450

Company	Rank	*Percentage Growth In Stockholder' Equity 1983/1975*
Family Dollar Stores, Inc.	70	448
PHH Group, Inc.	71	442
Loctite Corporation	72	434
National Convenience Stores, Inc.	73	434
Kansas Gas & Electric Company	74	426
Camco, Inc.	75	423
Hewlett-Packard Company	76	416
Versa Technologies, Inc.	77	412
Barry Wright Corporation	78	410
General Microwave Corporation	79	392
Extex, Inc.	80	388
Grow Group, Inc.	81	386
Johnson Controls, Inc.	82	385
Gelman Sciences, Inc.	83	384
Lear Siegler, Inc.	84	381
Farmer's Group, Inc.	85	378
Stewart Information Services Corp.	86	372
MEI Corporation	87	372
Research Industries Corporation	88	370
Unitrode Corporation	89	368
Vari-Care, Inc.	90	365
Vishay Intertechnology, Inc.	91	361
Astronics Corporation	92	359
Holly Corporation	93	357
Mayflower Corporation	94	352
Bowne & Co., Inc.	95	342
EG & G, Inc.	96	342
Zero Corporation	97	340
Cooper Tire & Rubber Company	98	331
Carlisle Corporation	99	325
John H. Harland Company	100	323
Airbourne Freight Corporation	101	322

The average 101 company increased stockholders' equity by 2,250 percent. The amazing results accomplished by the Chilton Corporation skew the average upward. When you eliminate Chilton's results, the remaining 100 companies *merely* averaged a 957 percent increase in stockholders' equity.

To put these results into some sort of perspective, we created the following comparison:

	Annual Compounded Rate of Growth, 1975–83
Standard and Poor's 500 Stock Price Index	+ 8.1%
America's 101 Best Performing Companies	
With Chilton Corporation	+ 162.4%
Without Chilton Corporation	+ 118.5%

Even without Chilton's results, the remaining 101 companies increased their owners' wealth almost *15 times* as fast as did the companies that make up Standard & Poor's broad based stock index.

America's Best Performing Companies, indeed!

Where Are They Located?

One of the clearest images that emerges about America's 101 Best Performing Companies is their exceptional diversity. That holds true for their scope of operations as well. Some operate on a worldwide basis. Digital Equipment Corporation and the Hewlett-Packard Company sell their computers virtually everywhere in the world. Even service businesses have international operations. Hospital Corporation of America, for example, owns and/or operates hospitals in Australia, Brazil, India, Malaysia, Republic of Panama, Saudi Arabia, United Kingdom, and the Virgin Islands.

Some, like The Limited, Inc., operate throughout the United States. Others, like National Convenience Stores, operate only in a section of the United States. A few, like MCORP, operate in only one state, and Kansas Gas & Electric Company's business is limited to just 22 counties in Kansas.

Summarizing the operating scope of the 101 companies is impossible. What we can do, however, is to summarize where their headquarters are located. That information is presented in Table 2–7 and on the map that follows.

The diversity continues in Table 2–7. Over half of the companies are headquartered in just four states, but the other "half" are located in 24 other states and the District of Columbia. In total, the 101 companies have headquarters in states that account for 83 percent of the U.S. population. They are literally everywhere.

Of the four states that account for the majority of the headquarters, two of the states—Texas and California—are in the Sun Belt, just as conventional wisdom would expect top performers to be located. But the other two states of the Big Four are Massachusetts and New York, moribund areas that the conventional wisdom would *know* were devoid of vitality.

Table 2–7.   America's 101 Best Performing Companies Headquarters Location

State	Number of Companies	% of U.S. Population
Texas	17	6.75%
California	15	10.76
Massachusetts	12	2.45
New York	11	7.53
	55	27.49%
Pennsylvania	4	5.06
Georgia	4	2.45
Michigan	4	3.88
Washington	3	1.85
Ohio	3	4.57
North Carolina	3	2.60
Wisconsin	3	2.02
Utah	2	.70
Minnesota	2	1.77
Connecticut	2	1.33
Virginia	2	2.37
Maryland	1	1.84
Tennessee	1	2.00
Kentucky	1	1.59
Kansas	1	1.03
Indiana	1	2.35
South Carolina	1	1.40
Florida	1	4.59
New Mexico	1	.60
Alabama	1	1.69
Oklahoma	1	1.42
New Hampshire	1	.41
District of Columbia	1	.26
Illinois	1	4.89
New Jersey	1	3.18
	101	83.34%

Geographic Location of the Headquarters of the 101 Best Performing Companies
(Keyed to the Growth in Stockholder's Equity Table)

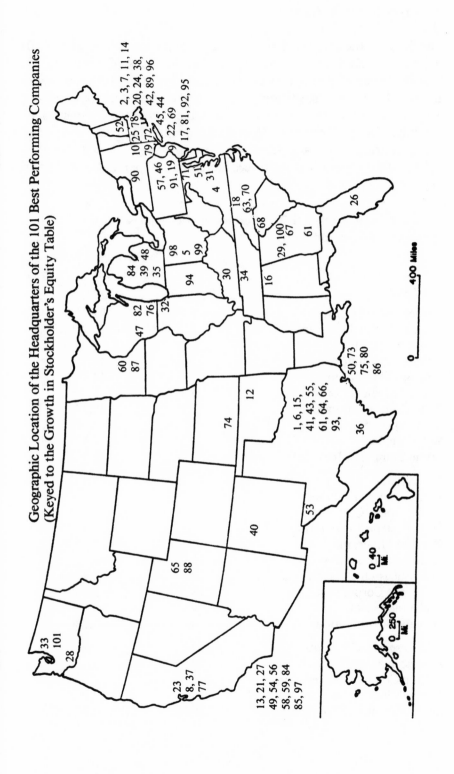

Increases In Stock Prices

The data on the increased stockholders' equity found among the 101 companies would lead one to suspect that the stock of America's 101 Best Performing Companies would be a good investment. That would be an exactly correct suspicion! Stock market investors have clearly demonstrated that they recognize the value that these companies are creating. The stock prices of 55 of the companies increased over 1,000 percent during the decade between 1975 and 1984 (Table 2–8). Seventy-eight of the companies' stock prices increased 500 percent or more during that time period.

Table 2–8. America's 101 Best Performing Companies Ranked by Increase in Year-end Stock Price

Company	Rank	Percentage Increase In Year-end Stock Price 1975/83
Gerber Scientific, Inc.	1	97,750%
Dranetz Technologies, Inc.	2	56,250
State o Maine, Inc.	3	34,900
Aeroflex Laboratories, Inc.	4	15,152
Analogic Corporation	5	14,300
Charter Medical Corporation	6	14,220
Pulte Home Corporation	7	10,347
Electrospace Systems, Inc.	8	8,400
Vari-Care, Inc.	9	7,611
Prime Computer, Inc.	10	5,975
SCI Systems, Inc.	11	5,413
Wang Laboratories, Inc.	12	5,208
D O C Optics Corporation	13	4,821
Porta Systems Corporation	14	4,579
Herman Miller, Inc.	15	4,409
Astronics Corporation	16	4,025
Adams Russell Company	17	3,719
Pic'n Save Corporation	18	3,569
Alpha Industries, Inc.	19	3,313
Dynatech Corporation	20	3,230
RAI Research Corporation	21	3,130
Advanced Micro Devices, Inc.	22	3,024
Auxton Computer Enterprises	23	2,937
Limited, Inc.	24	2,891
Lear Petroleum Corporation	25	2,876

Company	Rank	*Percentage Increase In Year-end Stock Price 1975/83*
National Medical Enterprises	26	2,846
General Microwave Corporation	27	2,800
Humana, Inc.	28	2,691
Plenum Publishing Corporation	29	2,483
Chilton Corporation	30	2,311
Unitrode Corporation	31	2,311
Whitehall Corporation	32	2,207
Logicon, Inc.	33	2,200
National Convenience Stores	34	2,138
Family Dollar Stores	35	2,094
Teleflex, Inc.	36	2,060
MEI Corporation	37	2,036
Versa Technologies, Inc.	38	1,951
Pacific Scientific Company	39	1,824
Waste Management, Inc.	40	1,814
Telex Corporation	41	1,694
Dreyfuss Corporation	42	1,686
Barry Wright Corporation	43	1,482
Washington Post Company	44	1,393
Apogee Enterprises	45	1,386
Piedmont Aviation, Inc.	46	1,340
Texas Oil & Gas Corporation	47	1,337
American Medical International	48	1,284
Luby's Cafeterias, Inc.	49	1,243
Nucor Corporation	50	1,208
Community Psychiatric Centers	51	1,197
James River Corp. of Virginia	52	1,194
G. Heileman Brewing Company	53	1,184
M/A Com, Inc.	54	1,172
Carlisle Corporation	55	1,132
Gray Communications System	56	962
Vishay Intertechnology, Inc.	57	916
Stewart Information Services	58	911
Teradyne, Inc.	59	891
Aydin Corporation	60	866
Standard-Pacific Corporation	61	850
Hospital Corporation of America	62	821
Transtechnology Corporation	63	808
California Microwave, Inc.	64	799
EG & G, Inc.	65	796

Company	Rank	*Percentage Increase In Year-end Stock Price 1975/83*
Multimedia, Inc.	66	786
John H. Harland Company	67	722
Bowne & Co., Inc.	68	706
Cooper Tire & Rubber Company	69	683
Tandy Corporation	70	646
Lear Siegler, Inc.	71	638
Allied Bancshares, Inc.	72	587
Johnson Controls, Inc.	73	537
Pacific Telecom, Inc.	74	511
Mayflower Corporation	75	506
Tyco Laboratories, Inc.	76	504
American Stores Company	77	500
Communications Industries, Inc	78	481
E-Systems, Inc.	79	475
Grow Group, Inc.	80	423
Smithfield Foods, Inc.	81	408
Cox Communications, Inc.	82	405
Zero Corporation	83	399
Camco Incorporated	84	386
PHH Group, Inc.	85	374
Entex, Inc.	86	346
Alaska Air Group, Inc.	87	338
Holly Corporation	88	277
SmithKline Beckman Corp.	89	254
Research Industries Corporation	90	220
Hewlett-Packard Company	91	187
Farmer's Group, Inc.	92	161
Data Products Corporation	93	156
Digital Equipment Corporation	94	143
Loctite Corporation	95	135
MCORP	96	110
Airbourne Freight Corporation	97	108
Gelman Sciences, Inc.	98	94
Public Service Co. of New Mexico	99	31
El Paso Electric Company	100	28
Kansas Gas & Electric Company	101	− 8

In fact, 98 of the 101 companies' stock prices outperformed Standard & Poor's 500 Stock Index. The three companies whose stock price increase did not beat the S & P 500 are the three utility companies in the group.

The following is the specific comparison of how the year-end closing stock price of the average 101 company increased between 1975 and 1984, compared with the increase in the S & P 500 over the same time.

	Increase in Year-End Stock Price 1975 through 1984
Standard & Poor's 500 Stock Index	+ 82%
Average of *America's 101* *Best Performing Companies'* Stock Prices	+ 3,937%

Let's put it another way. Had you invested $100 in something called the S & P 500 Index back in 1975, you would have $182 in your account by the end of 1984. If you had invested it, instead, in something called America's 101 Best Performing Companies, you would have had $4,037!! Some difference! Had you invested the money in Gerber Scientific Company, one of the 101, you would have ended up with $97,850!!

What Businesses Are They In?

The diversity continues. Conventional wisdom would lead you to believe companies turning in hot performances would be in fast growing high technology businesses. Nothing could be further from the truth. America's 101 Best Performing companies are in such diverse businesses that we have had to rely on Standard Industrial Classification (SIC)[2] codes to provide a structure to accommodate the 101 companies.

SIC codes are a "road map" through the U.S. economy. Businesses are grouped in categories, called Major Groups, of similar or related activities. Each Major Group is further subdivided into more specific categories. We have included 70 Major Groups that cover the for-profit economic segments of the economy. America's 101 Best Performing Companies are frequently active in many SIC code categories. Barry Wright Corporation reports sales in six different SIC codes, and so does E. G & G, Inc. A few companies, such as utilities, do business in only one SIC code.

[2] *The Standard Industrial Classification Manual* (SIC) is one of the most important tools that has been developed to promote the comparability of statistics describing various facets of the economy. The SIC defines industries in accordance with the composition and structure of the economy and covers the entire field of economic activities.

In an effort to focus on the core businesses of the 101 companies, we have assigned each company that reports multiple SIC code businesses a single SIC code based on the industry that accounted for the largest *single* segment of their sales in the most recent available year.

The results of this activity are displayed in Table 2-9. The 101 companies have core businesses in 33 out of the 70 SIC code categories, just about half of all of the areas of business activity. (Remember that we have a tiny fraction of *all* businesses here.) It is interesting also to note the general areas of business that have no representation by the 101 companies.

None of the 101 has a core business in agriculture, forestry, or fishing—the primary industries. Nor does any of them have a core business in the extractive industries—mining and oil and gas extraction. None of the 101 companies is active in the wholesale trades. Finally, there is no representation in activities that are essentially sole proprietorships, such as insurance agents, real estate agents, personal services, automotive repair and service stations, movie theaters, legal services, educational services, and social services.

Turning to those areas of economic activity where the 101 companies are represented, probably the most striking observation is how many *low-tech* businesses are represented: construction, glass manufacturing, food packing and beverages, clothing and furniture, packaging, printing and publishing, transportation, refuse collecting, retailing, and health care. That is not to say that these industries do not make use of high technology in performing their functions. Anyone who has ever seen a CAT scanner in a hospital understands that this machine represents extreme high tech brought to focus on providing better health care. However, despite all the equipment, health care is basically provided by low-tech doctors, nurses, aides, and orderlies.

In fact, two of the companies are in industries in which the conventional wisdom says the United States is completely uncompetitive: steel and tires.

That doesn't mean that high technology is not represented. Far from it. The single four digit SIC code with the most companies represented is computers—15 companies manufacture some sort of electrical and electronic machinery.

The point seems to be that outstanding performance is not defined by industry or type of business. The opportunity to become one of America's Best Performing Companies can be found in many, many sectors of the U.S. economy. That is good news, indeed. It means that we have the ability to compete in a wide variety of the world's markets since, in the end, it is not products or services that determines performance, but people!

Table 2-9. America's 101 Best Performing Companies Organized by Standard Industrial Classification Codes

SIC Code	*Company*
Major Group 01 Agricultural Production— Crops	None
Major Group 02 Agricultural Production— Livestock	None
Major Group 07 Agricultural Services	None
Major Group 08 Forestry	None
Major Group 09 Fishing, Hunting and Trapping	None
Major Group 10 Metal Mining	None
Major Group 11 Anthracite Mining	None
Major Group 12 Bituminous Coal and Lignite Mining	None
Major Group 13 Oil & Gas Extraction	None
Major Group 14 Mining and Quarrying of Nonmetallic Minerals	None
Major Group 15 Building Construction— General Contractors and Operative Builders	SIC 1521 General Building Contractors— *Residential Buildings* Pulte Home Corporation Standard-Pacific Corporation SIC 1541 General Building Contractors— *Nonresidential Buildings* Research Industries Corporation
Major Group 16 Other Construction	None

SIC Code	Company
Major Group 17 Special Trade Contractors	SIC 1793 *Glass and Glazing Work* Apogee Enterprises
Major Group 20 SIC 2011 Manufacturing— Food and kindred Products	*Meat Packing Plants* Smithfield Foods, Inc. SIC 2082 *Malt Beverages* G. Heileman Brewing Company SIC 2086 *Bottled and Canned Soft Drinks* MEI Corporation
Major Group 21 Tobacco Manufacturers	None
Major Group 22	SIC 2253 *Knit Outerwear Mills* State o Maine, Inc.
Major Group 23 Apparel and Other Finished Products	None
Major Group 24 Lumber and Wood Products	None
Major Group 25 Furniture and Fixtures	SIC 2521 *Wood Office Furniture* Herman Miller, Inc.
Major Group 26 Paper and Allied Products	SIC 2641 *Paper Coating and Glazing* Tyco Laboratories, Inc. SIC 2647 *Sanitary Paper Products* James River Corp. of Virginia SIC 2561 *Folding Paperboard Boxes* Astronics Corporation
Major Group 27 Printing, Publishing and Allied Industries	SIC 2711 *Newspapers* Washington Post Company SIC 2721 *Periodicals*

	Plenum Publishing Corporation
	SIC 2753
	Engraving and Plate Printing
	Bowne & Co., Inc.
	SIC 2782
	Blankbooks, Looseleaf Binders
	John H. Harland Company
Major Group 28 Chemicals and Allied Products	28 SIC 2834 *Pharmaceutical Preparations* SmithKline Beckman Corporation SIC 2851 *Paints, Varnishes, Lacquers,* *Enamels* Grow Group, Inc. SIC 2891 *Adhesives and Sealants* Loctite Corporation
Major Group 29 Petroleum Refining	SIC 2911 *Petroleum Refining* Holly Corporation
Major Group 30 Rubber and Miscellaneous Plastics Products	SIC 3011 *Tires and Inner Tubes* Cooper Tire & Rubber Company SIC 3069 *Fabricated Rubber Products, NEC* Transtechnology Corporation Versa Technologies, Inc. Carlisle Corporation SIC 3079 *Miscellaneous Plastics Products* RAI Research Corporation
Major Group 31 Leather and Leather Products	None
Major Group 32 Stone, Clay, Glass and Concrete Products	None
Major Group 33 Primary Metal Industries	SIC 3312 *Blast Furnaces, Steel Works and* *Rolling Mills* Nucor Corporation

Major Group 34 Fabricated Metal Products	SIC 3469 *Metal Stampings, NEC* Zero Corporation SIC 3499 *Fabricated Metal Products, NEC* Barry Wright Corporation
Major Group 35 Machinery, except Electrical	SIC 3533 *Oil Field Machinery and Equipment* Camco Incorporated SIC 3559 *Special Industry Machinery, NEC* Gerber Scientific, Inc. SIC 3569 *General Industrial Machinery NEC* Pacific Scientific Company Gelman Sciences, Inc. SIC 3573 *Electronic Computing Equipment* Data Products Corporation Digital Equipment Corporation Dynatech Corporation Hewlett-Packard Company Prime Computer, Inc. Telex Corporation Wang Laboratories, Inc.
Major Group 36 Electrical and Electronic Machinery, Equipment and Supplies	SIC 3621 *Motors and Generators* Aeroflex Laboratories, Inc. SIC 3661 *Telephone and Telegraph Apparatus* Porta Systems Corporation SIC 3662 *Radio and Television Transmitting,* *Signaling and Detection Equipment* Aydin Corporation California Microwave, Inc. Communications Industries, Inc Electrospace Systems, Inc. SCI Systems, Inc. Whitehall Corporation SIC 3674 *Semiconductors and Related* *Devices*

	Advanced Micro Devices, Inc.
	E-Systems, Inc.
	M/A Com, Inc.
	Unitrode Corporation
	Vishay Intertechnology, Inc.
	SIC 3679
	Electronic Components, NEC
	Alpha Industries, Inc.
	Analogic Corporation
Major Group 37 Transportation Equipment	SIC 3714 *Motor Vechicle Parts and Accessories* Teleflex, Inc. SIC 3721 *Aircraft* Lear Siegler, Inc.
Major Group 38 Measuring, Analyzing and Controlling Instruments	SIC 3822 *Automatic Controls* Johnson Controls, Inc. SIC 3823 *Instruments for Process Variables* EG & G, Inc. SIC 3825 *Instruments for Measuring Electricity* Dranetz Technologies, Inc. General Microwave Corp. Teradyne, Inc.
Major Group 39 Miscellaneous Manufacturing	None
Major Group 40 Railroad Transportation	None
Major Group 41 Local, Suburban and Interurban Passenger Transportation	None
Major Group 42 Motor Freight Transportation and Warehousing	SIC 4213 *Trucking, Except Local* Mayflower Corporation
Major Group 44 Water Transportation	None
Major Group 45	SIC 4511

SIC Code	Company
Transportation by Air	*Air Transportation, Certified Carriers* Alaska Air Group, Inc. Piedmont Aviation, Inc.
Major Group 46 Pipelines, Except Natural Gas	None
Major Group 47 Transportation Services	SIC 4712 *Freight Forwarding* Airbourne Freight Corporation
Major Group 48 Communication	SIC 4811 *Telephone Communications* Pacific Telecom, Inc. SIC 4833 *Television Broadcasting* Adams Russell Company Cox Communications, Inc. Gray Communications Systems, Inc. Multimedia, Inc.
Major Group 49 Electric, Gas and Sanitary Services	SIC 4911 *Electric Services* El Paso Electric Company Kansas Gas & Electric Company Public Service Co. of New Mexico SIC 4922 *Natural Gas Transmission* Lear Petroleum Corporation Texas Oil & Gas Corporation SIC 4923 *Natural Gas Transmission and* *Distribution* Entex, Inc. SIC 4953 *Refuse Systems* Waste Management, Inc.
Major Group 50 Wholesale Trade—Durable Goods	None
Major Group 51 Wholesale Trade—Nondurable Goods	None
Major Group 52 Building Materials, Hardware Garden supply and Mobile Home	None

Retailers

Major Group 53 General Merchandise Stores	SIC 5331 *Variety Stores* Family Dollar Stores Pic'n Save Corporation
Major Group 54 Food Stores	SIC 5411 *Grocery Stores* American Stores Company National Convenience Stores
Major Group 55 Automobile Dealers and Gasolene Service Stations	None
Major Group 56 Apparel and Accessory Stores	SIC 5621 *Women's Ready-to-Wear Stores* Limited, Inc.
Major Group 57 Furniture, Home Furnishings and Equipment Stores	SIC 5732 *Radio and Television Stores* Tandy Corporation
Major Group 58 Eating and Drinking Places	SIC 5812 *Eating Places* Luby's Cafeteria's, Inc.
Major Group 59 Miscellaneous Retail	Sic 5999 *Retail Stores, NEC* D O C Optics Corporation
Major Group 60 Banking	SIC 6025 *National Banks* Allied bancshares, Inc. MCORP
Major Group 61 Credit Agencies Other Than Banks	None
Major Group 62 Security and Commodity Brokers, Dealers, Exchanges and Services	SIC 6211 *Security Brokers and Dealers* Dreyfuss Corporation
Major Group 63 Insurance	SIC 6331 *Fire, Marine and Casualty* *Insurance* Farmers' Group, Inc.

SIC Code	Company
	SIC 6361 *Title Insurance* Stewart Information Services, Inc.
Major Group 64 Insurance Agents	None
Major Group 65 Real Estate	None
Major Group 67 Holding and Other Investment Offices	None
Major Group 70 Hotels and Lodging Places	None
Major Group 72 Personal Services	None
Major Group 73 Business Services	SIC 7321 *Consumer Credit Reporting* Chilton Corporation SIC 7379 *Computer Related Services, NEC* Auxton Computer Enterprises SIC 7392 *Management, Consulting and* *Public Relations* PHH Group, Inc.
Major Group 75 Automotive Repair and Services	None
Major Group 78 Motion Pictures	None
Major Group 79 Amusement and Recreation Services	None
Major Group 80 Health Services	SIC 8051 *Skilled Nursing Care Facilities* Vari-Care, Inc. SIC 8062 *General Medical and Surgical* *Hospitals* American Medical International Charter Medical Corporation Hospital Corporation of America

	Humana, Inc.
	National Medical Enterprises, Inc.
	SIC 8063
	Psychiatric Hospitals
	Community Psychiatric Centers
Major Group 81	
Legal Services	None
Major Group 82	
Educational Services	None
Major Group 83	
Social Services	None
Major Group 89	SIC 8911
Miscellaneous Services	*Engineering, Architectural and*
	Surveying
	Logicon, Inc.

Length of Time in Business

In 1775, Robert Bowne opened a store a few blocks from Wall Street in New York and began to sell writing paper, account books, quill pens, bolting cloths, furs, nails and cutlery. As stationery sales began to represent a more significant part of the store's volume, Robert Bowne began to print his own stationery. By the 1820s, Bowne & Co. was exclusively a stationer and a printer. Now, *210 years later,* Bowne & Co. Inc. is one of the country's premier financial document printers and one of America's 101 Best Performing Companies.

In 1830, a pair of brothers who had recently emigrated from Germany anglicized their name to Smith and began to sell patent medicines from the tailgate of a horse drawn wagon. Now, *150 years later,* SmithKline & Beckman Corporation is one of the world's leading suppliers of prescription and proprietary products for human and animal health, as well as diagnostic and analytical products and services that facilitate the detection and treatment of disease, *and* one of America's 101 Best Performing Companies.

In 1883, Warren Seymour Johnson applied for U.S. Patent #281,884 on a device that he described as an "electric tele-thermo-scope." The patent was granted, and in 1885 the Johnson Electric Service Company was incorporated with a charter "to manufacture, sell, and deal in electric and pneumatic apparatus, and to construct and apply the same to public and private buildings in order to regulate temperature or control gasses." Over *100 years later,* Johnson Controls, Inc.'s major business is the design, installation, and service of control systems for commercial buildings, and it is one of America's 101 Best Performing Companies.

This fascinating exercise could go on, but we'll try to make the point in another way.

- In 1975, the Vietnam War ended and, obviously, all of America's 101 Best Performing companies were in business.
- In 1953, the Korean War ended, and 45 of the companies were already in business.
- In 1945, World War II ended, and 31 of the companies were in business.
- In 1918, World War I ended, and 17 of the companies were in business.
- In 1898, the Spanish-American War ended, and 11 of America's· Best were already at work.
- In 1865, the Civil War ended, and 3 of America's Best were doing business.
- In 1781, the Revolutionary War was over, and Robert Bowne had already been selling stationery in New York City for six years.

The conventional wisdom would have you believe that growth companies have to be young companies, because old companies get senile and lose their abilities to compete. Table 2–10 should dispel that nonsense forever. The table displays the year that each of America's 101 Best Performing Companies was founded. The history of these companies is nothing less than the history of the United States. Their performance indicates that they are also the future of the United States.

Table 2–10. America's 101 Best Performing Companies Ranked by Longevity

Company	Rank	Year Founded
Bowne & Co., Inc.	1	1775
SmithKline Beckman Corporation	2	1830
G. Heileman Brewing Company	3	1853
Johnson Controls, Inc.	4	1885
Multimedia, Inc.	5	1888
MCORP	6	1890
Smithfield Foods, Inc.	7	1890
MEI Corporation	8	1895

Company	Rank	Year Founded
Stewart Information Services	9	1896
Chilton Corporation	10	1897
Gray Communication Systems	11	1897
Tandy Corporation	12	1899
El Paso Electric Company	13	1901
Kansas Gas & Electric Company	14	1909
Cooper Tire & Rubber Company	15	1914
Carlisle Corporation	16	1917
Pacific Scientific Company	17	1918
John H. Harland Company	18	1923
Farmer's Group, Inc.	19	1927
Mayflower Corporation	20	1927
Herman Miller, Inc.	21	1930
Grow Group, Inc.	22	1934
Alaska Air Group, Inc.	23	1937
Aeroflex Laboratories, Inc.	24	1938
American Stores Company	25	1939
Hewlett-Packard Company	26	1939
Piedmont Aviation, Inc.	27	1940
Teleflex, Inc.	28	1943
Barry Wright Corporation	29	1943
EG & G, Inc.	30	1945
Luby's Cafeterias, Inc.	31	1945
Camco Incorporated	32	1946
Communications Industries, Inc.	33	1946
PHH Group, Inc.	34	1946
Plenum Publishing Company	35	1946
Public Service Co. of New Mexico	36	1946
Holly Corporation	37	1947
Washington Post Company	38	1947
Gerber Scientific, Inc.	39	1948
Apogee Enterprises	40	1949
M/A Com, Inc.	41	1950
Pic'n Save Corporation	42	1950
Wang Laboratories	43	1951
Zero Corporation	44	1952
Loctite Corporation	45	1953
Lear Siegler, Inc.	46	1954
Texas Oil & Gas Corporation	47	1954
General Microwave Corporation	48	1955
Nucor Corporation	49	1955
Pacific Telecom, Inc.	50	1955
American Medical International	51	1956

Company	Rank	Year Founded
Pulte Home Corporation	52	1956
Digital Equipment Corporation	53	1957
Adams Russell Company	54	1958
RAI Research Corporation	55	1958
Dynatech Corporation	56	1959
Family Dollar Stores	57	1959
Gelman Sciences, Inc.	58	1959
National Convenience Stores	59	1960
Teradyne, Inc.	60	1960
Unitrode Corporation	61	1960
D O C Optics Corporation	62	1961
Humana, Inc.	63	1961
Logicon, Inc.	64	1961
SCI Systems, Inc.	65	1961
Standard-Pacific Corporation	66	1961
Data Products Corporation	67	1962
Dranetz Technologies, Inc.	68	1962
Tyco Laboratories, Inc.	69	1962
Vishay Intertechnology, Inc.	70	1962
Whitehall Corporation	71	1962
Limited, Inc.	72	1963
Telex Corporation	73	1963
Cox Communications, Inc.	74	1964
E-Systems, Inc.	75	1964
Dreyfuss Corporation	76	1965
Alpha Industries, Inc.	77	1966
Entex, Inc.	78	1966
State o Maine, Inc.	79	1966
Aydin Corporation	80	1967
Airbourne Freight Corporation	81	1968
Analogic Corporation	82	1968
Astronics Corporation	83	1968
California Microwave, Inc.	84	1968
Lear Petroleum Corporation	85	1968
Research Industries Corporation	86	1968
Vari-Care, Inc.	87	1968
Waste Management, Inc.	88	1968
Advanced Micro Devices, Inc.	89	1969
Auxton Computer Enterprises	90	1969
Charter Medical Corporation	91	1969
Community Psychiatric Centers	92	1969
Hospital Corporation of Amearica	93	1969

Company	Rank	Year Founded
James River Corp. of Virginia	94	1969
National Medical Enterprises	95	1969
Porta Systems Corporation	96	1969
Electrospace Systems, Inc.	97	1970
Versa Technologies, Inc.	98	1971
Prime Computer, Inc.	99	1972
Allied Bancshares, Inc.	100	1971
Transtechnology Corporation	101	1974

Research and Development Expenditures

One of the reasons frequently advanced for the United States' declining competitive abilities is a failure to invest in research and development and, as a result, innovation is increasingly coming from other countries. A failure to invest in research and development is also cited as a reason for our declining productivity. We haven't invested enough in finding ways to do the work better.

These are difficult charges to analyze, but they seem substantial enough that we should examine how America's 101 Best Performing Companies deal with research and development investments.

Generally Accepted Accounting Principles indicate that publicly owned companies should specify their expenditures for research and development when they become "significant." Thirty-one of the America's 101 Best Performing Companies specify their research and development expenditures specifically on their income statements. These data are presented in Table 2–11.

In total, these 31 companies spent over $2 billion on research and development in their most recent fiscal year.

This expenditure averages 6.8 percent of the group's total sales and the median expenditure is 6.7 percent of sales. By way of comparison, *Business Week's* annual survey of research and development expenditures by all U.S. businesses indicates that in 1984, an average U.S. business spent 2.3 percent of sales on R & D.[3] Since that is only about one-third of the percentage of sales that America's 101 Best Performing Companies invest in R & D, those charges about starving R & D may well have substance.

[3] "R & D Scoreboard," *Business Week*, March 22, 1985, p. 192.

Table 2–11.   America's 101 Best Performing Companies Most Recent Annual Research & Development Expenditures

Company	Percent of Annual Sales	Total R & D Expenditure
Advanced Micro Devices, Inc.	17.3%	$101,335,000
Analogic Corporation	12.6	17,845,000
Teradyne, Inc.	11.3	44,218,000
Digital Equipment Corporation	11.2	630,696,000
Porta Systems Corporation	10.5	3,109,000
Research Industries Corporation	10.3	599,000
Prime Computer, Inc.	10.2	64,062,000
Electrospace Systems, Inc.	10.2	8,111,000
Hewlett-Packard Company	9.7	592,000,000
SmithKline Beckman Corporation	9.4	279,200,000
Dynatech Corporation	8.1	12,111,000
Alpha Industries, Inc.	7.4	4,476,000
Data Products Corporation	7.2	28,816,000
Wang Laboratories	7.0	160,500,000
EG & G, Inc.	6.8	73,700,000
Gelman Sciences, Inc.	6.7	2,899,000
Gerber Scientific, Inc.	6.1	10,594,000
Aydin Corporation	5.8	8,047,000
Dranetz Technologies, Inc.	5.7	1,552,000
Unitrode Corporation	5.5	8,813,000
Pacific Scientific Corporation	4.8	4,453,000
M/A Com, Inc.	4.3	33,598,000
Telex Corporation	4.2	14,927,000
Adams Russell Company	4.2	4,620,000
Whitehall Corporation	3.9	2,531,000
Herman Miller, Inc.	3.4	13,943,000
General Microwave Corporation	3.2	388,000
Loctite Corporation	3.1	7,610,000
California Microwave, Inc.	3.1	3,492,000
Grow Group, Inc.	2.4	6,872,000
RAI Research Corporation	2.3	165,000

Total R & D Expenditures: $2,145,282,000
Average R & D Expenditures As a % of Annual Sales: 6.8%

3

PROFILES OF AMERICA'S 101 BEST PERFORMING COMPANIES

This chapter contains brief, descriptive profiles of each of America's Best Performing Companies. The Statement of Income shown for each company is the most recent two years available. None of the data in the Income Statements is re-stated.

In the Stockholder's Equity, Jobs, and Labor Productivity table, Stockholder's Equity and Net Sales are *not* re-stated numbers. The Index of Labor Productivity is described in Chapter One.

In the Capital Productivity table, the Total Invested Capital and the Net Income, or Funds From Operations, data are also *not* re-stated numbers. The Index of Capital Productivity is described in Chapter One.

In the Stock Prices and Earnings Per Share table, the numbers *are* re-stated to reflect any stock splits and/or stock dividends that occurred in any of the years 1975 through 1984. Adjustments were made from 1984 backward to 1975.

There are significant differences in the way the 101 companies report similar kinds of financial data in their financial statements. This is so even among companies engaged in similar businesses and operating in the same industries. It includes the inconsistent reporting and restating of items such as the results from foreign operations, the results of subsidiaries, interest income, extraordinary items, and so forth. Although efforts were made to limit these inconsistencies as much as possible, they could not be completely eliminated.

Also, in constructing the historical financial tables for the 101 companies whose fiscal years do not coincide with the calendar year, decisions had to be made on which year to show certain financial data. Inevitably, therefore, some of the 101 companies that report on a fiscal year basis may show discrepancies in year-to-year comparisons between their most recent Statements of Income figures and their Net Sales and Net Income data shown in the 1983/75 historical tables.

ADAMS-RUSSELL CO., INC.

Corporate Headquarters: 1380 Main Street
                          Waltham, MA 02154

Telephone: (617) 894-8540
Incorporated in Massachusetts
American Stock Exchange—AAR

Business: Manufactures telecommunications products in the areas of defense electronics, intelligence collection and analysis, communications, entertainment and CATV advertising.

Officers:
John J. Lynch, President & Chief Financial Officer
Joseph S. Batal, Vice President, Human Resources
John Brockman, Vice President, Cable Services
Kennett F. Burnes, Clerk (Partner, Choate, Hall & Stewart)
James J. Connolly, Group Vice President, Electronics & Instruments
William C. Henchy, Vice President
Trevor Lambert, Vice President, Corporate Development
Harold H. Leach, Group Vice President, Aerospace Products
David J. MacLachlan, Vice President, Finance, and Secretary

Statement of Income (Year ends 8/30—$ figures in 000's)

	1984	1983
Net Sales	$109,663	$91,883
Costs and Expenses		
Cost of Sales	$ 64,912	$56,156
Selling, General and Administrative Expenses	24,610	21,547
Research & Development Expense	4,620	2,719
Total	$ 94,142	$80,332
Operating Income	$ 15,521	$11,551
Other Income (Expense)		
Interest Expense	$ (4,603)	$(3,530)
Interest Income and Other Income	195	518
Total	$ (4,408)	$(3,012)
Income from Continuing Operation before Income Taxes	$ 11,113	$ 8,539
Provision for Income Taxes	3,293	1,922
Income from Continuing Operations	$ 7,820	$ 6,617
Income from Discontinued Operations	$ —	$ 3,163
Net Income	$ 7,820	$ 9,780

56

Stockholder's Equity, Jobs, and Labor Productivity ($ figures in 000's)

Year	Stockholder's Equity	Net Sales	Number of Employees	Index of Labor Productivity
1975	$ 3,348	$14,517	510	28.456
1976	4,819	15,882	470	33.791
1977	5,843	17,639	510	34.586
1978	6,238	24,111	520	46.367
1979	8,146	28,387	600	47.312
1980	17,549	36,099	738	48.915
1981	26,472	59,937	1,100	54.488
1982	33,257	71,859	1,300	55.276
1983	43,488	91,883	1,370	67.068
Change, 1983/1975	+1,199 %	+533 %	+169 %	+136 %

Capital Productivity ($ figures in 000's)

Year	Total Invested Capital	Net Income	Index of Capital Productivity
1975	$13,279	$ 385	.029
1976	12,887	633	.049
1977	14,099	1,059	.075
1978	17,336	1,461	.084
1979	20,635	1,097	.092
1980	30,074	2,712	.090
1981	42,446	5,108	.120
1982	70,317	6,003	.085
1983	83,148	9,780	.118
Change, 1983/1975	+527 %	+2,440 %	+306 %

Stock Prices and Earnings per Share[*]

Year	Stock Prices			Earnings[**] Per Share
	High	Low	Close	
1975	$ .794	$ .238	$ .635	$ .098
1976	1.706	.635	1.230	.159
1977	2.024	1.190	1.984	.273
1978	4.841	1.905	3.333	.375
1979	9.008	3.214	8.056	.476
1980	18.667	6.222	17.611	.627
1981	19.317	11.750	13.333	.860
1982	22.667	12.083	20.250	1.000
1983	30.875	20.000	25.500	1.610
1984	25.500	15.875	24.250	1.280

Change, 1975–84 +3,719%; change, S&P 500 Index, 1975–84 +82%

[*]Adjusted for stock splits and stock dividends   [**]Includes extraordinary items

57

The company develops products for several specialized markets within the telecommunications field. Its Electronic Products group designs, manufactures, and markets a wide range of electronic products subassemblies and systems, directed at five specialized markets: electronic warfare; command, control, and communications; intelligence collection; missile electronics; and radar and telemetry applications. Its Telecommunications group owns and operates cable television systems located primarily in the northwestern United States and has more than 134,000 basic subscribers; this group also manufactures automatic advertising insertion equipment for the CATV industry. The company has enjoyed consistent growth in net income from continuing operations, and it set a new record during fiscal 1985. Fiscal 1983 results reflected the sale of a television tion at a significant gain. The company's stated objective is to continue to grow at a rate in excess of 20 percent.

Basically, what Adams-Russell has done is develop an offset to its defense electronics business that shares much of the technological base but responds to completely different market conditions. That offset is Adams-Russell's growing position in cable television.

Cable television as an industry is currently in a period of shakeout, which appears to be passing quickly as mergers and acquisitions rationalize the industry. How much of the $22 billion currently being spent on TV advertising can be diverted to CATV remains to be determined. However large the business becomes, Adams-Russell will be a significant player.

ADVANCED MICRO DEVICES, INC.

Corporate Headquarters: 901 Thompson Place
Sunnyvale, CA 94088
Telephone: (408) 732-2400
Incorporated in Delaware
New York Stock Exchange—AMD

Business: Manufactures complex proprietary and industry standard integrated circuits for producers of electronic systems.

Officers:

W. J. Sanders III, President and Chief Executive Officer
Anthony B. Holbrook, Executive Vice President and Chief Operating Officer
James B. Downey, Senior Vice President, Operations
Richard Previte, Senior Vice President, Finance and Treasurer
George M. Scalise, Senior Vice President, Chief Accounting Officer and Secretary
Stephan Zelencik, Senior Vice President, Sales and Marketing
Gene Conner, Vice President and Group Executive
James N. Miller, Vice President and Group Executive
Thomas W. Armstrong, Vice President, General Counsel
Marvin Burkett, Vice President, Controller
Stanley Winvick, Vice President, Human Resources
Vice Presidents: Benjamin M. Anixter, Glen Balzer, Frank Barone, Donald M. Brettner, James A. Cunningham, Brian Currie, Frank DiGesualdo, J. Philip Downing, John East, W. Curtis Francis, Clive Ghest, Alfred G. Lapierre, David A. Laws, James D. Lynch, W. Richard Marz, David Simpson, Terry Smith, Elliot Sopkin

Statement of Income (Year ends 3/31—$ figures in 000's)

	1985	1984
Net Sales	$931,079	$583,346
Expenses:		
Cost of Sales	$428,181	$276,522
Research and Development	164,200	101,335
Marketing, General and Administrative	158,901	108,206
	$751,282	$486,063
Operating Income	$179,797	$ 97,283
Interest (Income) Expense, Net	(2,025)	851
Income before Taxes on Income	$181,822	$ 96,432
Provision for Taxes on Income	46,453	25,321
Net Income	$135,369	$ 71,111

Stockholder's Equity, Jobs, and Labor Productivity ($ figures in 000's)

Year	Stockholder's Equity	Net Sales	Number of Employees	Index of Labor Productivity
1975	$ 11,641	$ 34,387	1,927	17.845
1976	16,932	62,116	2,947	21.078
1977	45,016	92,331	4,523	20.414
1978	57,534	148,276	6,632	22.358
1979	87,513	225,593	7,976	28.284
1980	118,600	309,391	9,915	31.204
1981	131,974	281,580	9,904	28.431
1982	183,354	358,345	10,521	34.060
1983	278,574	583,346	13,067	44.643
Change, 1983/1975	+2,293 %	+1,596 %	+578 %	+150 %

Capital Productivity ($ figures in 000's)

Year	Total Invested Capital	Net Income	Index of Capital Productivity
1975	$ 15,813	$ 1,434	.091
1976	25,492	4,474	.176
1977	51,804	5,037	.097
1978	63,951	10,955	.171
1979	102,030	23,277	.228
1980	147,554	24,684	.167
1981	168,794	8,950	.053
1982	220,656	20,983	.095
1983	305,999	71,111	.232
Change, 1983/1975	+1,835 %	+4,859 %	+156 %

Stock Prices and Earnings per Share[*]

Year	Stock Prices			Earnings[**] Per Share
	High	Low	Close	
1975	$ 1.093	$ .139	$ .944	$ .040
1976	2.491	.907	1.870	.121
1977	2.185	1.259	1.648	.131
1978	3.153	1.292	2.417	.247
1979	6.396	2.021	6.042	.490
1980	14.833	4.500	11.500	.517
1981	12.083	4.667	5.875	.183
1982	14.000	5.188	12.563	.390
1983	35.500	12.125	33.625	1.230
1984	41.125	25.125	29.500	2.320

Change, 1975–84 +3,024%; change, S&P 500 Index, 1975–84 +82%

[*]Adjusted for stock splits and stock dividends   [**]Includes extraordinary items

Note: The fiscal year financial results in the tables above are shown in the year in which most of the results were achieved.

This company, founded in 1969, is a leading manufacturer of complex proprietary and industry-standard integrated circuits (ICs). The ICs are sold principally to producers of electronic systems for commercial and military computations, communications firms, and instrumentation markets. The company's product portfolio includes microprocessors, peripherals, memory devices, analogs and logic procedures using advanced biopolar and MOS large scale integrated circuit technologies. The company's outstanding growth to nearly billion dollar status has been accomplished by aggressive technological leadership and investment. During the last five years, research and development expenditures have consistently exceeded 15 percent of sales. At press time, the company is facing its greatest challenges ever, as it contends with significant falloff in demand for its products and unprecedented pricing pressures. Its short term response has been to launch a cost reduction program called STAUNCH (Stress Those Actions Urgently Needed to Check Hemorrhaging). This innovative program represents a "no layoff" approach to reducing costs, and includes four-day work weeks and pay cuts for executives.

Some of the 101 Best Performing Companies are the lengthened shadow of a single man. Advanced Micro Devices is one. ADM's substance and style is a direct reflection of its flashy founder and chairman, W. J. "Jerry" Sanders, III. The STAUNCH program is pure "we're all in this together" Sanders and ADM employees love it.

While founder/managers can sometimes stifle growth after their companies reach a certain size, Sanders has found ways to accelerate growth. He has created 13 relatively independent, entrepreneurial "companies" within ADM. Each of these groups finds market needs and develops products to meet those needs. ADM is market driven in an industry where companies are frequently technology driven and out of touch with their markets.

AIRBORNE FREIGHT CORPORATION

Corporate Headquarters: 190 Queen Anne Avenue North
Seattle, WA 98111
Telephone: (206) 285-4600
Incorporated in Delaware
New York Stock Exchange—ABF

Business: An air transport company providing over-night delivery service for small packages and documents throughout the United States.

Officers:
Robert S. Cline, Chairman and Chief Executive Officer
Robert G. Brazier, President and Chief Operating Officer
Kent W. Freudenberger, Executive Vice President, Marketing Division
Roy C. Liljebeck, Executive Vice President, Chief Financial Officer and Treasurer
Raymond T. Van Bruwaene, Executive Vice President, Operations Division
John J. Cella, Senior Vice President, International Division
Frank C. Steele, Senior Vice President, Sales
David A. Billings, Vice President, Corporate Systems
James J. Guiod, Vice President, Eastern Sales Division
Hal D. McClellan, Vice President, Human Resources
Lanny H. Michael, Controller
Earl L. Richardson, Vice President, Mid-Continent Region
Thomas W. Rooney, Vice President, Corporate Marketing
David H. Scheevel, Vice President, Revenue and Property Control
Don A. Smith, Vice President, Operations, Division II
Harry K. Sprague, Assistant Vice President, Traffic
Jack Wilbourne, Secretary
J. Vernon Williams, Assistant Secretary
William E. York, Vice President, Southeast Region

Statement of Income (Year ends 12/31—$ figures in 000's)

	1984	1983
Revenues	$417,854	$334,777
Operating Expenses:		
Transportation Purchased	$156,498	$114,411
Station and Ground Operations	107,706	89,181
Flight Operations and Maintenance	50,959	46,520
General and Administrative	34,600	27,407
Sales and Advertising	29,359	23,762
Depreciation and Amortization	15,889	14,359
	$395,011	$315,640
Operating Income	$ 22,843	$ 19,137
Interest Expense, Net	$ (1,621)	$ (1,838)
Contribution to Profit Sharing Plan	(1,486)	(1,778)
Earnings before Income Taxes	$ 19,736	$ 15,521
Income Taxes	8,907	6,590
Net Earnings	$ 10,829	$ 8,931

Stockholder's Equity, Jobs, and Labor Productivity ($ figures in 000's)

Year	Stockholder's Equity	Net Sales	Number of Employees	Index of Labor Productivity
1975	$16,216	$113,011	1,900	59.479
1976	19,711	132,882	2,058	64.569
1977	23,634	150,387	2,050	73.360
1978	28,768	187,915	2,286	82.203
1979	33,986	246,379	2,297	107.261
1980	42,537	286,616	3,127	91.658
1981	42,234	279,698	2,787	100.358
1982	43,061	295,213	2,947	100.174
1983	68,458	334,777	3,304	101.325
Change, 1983/1975	+322 %	+196 %	+74 %	+71 %

Capital Productivity ($ figures in 000's)

Year	Total Invested Capital	Funds from Operations	Index of Capital Productivity
1975	$16,216	$ 5,010	.309
1976	19,711	6,723	.341
1977	23,634	7,928	.335
1978	28,768	10,670	.371
1979	33,986	12,263	.361
1980	62,447	14,809	.237
1981	68,974	15,953	.231
1982	76,340	20,662	.271
1983	78,619	29,232	.372
Change, 1983/1975	+385 %	+484 %	+20 %

Stock Prices and Earnings per Share[*]

	Stock Prices			Earnings[**]
Year	High	Low	Close	Per Share
1975	$ 9.333	$ 3.250	$ 8.917	$ .847
1976	15.125	8.625	14.500	1.220
1977	16.000	11.500	15.750	1.450
1978	26.750	14.375	17.875	1.960
1979	28.250	17.625	26.500	2.170
1980	27.000	16.125	20.250	1.710
1981	22.125	9.125	9.750	.660
1982	17.500	7.750	14.250	.770
1983	30.875	13.625	29.750	1.600
1984	30.500	13.000	18.500	1.850

Change, 1975–84 +108%; change, S&P 500 Index, 1975–84 +82%

[*]Adjusted for stock splits and stock dividends   [**]Includes extraordinary items

CORPORATE PROFILE—AIRBORNE FREIGHT CORPORATION

The company provides integrated air and ground freight transportation, principally providing door-to-door express, next morning delivery of small packages and documents throughout the United States. It operates under the tradename "Airborne Express." The company is the number two carrier in the overnight express industry, following only Federal Express. It operates its own airline and a fleet of ground transportation vehicles. Each weeknight the airline flies approximately 54,000 air miles, serving 115 major cities in the United States. It provides next day service to over 20,300 cities, of which 8,746 receive service before noon. The company also provides air freight services for shipments of any size on a worldwide basis, using a combination of commercial air carriers, its airline and its own or independent ground transportation services. In all instances the company's commitment begins with pickup at point of origin and extends through final delivery. Domestic revenues represent about 80 percent of the total. The company during 1985 experienced pressure on operating income due to increasing competition and the maturing of the overnight express industry. Its stated goal is to be a "low cost producer" and to achieve an improving return on shareholder equity. Industry conditions will test management's ability to continue its record of recent growth.

ALASKA AIRGROUP, INC.

Corporate Headquarters: 19300 Pacific Highway South
                          Seattle, WA 98188
Telephone: (206) 433-3200
Incorporated in Alaska
New York Stock Exchange—ALK

Business: Provides passenger and freight air transportation services.
Officers:

Bruce R. Kennedy, Chairman, Chief Executive Officer and President
Gus Robinson, Executive Vice President, Chief Operating Officer
Robert E. Gray, Senior Vice President
James A. Johnson, Senior Vice President
G. Edward Bollinger, Vice President
John F. Kelly, Vice President
Marjorie E. Laws, Corporate Secretary
Kenneth F. Skids, Vice President
Raymond J. Vecci, Vice President
Douglas L. Versteeg, Vice President
J. Ray Vingo, Vice President
Jan David Blais, Staff Vice President
Patrick L. Glenn, Staff Vice President
William L. McKay, Regional Vice President
Robert H. Putman, Staff Vice President

Statement of Income (Year ends 12/31—$ figures in 000's)

	1984	1983
Operating Revenues		
Passenger	$312,244	$240,305
Freight and Mail	32,387	26,503
Public Service	3,604	3,587
Contract Service and Other, Net	11,407	10,239
Total Operating Revenues	$361,642	$280,634
Operating Expenses		
Wages and Benefits	$111,515	$ 88,291
Aircraft Fuel	87,196	69,713
Aircraft Maintenance	13,685	9,277
Aircraft Rent	17,263	11,572
Commissions	24,381	17,456
Depreciation and Amortization	12,098	10,748
Other	61,503	42,675
Total Operating Expenses	$327,641	$249,732
Operating Income	$ 34,001	$ 30,902
Other Income (Expense)		
Interest Expense	$ (9,264)	$ (6,860)
Interest Capitalized	3,926	1,153
Interest Income	5,780	4,280
Other, Net	(413)	(1,190)
	$ 29	$ (2,617)
Income before Income Tax Expense	$ 34,030	$ 28,285
Income Tax Expense	10,122	12,557
Net Income	$ 23,908	$ 15,728

Stockholder's Equity, Jobs, and Labor Productivity ($ figures in 000's)

Year	Stockholder's Equity	Net Sales	Number of Employees	Index of Labor Productivity
1975	$ 9,122	$ 66,620	1,238	53.813
1976	15,726	69,475	1,212	57.323
1977	19,894	76,518	1,305	58.634
1978	25,892	86,246	1,339	62.917
1979	12,664	98,200	1,343	73.120
1980	17,785	130,850	1,424	91.889
1981	29,876	181,960	1,573	115.677
1982	70,187	234,524	1,840	127.459
1983	86,608	280,634	2,245	125.004
Change, 1983/1975	+ 849 %	+ 321 %	+ 81 %	+ 132 %

Capital Productivity ($ figures in 000's)

Year	Total Invested Capital	Funds from Operations	Index of Capital Productivity
1975	$ 42,677	$ 9,532	.223
1976	44,704	10,358	.232
1977	45,877	10,762	.235
1978	63,781	11,676	.183
1979	41,654	7,906	.190
1980	59,910	8,103	.135
1981	91,879	18,539	.202
1982	125,956	32,059	.255
1983	160,163	83,453	.240
Change, 1983/1975	+ 275 %	+ 303 %	+ 8 %

Stock Prices and Earnings per Share[*]

| | Stock Prices | | | Earnings[**] |
Year	High	Low	Close	Per Share
1975	$ 4.850	$ 2.145	$ 3.451	$1.194
1976	4.995	3.428	3.918	1.544
1977	4.011	2.571	2.879	.691
1978	6.587	2.700	4.211	1.443
1979	6.463	3.855	4.535	.689
1980	5.119	3.095	3.929	1.038
1981	8.375	3.750	6.125	1.060
1982	14.375	4.625	13.250	1.260
1983	18.625	10.375	14.125	1.450
1984	17.250	9.250	15.125	2.190

Change, 1975–84 + 338%; change, S&P 500 Index, 1975–84 + 82%

[*]Adjusted for stock splits and stock dividends   [**]Includes extraordinary items

66

This outstanding company is the holding company for Alaska Airlines, which has historically provided air transportation service between the major cities in Alaska, and 11 cities in Washington, Oregon, California, and Idaho. During early 1985 the company inaugurated services between Seattle/Portland and Phoenix, Arizona. The company is increasing its continental U.S. airline activities by expanding its frequency of flights between Seattle and the various Los Angeles airports. The company's service pattern is based on two principal hubs: Anchorage and Seattle. For each of the last 11 years, the company carried more passengers between Alaska and the lower 48 states than any other airline. At yearend 1985, the company's fleet consisted of 11 owned and 16 leased Boeing jets. Included among the leased aircraft are three B727-200s, currently operated on the company's interchange routes with American Airlines, which provides through-plane service from Alaska to Chicago, Washington D.C., Dallas/Ft. Worth, and Houston. Over 60 small Alaskan communities are also served through contracts with local air carriers.

Alaska Airlines is one of a small group of regional airlines that have used deregulation to run circles around their major airline competitors. (Piedmont Aviation, another of America's 101 Best Performing Companies, is a second one.) Alaska Air's key to success is quite straightforward. It has studied the *entire* travel experience faced by passengers and provides the highest quality experience at every step of the way. It provides nothing more than what the larger airlines promise. The difference is that Alaska Airline delivers. It shows in the numbers.

ALLIED BANCSHARES, INC.

Corporate Headquarters: 1000 Louisiana
Houston, TX 77002
Telephone: (713) 224-6611
Incorporated in Texas
Over the Counter—ALBN

Business: Holding company for commercial banks, insurance and leasing companies.
Officers:
Walter M. Mischer, Chairman
Gerald H. Smith, Chief Executive Officer
D. Kent Anderson, President
Jay C. Crager, Jr., Executive Vice President, Chief Financial Officer and Secretary
Paul W. Carlisle, Jr., Senior Vice President—Operations
Robert B. Goldstein, Senior Vice President—Credit Administration
Andrew P. Greenwood, Senior Vice President—Marketing
Thomas Y. Hamilton, Senior Vice President—Human Resources
Frank C. McDowell, Senior Vice President—Real Estate
Thomas C. Clausen, Treasurer
Ernest Pekmezaris, Controller
Richard A. Durham, General Auditor
Gerald D. Billings, Vice President—Compliance
John R. Booth, Jr., Vice President—Portfolio Management
Robert B. Canning, Jr., Vice President—Investments
Charles G. Cooper, Vice President—Credit Administration
R. Wayne Crawford, Vice President—Corporate Planning
Henry M. Ellis, Vice President—Insurance
John J. Hanby, Jr., Vice President—Retail Lending
Carol Herder, Vice President—Leasing
Laura A. Horstman, Vice President—Facilities Coordinator
Debra D. Mathis, Vice President—Taxes
J. C. Pollard, Jr., Vice President—Financial Planning
Sherman L. Smith, Vice President—Funding Management
Betty A. Williams, Vice President—Financial Systems
Dianne Kendall, Compliance Officer

Statement of Income (Year ends 12/31—$ figures in 000's)

	1984	1983
Total Interest Income	$1,012,759	$749,285
Total Interest Expense	687,682	453,643
Net Interest Income	$ 325,077	$295,642
Provision for Possible Loan Losses	$ 64,296	$ 69,236
Net Interest Income after Provision for Possible Loan Losses	$ 260,781	$226,406
Total Non-Interest Income	$ 70,870	$ 69,302
Total Non-Interest Expenses	211,948	182,084
Earnings before Federal Income Taxes	$ 119,703	$113,624
Federal Income Taxes	$ 921	$ 10,393
Net Earnings	$ 118,782	$103,231

Stockholder's Equity, Jobs, and Labor Productivity ($ figures in 000's)

Year	Stockholder's Equity	Net Sales	Number of Employees	Index of Labor Productivity
1975	$ 65,963	$ 73,316	824	88.976
1976	76,661	79,069	859	92.048
1977	95,437	99,824	1,050	95.070
1978	116,896	139,566	1,250	111.653
1979	132,812	196,077	1,575	124.493
1980	161,674	294,351	1,900	154.922
1981	268,683	530,471	3,000	176.824
1982	368,541	709,828	3,450	205.747
1983	457,035	784,815	3,700	212.112
Change, 1983/1975	+593 %	+971 %	+349 %	+138 %

Capital Productivity ($ figures in 000's)

Year	Total Invested Capital	Net Income	Index of Capital Productivity
1975	$1,001,215	$12,131	.012
1976	1,136,008	13,590	.012
1977	1,440,086	17,163	.012
1978	1,781,795	22,891	.013
1979	2,260,305	28,415	.013
1980	2,855,186	37,295	.013
1981	4,441,289	62,917	.014
1982	6,010,628	82,348	.014
1983	7,895,070	98,776	.013
Change, 1983/1975	+689 %	+714 %	+3 %

Stock Prices and Earnings per Share[*]

Year	Stock Prices			Earnings[**] Per Share
	High	Low	Close	
1975	$ 3.556	$ 2.933	$ 3.111	$ .553
1976	5.356	3.156	5.222	.620
1977	5.534	5.022	5.200	.724
1978	7.440	4.960	6.267	.915
1979	9.200	6.267	9.200	1.129
1980	14.560	7.307	14.027	1.434
1981	21.840	13.840	20.960	1.933
1981	21.120	13.360	18.880	2.227
1983	27.500	16.700	21.900	2.544
1984	25.750	20.375	21.375	2.890

Change, 1975–84 +587%; change, S&P 500 Index, 1975–84 +82%

[*]Adjusted for stock splits and stock dividends   [**]Includes extraordinary items

This company is a multibank holding company. At yearend 1984, Allied owned 50 commercial banks and 6 bank-related subsidiaries. The subsidiaries include a credit life and accident and health insurance underwriting company, an insurance agency, a trust company, two leasing companies, and a small business investment corporation. Of the banks owned at yearend 1984, 34 were state banks incorporated under the Texas Banking Code, and 16 were national banking associations organized under the laws of the United States. Although Allied was incorporated during 1971, its active corporate existence dates from December 1972, when its first three banks were acquired. In total, through the end of 1984, five banks were started, and the 45 other banks were acquired as ongoing operating units. This firm has shown impressive performance during the last decade.

Allied Bancshare's management brings a wondrous commodity to managing its business, "common sense." Allied lends money to people and businesses it understands. That means small to medium sized businesses and the executive/professional segment of the consumer market. It also means doing business in East Texas only—Allied does not have a single dollar loaned in the international market.

Allied holds a high-quality, widely diversified portfolio. It could legally make loans up to $100 million, but its self-imposed limit is $30 million. In fact, in a loan portfolio that exceeded $6.9 billion on January 1, 1985, only 30 customers had loans over $15 million. Allied also understands that it is in a service business, and that in a service business, people are crucial. Allied encourages its employees to share in the ownership of the bank, thus giving them an added incentive to satisfy customers. Over 80 percent of Allied Bancshare's employees own stock in the bank.

ALPHA INDUSTRIES, INC.

Corporate Headquarters: 20 Sylvan Road
                                 Woburn, MA 01801
Telephone: (617) 935-5150
Incorporated in Delaware
American Stock Exchange—AHA

Business: Manufactures microwave ceramic and semiconductor devices, microwave components and multi-function systems.

Officers:
- George S. Kariotis, Chairman and Chief Executive Officer
- Martin J. Reid, President and Chief Operating Officer
- Allan L. Coon, Senior Vice President/Treasurer and Chief Financial Officer
- Constantine Kamnitsis, Senior Vice President
- Robert E. Goldwasser, Ph.D., Vice President
- Howard J. Hall, Vice President
- James C. Korcuba, Vice President
- Frank A. Leith, Vice President
- Donald E. Paulson, Secretary
- John A. Hanna, Jr., Assistant Treasurer
- Paul E. Vincent, Controller

Statement of Income (Year ends 3/31—$ figures in 000's)

	1985	1984
Sales	$69,278	$60,148
Cost of Sales	50,563	38,437
Selling and Administrative Expense	15,618	12,814
	$66,181	$51,251
Operating Income	$ 3,097	$ 8,897
Interest Expense	$ (370)	$ (390)
Interest and Other Income	1,216	1,502
	$ 846	$ 1,112
Income before Income Taxes	$ 3,943	$10,009
Income Taxes	$ 254	$ 4,455
Net Income	$ 3,689	$ 5,554

Stockholder's Equity, Jobs, and Labor Productivity ($ figures in 000's)

Year	Stockholder's Equity	Net Sales	Number of Employees	Index of Labor Productivity
1975	$ 2,612	$ 7,838	325	24.117
1976	3,542	10,077	360	27.992
1977	4,806	12,171	460	26.459
1978	5,982	16,374	525	31.189
1979	8,315	21,799	610	35.736
1980	18,737	29,579	780	37.922
1981	40,068	45,371	1,013	44.789
1982	45,581	52,219	1,120	46.624
1983	51,420	60,148	1,263	47.623
Change, 1983/1975	+ 1,869 %	+ 667 %	+ 289 %	+ 98 %

Capital Productivity ($ figures in 000's)

Year	Total Invested Capital	Net Income	Index of Capital Productivity
1975	$ 3,988	$ 180	.045
1976	4,975	775	.156
1977	6,193	1,148	.185
1978	7,448	1,334	.179
1979	10,442	1,873	.179
1980	21,369	2,775	.130
1981	42,768	4,515	.106
1982	49,979	5,213	.104
1983	55,540	5,554	.100
Change, 1983/1975	+ 1,293 %	+ 2,986 %	+ 122 %

Stock Prices and Earnings per Share[*]

Year	Stock Prices High	Low	Close	Earnings[**] Per Share
1975	$ .625	$ .208	$ .333	$.050
1976	.792	.333	.750	.210
1977	1.667	.667	1.458	.303
1978	3.083	1.292	2.250	.347
1979	6.438	2.188	6.188	.475
1980	15.125	5.188	13.313	.580
1981	19.688	10.125	14.000	.740
1982	20.000	9.250	17.625	.750
1983	28.125	16.250	21.625	.790
1984	22.250	9.500	11.375	.520

Change, 1975–84 + 3,313%; change, S&P 500 Index, 1975–84 + 82%

[*]Adjusted for stock splits and stock dividends   [**]Includes extraordinary items

Note: The fiscal year financial results in the tables above are shown in the year in which most of the results were achieved.

72

The company is a leading supplier of microwave ceramic and semiconductor devices, microwave and millimeter wave components, and multifunction subsystems that are sold to manufacturers of sophisticated electronics systems. These products generate, amplify, detect, and control microwave energy. Worldwide, Alpha services over 1,000 customers in three basic markets. The largest is the military defense electronics market, which accounts for approximately 60 percent of Alpha's sales. The balance of sales consists of microwave products sold to the telecommunications industry and for commercial avionics, marine radar, and radar and motion detection applications. Approximately 16 percent of sales comes from international business. Like others serving the volatile military/high-tech markets, Alpha has recently experienced volume and earning problems.

Alpha's current operating problems stem from very special circumstances. In February 1985, the Air Force suspended Alpha's security clearance and suspended the company as a supplier after a grand jury indicted the company on bribery charges.

Good managements recover from such ordeals by fire stronger than ever. Alpha's markets are still growing at 20 percent or more annually, and the company has a substantial order backlog. Alpha has performed well in the past, and we think that it will perform again in the future.

AMERICAN MEDICAL INTERNATIONAL, INC.

Corporate Headquarters: 414 North Camden Drive
Beverly Hills, CA 90210

Telephone: (213) 278-6200
Incorporated in Delaware
New York Stock Exchange—AMI

Business: Owns, manages and operates hospitals and provides health care services worldwide.

Officers:
Royce Diener, Chairman and Chief Executive Officer
Walter L. Weismand, President and Chief Operating Officer
Executive Vice Presidents
R. Bruce Andrees, Chief Financial Officer
Thomas E. Donahue, Jr., Secretary and General Counsel
Charles P. Reilly, Corporate Development
Senior Vice Presidents
Robert L. Bohlman, Eastern U.S. Division Hospitals
Jennifer S. Flinton, Marketing and Communications
H. D. Foitik, Central U.S. Division Hospitals
Revell Lamprecht, President, Professional Hospital Services
Neal L. Maslan, Western U.S. Division Hospitals
John H. Moxley, III, M. D., Alternative Services and Strategic Planning
Conraid L. Pope, Hospital Operations—Quality Assurance
Fermo Rossi, Construction and Engineering

Statement of Income (Year ends 8/31—$ figures in 000's)

	1984	1983
Operating Revenues	$2,422,716	$2,217,862
Less: Provisions for Contractual		
Allowances and Uncollectable Accounts	459,172	457,312
Net Operating Revenues	$1,963,544	$1,760,550
Operating Costs and Expenses		
Operating Expenses	$1,471,505	$1,374,196
Depreciation and Amortization	115,779	85,680
Interest Expense, Net	96,982	67,233
Income from Operations	$ 279,278	$ 233,441
Less: Merger Costs	26,516	—
Income before Taxes	$ 252,762	233,441
Provision for Income Taxes	115,700	104,100
Net Income	$ 137,062	$ 129,341

Note: The above data has been restated to reflect recent merger and acquisition activity and pooling of income from subsidiary companies. These changes are not reflected in the tables on the following pages.

Stockholder's Equity, Jobs, and Labor Productivity ($ figures in 000's)

Year	Stockholder's Equity	Net Sales	Number of Employees	Index of Labor Productivity
1975	$ 72,447	$ 202,712	11,000	18.428
1976	81,585	250,257	12,000	20.855
1977	94,197	289,964	13,000	22.305
1978	109,760	354,911	13,000	27.301
1979	129,737	449,350	16,000	28.084
1980	157,201	537,059	18,000	29.837
1981	306,337	913,536	27,000	33.835
1982	365,749	1,154,689	30,000	38.490
1983	449,238	1,339,603	32,000	41.863
Change, 1983/1975	+520 %	+561 %	+191 %	+127 %

Capital Productivity ($ figures in 000's)

Year	Total Invested Capital	Net Income	Index of Capital Productivity
1975	$ 238,014	$ 5,228	.022
1976	248,831	8,667	.035
1977	240,915	13,110	.054
1978	270,508	18,619	.069
1979	327,765	25,331	.077
1980	411,718	32,386	.079
1981	707,078	50,807	.072
1982	891,933	78,811	.088
1983	1,159,559	101,507	.088
Change, 1983/1975	+387 %	+1,842 %	+299 %

Stock Prices and Earnings per Share[*]

Year	Stock Prices			Earnings[**] Per Share
	High	Low	Close	
1975	$ 1.758	$ .849	$ 1.455	$ .218
1976	3.364	1.424	3.364	.352
1977	4.727	2.636	4.727	.504
1978	9.500	4.033	8.334	.675
1979	11.167	6.333	10.134	.864
1980	21.501	9.292	21.251	1.060
1981	24.501	16.188	19.500	1.200
1982	29.907	13.688	27.469	1.688
1983	37.250	20.625	24.000	2.050
1984	28.125	20.125	20.125	1.640

Change, 1975–84 +1,284%; change, S&P 500 Index, 1975–84 +82%

[*]Adjusted for stock splits and stock dividends   [**]Includes extraordinary items

AMI provides health care services to more than 500 communities around the world through its acute care hospitals and alternative health care delivery systems. More than 150 hospitals and health care centers are owned, managed, or are being developed by AMI. Through its alternative services divisions, AMI operates free-standing outpatient surgery centers, industrial medicine clinics, substance abuse treatment centers, and psychiatric care facilities. Other AMI subsidiaries contract with AMI and non-AMI hospitals and organizations to provide services such as computerized management information systems, medical records consulting, hospital design and development, respiratory therapy, durable medical equipment, diagnostic imaging, and dietary and pharmaceutical services.

In 1960, the United States spent $19.6 billion on health care. That represents 5.3 percent of our Gross National Product. A series of federal government programs in the 1960s caused a literal explosion in health care spending. By 1982, we were spending $179.5 billion on health care, a full 10.5 percent of our Gross National Product. By 1985, just four companies, Hospital Corporation of America, American Medical International, Humana, and National Medical Enterprises (all four on the 101 Best Performing roster) owned, or managed, a full 12 percent of *all* U.S. hospitals.

By 1983, Congress began to understand that a high-priority task was to get health care spending under control, and it began to pass a series of bills to that end. This slowdown in health care spending is causing some substantial restructuring in the industry, and American Medical International is experiencing some of the pain.

AMI is meeting the challenge with cost-cutting efforts, international expansion, and innovative new programs like home health care. It is also experimenting with high-risk programs like health insurance.

AMERICAN STORES CO.

Corporate Headquarters: PO Box 27447, 709 East South Temple
Salt Lake City, UT 84127
Telephone: (801) 539-0112
Incorporated in Delaware
New York Stock Exchange—ASC

Business: A holding company for retail stores selling food and/or drugs under the Acme Markets, Alpha Beta, Buttrey Food, Jewel, Osco, Sav-on and Skaggs names.

Officers:

L.S. Skaggs, Chairman of the Board
Richard G. Dunlop, Vice Chairman of the Board and Treasurer
Thomas H. Sunday, Executive Vice President, General Counsel and Secretary
Scott Bergeson, Executive Vice President and Assistant Secretary
Victor L. Lund, Office of the President
Michael T. Miller, Assistant Secretary
Frederick P. McBrier, Assistant Secretary
Alan D. Steward, Office of the President
Larry A. Hodges, Office of the President

Statement of Income (Year ends 2/2/85 and 1/28/84—$ figures in 000's)

	1985	1984
Net Sales	$12,118,793	$7,983,677
Cost of Goods	9,234,204	6,051,677
Gross Profit	$ 2,884,589	$1,932,000
Selling, General & Administrative Expense	$ 2,536,001	$1,697,484
Operating Profit	$ 348,588	$ 234,516
Non-Operating Income	$ 109,763	$ 17,228
Interest Expense	111,739	35,615
Income before Provision for Income Taxes	$ 346,613	$ 216,129
Provision for Income Taxes	154,521	98,227
Net Income	$ 185,525	$ 117,902

Stockholder's Equity, Jobs, and Labor Productivity ($ figures in 000's)

Year	Stockholder's Equity	Net Sales	Number of Employees	Index of Labor Productivity
1975	$ 80,323	$ 625,688	12,900	48.503
1976	106,504	782,444	15,381	50.871
1977	122,192	899,772	12,000	74.981
1978	137,715	1,089,909	13,648	79.859
1979	214,137	3,786,331	62,000	61.070
1980	243,868	6,419,882	62,800	102.227
1981	289,593	7,096,585	64,000	110.884
1982	357,455	7,507,769	62,449	120.222
1983	451,693	7,983,677	66,000	120.965
Change, 1983/1975	+462 %	+1,176 %	+412 %	+149 %

Capital Productivity ($ figures in 000's)

Year	Total Invested Capital	Funds from Operations	Index of Capital Productivity
1975	$ 95,568	$ 19,906	.208
1976	109,878	23,879	.217
1977	128,849	27,665	.215
1978	206,925	85,065	.169
1979	731,975	83,503	.114
1980	754,304	135,993	.180
1981	788,172	157,888	.200
1982	827,597	184,218	.223
1983	936,659	202,744	.216
Change, 1983/1975	+880 %	+919 %	+4 %

Stock Prices and Earnings per Share[*]

Year	Stock Prices			Earnings[**] Per Share
	High	Low	Close	
1975	$ 7.556	$ 2.278	$ 6.667	$ .593
1976	9.375	6.458	7.683	.727
1977	8.833	5.917	8.417	.853
1978	10.292	6.750	9.208	1.047
1979	11.500	7.833	8.875	1.453
1980	10.167	6.708	7.125	1.370
1981	9.917	6.917	9.833	1.807
1982	23.333	8.417	21.667	2.690
1983	44.000	19.250	39.625	3.610
1984	41.125	26.500	40.000	5.710

Change, 1975–84 +500%; change, S&P 500 Index, 1975–84 +82%

[*]Adjusted for stock splits and stock dividends   [**]Includes extraordinary items

Note: The fiscal year financial results in the tables above are shown in the year in which most of the results were achieved.

CORPORATE PROFILE—AMERICAN STORES COMPANY

American Stores Company is a holding company that conducts all of its operating activities through its wholly owned subsidiaries: Acme Markets, Inc.; Alpha Beta Co.; Buttrey Food Stores; Jewel Food Stores; Osco Drug, Inc.; Sav-on Drugs, Inc.; Skaggs Companies, Inc.; Skaggs Alpha Beta, Inc.; and Star Market Company. American Stores is one of the nation's leading retailers, operating combination drug/food stores, super drug centers, drug stores, food stores. The merchandise sold by the subsidiaries includes most food and nonfood items such as prescription drugs, tobacco products, housewares, health and beauty aids, and sundry merchandise for home and family use. The company operates 1,486 retail units in 40 states. The recent acquisition of Jewel Companies has added significantly to the size and stature of the company. The next several years will see the company concentrate its efforts on creating the first coast-to-coast drug chain under the name OSCO.

American Stores has a simple management secret. They just operate better stores than most of their competitors.

ANALOGIC CORP.

Corporate Headquarters: 8 Centennial Dr.
Peabody, MA 01961
Telephone: (617) 246-0300
Incorporated in Massachusetts
Over the Counter—ALOG

Business: Designs, manufactures and markets advanced, precision data conversion and computer based signal processing instruments and equipment.
Officers:

Bernard M. Gordon, Chairman of the Board and President
Bernard L. Friedman, Vice Chairman of the Board
John A. Tarello, Senior Vice President
Martyn E. Culverhouse, Vice President
C. Fredric Young, Vice President and Treasurer
Daniel Abenaim, Vice President
Edmund F. Becker, Jr., Vice President
M. Ross Brown, Vice President
Thomas J. Dempsey, Vice President
John McG. Dobbs, Vice President
Harold S. Goldberg, Vice President
Michael A. Koulopoulos, Vice President
Leopold Neumann, Vice President
Richard F. Powell, Vice President
Julian Soshnick, Vice President and General Counsel

Statement of Income (Year ends 7/31—$ figures in 000's)

	1984	1983
Net Sales	$141,312	$128,805
Cost of Sales	81,738	72,352
Gross Profit	59,574	56,463
Expenses and Other Charges (Income)		
General and Administrative	11,112	9,568
Selling	10,574	9,815
Research and Product Development	17,846	15,089
Interest Expense	660	—
Interest/Dividend Income	(4,530)	(2,228)
	35,664	32,335
Income from Operations	23,911	24,118
Gain from Sales of Investment and Marketable Securities, Net	1,311	—
Loss in Equity of Affiliated Company	(562)	(820)
Income before Taxes	24,660	23,298
Current	6,951	8,086
Deferred	1,202	118
	8,153	8,204
Net Income	$ 16,507	$ 15,094

Stockholder's Equity, Jobs, and Labor Productivity ($ figures in 000's)

Year	Stockholder's Equity	Net Sales	Number of Employees	Index of Labor Productivity
1975	$ 1,887	$ 8,625	255	33.824
1976	2,358	10,397	256	40.613
1977	3,636	16,744	420	39.867
1978	8,866	35,146	825	42.601
1979	13,779	48,615	1,100	44.195
1980	28,119	67,010	1,370	48.912
1981	56,923	82,861	1,500	55.241
1982	69,501	105,989	1,700	62.346
1983	113,416	128,805	1,900	67.792
Change, 1983/1975	+5,910 %	+1,393 %	+645 %	+100 %

Capital Productivity ($ figures in 000's)

Year	Total Invested Capital	Net Income	Index of Capital Productivity
1975	$ 2,011	$ 157	.078
1976	3,219	475	.148
1977	4,286	1,260	.294
1978	11,966	3,053	.255
1979	22,103	4,528	.205
1980	38,187	6,030	.158
1981	62,841	8,797	.140
1982	78,790	11,810	.150
1983	125,824	15,094	.120
Change, 1983/1975	+6,157 %	+9,514 %	+54 %

Stock Prices and Earnings per Share[*]

Year	Stock Prices			Earnings[**] Per Share
	High	Low	Close	
1975	$ .109	$ .047	$ .078	$ .017
1976	.391	.078	.391	.051
1977	2.188	.391	2.188	.131
1978	6.500	2.031	3.438	.233
1979	5.875	3.438	4.938	.343
1980	16.000	4.125	16.000	.440
1981	17.625	10.750	12.875	.535
1982	21.750	10.625	20.000	.700
1983	31.125	19.250	23.250	.850
1984	25.000	9.000	11.250	.900

Change, 1975–84 +14,300%; change, S&P 500 Index, 1975–84 +82%

[*]Adjusted for stock splits and stock dividends   [**]Includes extraordinary items

This high-growth firm is engaged in the design, manufacture, and marketing of advanced precision data conversion and computer-based signal processing instruments and equipment. These products are used to acquire, condition, translate, compute, interpret, store, transmit, or display critical data for medical, industrial, scientific testing and measurement, and other systems applications. The company markets directly to original equipment manufacturers and to end users through a sales network of both its own sales offices and independent distributors and manufacturers' representatives. This company is a high-growth, high-technology organization facing the continuing challenge to react quickly and respond successfully to changing market conditions while remaining consistently innovative in developing new products that have a competitive advantage and meet major market needs. Current conditions are testing management's ability to meet these challenges.

APOGEE ENTERPRISES, INC.

Corporate Headquarters: 7900 Xerxes Avenue South 1944
Minneapolis, MN 55431

Telephone: (612) 835-1874
Incorporated in Minnesota
Over the Counter—APOG

Business: Concentrates on the fabrication, installation and distribution of windows, curtainwall and automotive glass products.

Officers:

Russell H. Baumgardner, Chief Executive Officer
Donald W. Goldfus, President and Chief Operating Officer
Laurence J. Niederhofer, Vice Chairman
James L. Martineau, Vice President
Charles N. Nye, Vice President, Corporate Planning & Development
William G. Gardner, Treasurer and Chief Financial Officer
Darrell E. Sykes, Corporate Controller
Alfred L. Hoedeman, Secretary

Statement of Income (Year ends 3/2/85 and 3/3/84—$ figures in 000's)

	1985	1984
Net Sales	$219,605	$181,095
Cost of Sales	186,606	153,003
Gross Profit	$ 32,999	$ 28,092
Selling, General & Administrative Expenses	$ 20,756	$ 18,315
Operating Income	$ 12,243	9,741
Interest Expense	$ 1,191	$ 419
Income before Provision for Income Taxes	$ 11,052	$ 9,322
Provision for Income Taxes	5,232	4,153
Net Income	$ 5,820	$ 5,169

Stockholder's Equity, Jobs, and Labor Productivity ($ figures in 000's)

Year	Stockholder's Equity	Net Sales	Number of Employees	Index of Labor Productivity
1975	$ 7,147	$ 31,177	800	38.971
1976	8,312	38,599	961	40.165
1977	9,611	52,569	1,265	41.557
1978	11,931	74,208	1,391	53.349
1979	15,093	83,719	1,406	59.544
1980	19,071	106,263	1,673	63.516
1981	30,814	134,527	1,758	76.523
1982	38,194	167,510	1,944	86.168
1983	42,174	181,095	2,185	82.881
Change, 1983/1975	+490 %	+409 %	+173 %	+113 %

Capital Productivity ($ figures in 000's)

Year	Total Invested Capital	Net Income	Index of Capital Productivity
1975	$13,168	$1,245	.095
1976	14,153	1,279	.090
1977	19,721	1,455	.074
1978	22,386	2,477	.111
1979	28,747	3,456	.120
1980	33,983	4,496	.132
1981	44,010	6,397	.145
1982	46,476	7,699	.166
1983	53,747	5,169	.096
Change, 1983/1975	+308 %	+315 %	+2 %

Stock Prices and Earnings per Share[*]

Year	Stock Prices			Earnings[**] Per Share
	High	Low	Close	
1975	$ .614	$ .341	$ .587	$ .157
1976	.990	.597	.649	.161
1977	1.280	.640	1.178	.180
1978	2.419	1.075	1.766	.298
1979	4.320	1.632	3.840	.411
1980	7.680	2.580	6.960	.533
1981	9.200	5.680	9.200	.691
1982	15.000	7.100	13.500	.792
1983	14.750	9.750	10.375	.520
1984	11.750	6.875	8.875	.590

Change, 1975–84 +1,386%; change, S&P 500 Index, 1975–84 +82%

[*]Adjusted for stock splits and stock dividends   [**]Includes extraordinary items

Note: The fiscal year financial results in the tables above are shown in the year in which most of the results were achieved.

Stockholder's Equity, Jobs, and Labor Productivity ($ figures in 000's)

Year	Stockholder's Equity	Net Sales	Number of Employees	Index of Labor Productivity
1975	$ 1,008	$ 4,297	128	33.570
1976	1,268	6,895	226	30.509
1977	1,820	8,183	242	33.814
1978	2,191	8,791	253	34.474
1979	2,694	10,386	300	34.620
1980	3,563	13,043	350	37.266
1981	9,441	21,046	415	50.713
1982	14,367	28,701	470	61.066
1983	20,759	33,802	485	69.695
Change, 1983/1975	+ 1,959 %	+ 687 %	+ 279 %	+ 108 %

Capital Productivity ($ figures in 000's)

Year	Total Invested Capital	Net Income	Index of Capital Productivity
1975	$ 1,158	$ 87	.075
1976	1,756	489	.278
1977	2,236	550	.246
1978	2,926	366	.125
1979	3,572	577	.162
1980	5,561	864	.155
1981	15,298	2,081	.136
1982	19,244	3,177	.165
1983	23,108	3,880	.168
Change, 1983/1975	+ 1,896 %	+ 4,360 %	+ 124 %

Stock Prices and Earnings per Share[*]

Year	Stock Prices			Earnings[**] Per Share
	High	Low	Close	
1975	$ .200	$ .066	$ .066	$ .034
1976	.180	.033	.033	.192
1977	.395	.182	.395	.216
1978	1.518	.364	.729	.146
1979	2.237	.735	1.937	.230
1980	6.331	1.603	5.369	.333
1981	19.504	5.372	7.769	.628
1982	13.967	4.876	13.884	.780
1983	22.386	12.159	15.000	.909
1984	15.682	8.750	10.000	.955

Change, 1975–84 + 15,152%; change, S&P 500 Index, 1975–84 + 82%

[*]Adjusted for stock splits and stock dividends   [**]Includes extraordinary items

CORPORATE PROFILE—ARX, INC. (FORMERLY AEROFLEX LABORATORIES INCORPORATED)

Aeroflex Laboratories is a diversified, engineering-based corporation primarily serving the United States military community and principal military contractors with specialized products and services. Generally ARX custom designs products and services to meet contract specifications. The company mainly designs and manufacturers electronic and mechanical components used in weapons, communications, and surveillance systems by the Armed Forces, NASA, and other government agencies. The company also provides project support consulting services, including systems integration, systems analysis, product design, and engineering. A major corporate unit manufactures specialized paper envelopes for commercial use. The company recently raised $25 million through the sale of convertible debentures and intends to use the proceeds for strategically desirable acquisitions.

ASTRONICS CORPORATION

Corporate Headquarters: 80 South Davis Street
P. O. Box 587
Orchard Park, NY 14127

Telephone: (716) 662-6640
Incorporated in New York
Over the Counter—ATRO

Business: Designs, manufactures and sells systems related to image display, record retention, elastomer applications and packaging products.
Officers:

Kevin T. Keane, President and Chief Executive Officer
John M. Yessa, Vice President—Finance and Treasurer
Carlton P. Cooke, Jr., President, MOD-PAC Corporation
Burton N. Grossman, Vice President, MOD-PAC Corporation
Donald J. Skroch, Vice President, MOD-PAC Corporation

Statement of Income (Year ends 12/31—$ figures in 000's)

	1984	1983
Net Sales	$12,531	$11,770
Costs and Expenses:		
Cost of Product Sold	$ 7,500	$ 7,248
Selling, General and Administrative	3,293	2,956
Interest Expense, Net	97	76
Gain of Sale of Securities	—	(204)
	$10,890	$10,077
Income before Provision for Income Taxes	$ 1,641	$ 1,693
Provision for Income Taxes	482	771
Net Income	$ 1,159	$ 923

89

Stockholder's Equity, Jobs, and Labor Productivity ($ figures in 000's)

Year	Stockholder's Equity	Net Sales	Number of Employees	Index of Labor Productivity
1975	$1,165	$ 2,615	100	26.150
1976	1,388	3,346	123	27.203
1977	1,683	4,260	164	25.976
1978	2,032	6,622	165	40.133
1979	2,528	8,015	181	44.282
1980	3,090	8,839	192	46.036
1981	3,864	10,388	215	48.316
1982	4,462	11,076	200	55.380
1983	5,346	11,770	206	57.136
Change, 1983/1975	+359 %	+350 %	+106 %	+119 %

Capital Productivity ($ figures in 000's)

Year	Total Invested Capital	Net Income	Index of Capital Productivity
1975	$1,586	$144	.091
1976	1,751	279	.159
1977	3,087	321	.104
1978	3,358	410	.122
1979	3,547	548	.154
1980	6,301	603	.096
1981	7,578	820	.108
1982	7,831	652	.083
1983	9,271	923	.100
Change, 1983/1975	+485 %	+541 %	+10 %

Stock Prices and Earnings per Share*

Year	Stock Prices			Earnings** Per Share
	High	Low	Close	
1975	$ .560	$ .160	$ .160	$.082
1976	.960	.640	.640	.164
1977	1.280	.640	.640	.205
1978	1.840	1.040	1.040	.261
1979	1.920	1.088	1.856	.358
1980	3.200	1.792	2.304	.394
1981	3.200	1.792	3.200	.527
1982	3.712	2.432	3.200	.420
1983	6.720	3.360	5.760	.589
1984	7.400	5.000	6.600	.736

Change, 1975–84 +4,025%; change, S&P 500 Index, 1975–84 +82%

*Adjusted for stock splits and stock dividends **Includes extraordinary items

The company is engaged in the design, manufacture, and marketing of systems related to image display, record retention, elastomer applications, and packaging products. Its systems products include state-of-the-art or advanced technological components integrated into operating environments: electroluminescent instrument panels in general and military aviation; document processing; and a variety of products for the railroad, petroleum, and general industries. Its packaging products are primarily in the form of expendabale folding boxes manufactured in various sizes and configurations. Most of the company's products are marketed nationally and, to a lesser extent, internationally. This small company has achieved a rather consistent record of growth in its target market areas and, other than a dip in net income during 1982, has achieved continuous growth during our nine-year research period.

AUXTON COMPUTER ENTERPRISES, INC.

Corporate Headquarters: 851 Trafalgar Court
Maitland, FL 32751

Telephone: (305) 660-8400
Incorporated in New Jersey
Over the Counter—AUXT

Business: Provides data processing consulting services, proprietary applications software packages and information processing services.

Officers:

John P. Croxton, Chief Executive Officer
Cheryl E. Galloway, President and Chief Operating Officer
Richard Licursi, Vice President
Nicholas DiGravina, Vice President, Finance, Secretary/Treasurer
James R. Thompson, Vice President
Louis A. Venezia, Vice President

Consolidated Statement of Income (Year ends 12/31—$ figures in 000's)

	1984	1983
Revenues	$23,960	$19,514
Costs and Expenses		
Salaries and Employee Benefits	14,624	11,547
Other Costs and Expenses	6,197	4,848
Registration Costs	—	400
Total Costs and Expenses	20,841	16,795
Earnings before Taxes	$ 3,139	$ 2,719
Income Taxes	1,551	1,186
Earnings before Cumulative Effect of Change in Accounting Principle	1,588	1,533
Cumulative Effect on Prior Years (Dec. 31, 1983) of Changing the Method of Recognizing License Fees	(69)	—
Net Income	$ 1,519	$ 1,533

Stockholder's Equity, Jobs, and Labor Productivity ($ figures in 000's)

Year	Stockholder's Equity	Net Sales	Number of Employees	Index of Labor Productivity
1975	$ 422	$ 4,511	126	35.802
1976	611	4,751	129	36.829
1977	729	4,992	143	34.909
1978	918	6,335	180	35.194
1979	1,338	8,078	204	39.598
1980	1,624	9,041	162	55.809
1981	2,011	9,662	184	52.511
1982	2,800	12,532	258	48.574
1983	4,992	19,514	320	60.981
Change, 1983/1975	+ 1,083 %	+ 333 %	+ 154 %	+ 71 %

Capital Productivity ($ figures in 000's)

Year	Total Invested Capital	Net Income	Index of Capital Productivity
1975	$ 432	$ 87	.201
1976	611	221	.362
1977	729	213	.292
1978	918	302	.329
1979	2,052	604	.294
1980	2,323	413	.178
1981	3,078	320	.104
1982	2,883	790	.274
1983	5,048	1,533	.304
Change, 1983/1975	+ 1,069 %	+ 1,662 %	+ 51 %

Stock Prices and Earnings per Share[*]

Year	Stock Prices			Earnings[**] Per Share
	High	Low	Close	
1975	$ .480	$ .214	$ .214	$.021
1976	.613	.214	.214	.053
1977	.320	.008	.008	.053
1978	.580	.008	.008	.075
1979	1.015	.347	.855	.132
1980	2.030	.801	1.282	.085
1981	3.098	1.175	2.618	.064
1982	18.250	2.375	12.750	.160
1983	18.750	8.750	17.500	.300
1984	17.750	4.400	6.500	.300

Change, 1975–84 + 2,937%; change, S&P 500 Index, 1975–84 + 82%

[*]Adjusted for stock splits and stock dividends   [**]Includes extraordinary items

AUXCO provides data processing consulting services, proprietary applications software packages, and information processing services to domestic and international corporations, with special emphasis on the telecommunications industry. Data processing consulting services, offered through a network of seven branch locations throughout the United States, include management consulting, education, systems analysis and design, data base design, proprietary software development, systems testing, documentation, and user training. AUXCO currently offers four proprietary software packages that aid communications companies in business management through computerization of key operations. AUXCO's information processing services are offered to companies in the communications industry on a timesharing basis using AUXCO's computer facility in Maitland, Florida and a nationwide telecommunications network. These processing services use AUXCO's proprietary software packages and specialized programs. The company, while small, has turned in a strong performance over the last several years and is reaching a size level at which it will face new challenges if it is to maintain its growth record. It should be noted that the company had five customers who, during its latest fiscal year, each represented more than 10 percent of company sales.

AYDIN CORP.

Corporate Headquarters: 700 Dresher Rd.
                                        Horsham, PA 19044

Telephone: (215) 657-7510
Incorporated in Delaware
New York Stock Exchange—AYD

Business: Manufactures telecommunications equipment and systems, including avionics and ground equipment for data communication, radars, etc.
Officers:
    Ayhan Hakimoglu, President
    Wilbur L. Creech, Senior Vice President, U.S. Govt. Programs
    Palle S. Christensen, Vice President & President, Aydin Monitor Systems
    Louis Goetz, Vice President & President, Aydin Controls
    James A. Lohr, Vice President & President, Aydin Computer Systems
    B. Jack Miller, Vice President Corporate Marketing
    Robert M. Moyes, Vice President & President, Aydin Microwave
    Andrew Pungratz, Vice President, Aydin Raytor
    Augustus P. Schneidau, Vice President & President, Aydin Systems
    Eckhard Schulz, Vice President & President, Aydin Radar & EW
    John Vanderslice, Vice President & President, Aydin Vector

Statement of Income (Year ends 12/31—$ figures in 000's)

	1984	1983
Net Sales	$137,500	$152,911
Costs and Expenses		
Cost of Sales	90,811	101,158
Selling, General and Administrative	25,785	24,637
Research and Development	8,047	5,857
Interest Income, Net	(1,843)	(1,985)
	$122,800	$129,667
Income from Operations	$ 14,700	$ 23,244
Gain on Sale of Lease Rights	—	2,337
Income before Taxes	$ 14,700	$ 25,581
Federal and State	4,985	9,803
Additional Federal Resulting		
from 1984 Tax Legislation	750	—
Net Income	$ 8,965	$ 15,778

Stockholder's Equity, Jobs, and Labor Productivity ($ figures in 000's)

Year	Stockholder's Equity	Net Sales	Number of Employees	Index of Labor Productivity
1975	$ 4,444	$ 35,426	950	37.291
1976	7,012	42,413	1,000	42.413
1977	10,668	51,436	1,100	46.760
1978	15,137	47,443	1,100	43.130
1979	20,059	64,167	1,350	47.531
1980	27,768	102,908	1,600	64.318
1981	34,483	100,424	1,600	62.765
1982	45,675	124,308	2,000	62.154
1983	62,224	152,911	2,000	76.456
Change, 1983/1975	+ 1,300 %	+ 332 %	+ 111 %	+ 105 %

Capital Productivity ($ figures in 000's)

Year	Total Invested Capital	Net Income	Index of Capital Productivity
1975	$ 8,556	$ 1,278	.149
1976	10,602	2,557	.241
1977	13,859	3,457	.249
1978	16,651	2,676	.161
1979	22,442	4,062	.181
1980	31,360	7,319	.233
1981	38,176	6,321	.166
1982	51,652	10,284	.199
1983	67,853	15,778	.233
Change, 1983/1975	+ 693 %	+ 1,135 %	+ 56 %

Stock Prices and Earnings per Share[*]

Year	Stock Prices			Earnings[**] Per Share
	High	Low	Close	
1975	$ 3.188	$ .625	$ 2.188	$ .305
1976	4.188	1.813	3.750	.630
1977	7.125	3.313	6.125	.825
1978	9.625	3.938	5.750	.600
1979	11.250	5.000	10.875	.890
1980	34.407	9.281	34.126	1.583
1982	34.501	12.469	19.313	1.358
1982	44.125	13.125	37.750	2.190
1983	62.500	33.125	40.750	3.310
1984	43.750	18.000	21.125	1.950

Change, 1975–84 + 866%; change, S&P 500 Index, 1975–84 + 82%

[*]Adjusted for stock splits and stock dividends   [**]Includes extraordinary items

Aydin Corporation is a high-technology manufacturer of telecommunications equipment and systems. Its products include avionics and ground equipment for data communications; color terminals and computer systems; radar; electronic warfare equipment; and support components. Its products and systems are used in both military and industrial applications. Each of Aydin's 10 divisions is organized as a profit center, with dedicated engineering, manufacturing, marketing, and accounting functions. Vertical integration is a key element in the company's growth strategy. As such, Aydin's breadth of products includes the manufacture of printed circuit boards, electronic cabinets, amplifiers and other microwave components, microcircuits, frequency sources, and color monitors. Sales and marketing are handled by Aydin's combination of a direct sales force and manufacturers' representatives. The company has recently experienced a period of decreased earnings and at press time is suffering from a fall off in overseas orders. Aydin's export business accounted for 41 percent of the firm's 1984 revenues. Aydin's ability to sustain its long history of growth was tested during 1984 and is continuing to be challenged.

BOWNE & CO., INC.

Corporate Headquarters: 345 Hudson Street,
New York, NY 10014

Telephone: (212) 924-5500

American Stock Exchange—BNE

Business: Prints timely and accurate information and documents related to corporate and public financing throughout the world.

Officers:

Edmund A. Stanely, Jr., Chairman

Franz von Ziegesar, President

Richard H. Koontz, Executive Vice President

Carl R. Pite, Vice President—Finance and Secretary

Francis J. Sorg, Jr., Senior Vice President

Allen D. Marold, Vice President—Human Resources

James P. O'Neil, Vice President and Corporate Controller

James O. Volden, Treasurer

Albert G. Mather, Jr., President, Bowne of Boston, Inc.

Robert J. Baker, President, Bowne of New York City, Inc.

Nicholas S. Amatangelo, President, Bowne of Chicago, Inc.

Bala Williams, President, Bowne of Dallas, Inc.

Richard W. Rappel, President, Bowne of San Francisco, Inc.

Richard S. Bonfanti, President, Bowne of Los Angeles, Inc.

Rudolf Steinmetz, President, Bowne of Canada, Inc.

Vittorio Sanguineti, Managing Director, Bowne de Montreal, Inc.

Chester M. Humbert, President, Intergraphic Technology, Inc.

Stuart A. Leibowitz, President, Redler, Inc.

John H. Humpstone, Jr., General Manager, Legal Systems, Inc.

Statement of Income (Year ends 10/31—$ figures in 000's)

	1984	1983
Revenues		
Net Sales	$119,587	$109,193
Other	3,848	6,030
	$123,435	$115,223
Expenses		
Cost of Sales	$ 70,170	$ 57,957
Selling and Administrative	34,335	27,202
Depreciation and Amortization	3,096	1,693
Minority Interests	220	—
	$107,821	$ 86,852
Income from Continuing Operations before Income Taxes	$ 15,614	$ 28,371
Income Taxes	5,587	12,778
Income from Continuing Operations	$ 10,027	$ 15,593
Discontinued Operations		
Loss on Operations	—	(344)
Loss on Disposition	—	(403)
Net Income	$ 10,027	$ 14,846

Stockholder's Equity, Jobs, and Labor Productivity ($ figures in 000's)

Year	Stockholder's Equity	Net Sales	Number of Employees	Index of Labor Productivity
1975	$19,811	$ 45,318	1,037	43.701
1976	22,877	51,602	1,125	45.868
1977	26,467	58,863	1,200	49.053
1978	31,329	70,722	1,300	54.402
1979	39,338	78,921	1,400	56.372
1980	51,545	104,251	1,400	74.465
1981	66,988	120,143	1,350	88.995
1982	76,276	106,213	1,200	88.511
1983	87,538	109,193	1,200	90.994
Change, 1983/1975	+342 %	+141 %	+16 %	+108 %

Capital Productivity ($ figures in 000's)

Year	Total Invested Capital	Net Income	Index of Capital Productivity
1975	$20,732	$ 3,042	.147
1976	23,711	3,507	.148
1977	27,272	4,175	.153
1978	32,286	5,439	.168
1979	40,126	9,036	.225
1980	52,324	13,864	.265
1981	67,763	17,757	.262
1982	77,051	12,438	.161
1983	88,313	14,846	.168
Change, 1983/1975	+326 %	+388 %	+15 %

Stock Prices and Earnings per Share[*]

	Stock Prices			Earnings[**]
Year	High	Low	Close	Per Share
1975	$ 2.767	$ .881	$ 1.861	$ .315
1976	3.012	1.861	2.228	.364
1977	2.854	1.800	2.674	.434
1978	5.183	2.214	4.049	.561
1979	5.782	3.997	5.471	.925
1980	15.774	4.524	15.774	1.419
1981	19.881	11.310	16.310	1.819
1982	18.250	9.250	15.750	1.280
1983	24.250	14.125	16.875	1.520
1984	19.000	12.000	15.000	1.040

Change, 1975–84 +706%; change, S&P 500 Index, 1975–84 +82%

[*]Adjusted for stock splits and stock dividends   [**]Includes extraordinary items

This company, founded in 1775, specializes in the timely and accurate preparation and distribution of information for international, corporate and public financings. Bowne's financial printing companies located in nine major financial centers, with service facilities in eight others, operate around the clock. The facilities are linked by facsimile and electronic transmission devices. They convert raw textual and financial data required in major corporate transactions into a form that can be studied and revised by the parties to a transaction, submitted to government regulatory bodies, and finally printed and distributed to the investing public. The company's products include registration statements, proxy material, prospectuses, tax-exempt bond offering circulars, tender offer documents, loan agreements, and reports to stockholders. Through its other subsidiaries, the company augments its services to the financial, corporate, and commercial printing markets. This old, well-established company has experienced considerable variation in net income during the last several years due to the fluctuations in the activity level of the various financial markets it serves. As the oldest of the 101 firms profiled, its long-term viability is almost beyond questioning, and its overall record is impressive.

CALIFORNIA MICROWAVE, INC.

Corporate Headquarters: 990 Almanor Ave.
                              Sunnyvale, CA 94086
Telephone: (408) 732-4000
Incorporated in California
Over the Counter—CMIC

Business: Manufactures electronic communications equipment for commercial and government markets.

Officers:

Dr. David B. Leeson, President and Chief Executive Officer

Gilbert F. Johnson, Exec. Vice President and Chief Operating Officer, President, Microwave Div.

David E. Hershberg, Vice President/Company and President, Satellite Transmission Systems

George L. Spillane, Vice President, Finance, Chief Financial Officer and Secretary

Joseph Russell, Vice President/Company, President, Government Electronics Div.

Statement of Income (Year ends 6/30—$ figures in 000's)

	1985	1984
Net Sales	$105,359	$112,493
Cost of Goods	79,275	84,555
Gross Profit	26,084	27,938
Selling, General and Administrative Expenses	14,647	13,884
Research & Development Expenses	3,401	3,492
Operating Income	8,036	10,562
Non-Operating Income	492	128
Income before Provision for Income Taxes	$ 8,528	$ 10,690
Income Taxes	3,921	4,824
Net Income	$ 4,607	$ 5,866

Stockholder's Equity, Jobs, and Labor Productivity ($ figures in 000's)

Year	Stockholder's Equity	Net Sales	Number of Employees	Index of Labor Productivity
1975	$ 3,312	$ 10,753	352	30.548
1976	4,185	18,062	635	28.444
1977	5,826	26,061	725	35.946
1978	7,885	33,167	751	44.164
1979	10,233	40,036	865	46.284
1980	10,970	38,066	694	54.850
1981	20,056	56,971	994	57.315
1982	24,290	88,615	1,034	85.701
1983	30,283	101,209	1,193	84.836
Change, 1983/1975	+814 %	+841 %	+239 %	+178 %

Capital Productivity ($ figures in 000's)

Year	Total Invested Capital	Funds from Operations	Index of Capital Productivity
1975	$ 3,343	$ 640	.191
1976	5,461	941	.172
1977	6,652	1,691	.254
1978	9,885	2,312	.234
1979	14,475	3,048	.211
1980	18,212	1,375	.075
1981	24,022	4,115	.171
1982	28,675	5,826	.203
1983	37,554	8,101	.216
Change, 1983/1975	+1,023 %	+1,166 %	+13 %

Stock Prices and Earnings per Share[*]

Year	Stock Prices			Earnings[**] Per Share
	High	Low	Close	
1975	$ 1.259	$ .296	$ .988	$ .097
1976	2.074	.988	1.877	.152
1977	3.704	1.796	3.407	.261
1978	5.778	2.861	4.667	.320
1979	6.417	4.167	4.917	.390
1980	7.250	2.833	7.000	.027
1981	10.417	5.917	8.083	.353
1982	15.250	6.417	15.250	.520
1983	27.625	14.000	19.000	.650
1984	19.250	6.750	8.876	.500

Change, 1975–84 +799%; change, S&P 500 Index, 1975–84 +82%

[*]Adjusted for stock splits and stock dividends   [**]Includes extraordinary items

This company manufactures electronic communications equipment for commercial and government applications. It is one of the only independent companies to have surpassed the $100 million sales level in the transmission sector of the communications industry. The company is considered a world-class supplier of communications transmission capital equipment and systems. As such, the company has a record of success as a source of commercial satellite earth stations; its customers include many of the major U.S. communications carriers, cable and broadcast television networks, and private transmissions users. In addition, the company is a key supplier to the U.S. government of radar test equipment, electronic intelligence systems, and communications receivers. Fiscal 1985 saw the company experience a decline in net income. The company is well recognized for its strategic thinking and management practices, and these attributes will be tested by its changing external environment. The current situation in the telecommunications industry has caused a slowdown in customer orders and this, coupled with shorter product life cycles, will be challenging management's ability to return to the high growth rates achieved in the past.

CAMCO, INC.

Corporate Headquarters: 7030 Ardmore Street
                          Houston, TX 77054
Telephone: (713) 747-4000
Incorporated in Texas
American Stock Exchange—CAM

Business: Manufactures and supplies premium quality oil and gas well completion and control equipment for customers in 62 different countries.

Officers:

David M. Veit, Chairman of the Board
Gilbert H. Tausch, President and Chief Executive Officer
Dick M. Koons, Vice President, Operations
Merle C. Muckleroy, Vice President, Sales and Service
Robert J. Caldwell, Vice President, Engineering and Research
Donald W. Eastwood, Vice President, Western Hemisphere Sales
Stephen M. Fotiades, Vice President, Eastern Hemisphere Sales
Jack E. Hill, Vice President, Marketing
William U. Pursell, Vice President, Manufacturing
Stephen D. Smith, Vice President, Subsidiary Operations
Herbert S. Yates, Vice President, Finance
Roger A. Brown, Secretary and General Counsel

Statement of Income (Year ends 12/31—$ figures in 000's)

	1984	1983
Net Sales		
Products	$119,937	$113,762
Services	48,857	44,867
Total Sales	$168,794	$158,629
Cost of Sales		
Products	$ 70,295	$ 65,979
Services	35,603	33,717
Gross Margin	$ 62,896	$ 58,933
Selling, General and Administrative Expenses	$ 43,016	$ 37,109
Interest Income	(1,901)	(892)
Income before Income Taxes	$ 18,854	$ 19,140
Provision for Income Taxes	6,555	8,584
Net Income	$ 12,299	$ 10,556

Stockholder's Equity, Jobs, and Labor Productivity ($ figures in 000's)

Year	Stockholder's Equity	Net Sales	Number of Employees	Index of Labor Productivity
1975	$15,842	$ 34,208	1,216	28.132
1976	22,095	38,087	1,239	30.740
1977	23,756	46,254	1,314	35.201
1978	26,769	56,120	1,325	42.355
1979	32,182	76,163	1,665	45.744
1980	41,402	123,964	2,280	54.370
1981	59,886	176,080	2,475	71.143
1982	78,484	184,442	2,500	73.777
1983	82,877	158,629	2,300	68.969
Change, 1983/1975	+ 423 %	+ 364 %	+ 89 %	+ 145 %

Capital Productivity ($ figures in 000's)

Year	Total Invested Capital	Net Income	Index of Capital Productivity
1975	$25,440	$ 1,469	.058
1976	28,266	759	.027
1977	28,670	1,661	.058
1978	35,730	3,091	.087
1979	46,366	5,694	.123
1980	64,532	4,766	.074
1981	81,319	15,590	.192
1982	99,373	17,945	.181
1983	98,602	10,556	.107
Change, 1983/1975	+ 288 %	+ 619 %	+ 85 %

Stock Prices and Earnings per Share[*]

Year	Stock Prices			Earnings[**] Per Share
	High	Low	Close	
1975	$ 3.292	$ 1.667	$ 2.417	$ .353
1976	2.917	1.667	2.167	.150
1977	3.583	2.000	3.542	.287
1978	7.458	3.000	6.292	.530
1979	11.292	5.458	10.917	.967
1980	20.375	8.125	18.375	.690
1981	22.375	13.375	19.125	2.160
1982	19.500	8.000	14.000	2.480
1983	19.250	11.125	11.750	1.450
1984	14.250	9.875	11.750	1.680

Change, 1975–84 + 386%; change, S&P 500 Index, 1975–84 + 82%

[*]Adjusted for stock splits and stock dividends   [**]Includes extraordinary items

The company is a leading supplier of premium quality well completion and control equipment for use in critical energy industry applications. Camco has manufacturing facilities in the United States, United Kingdom, Mexico, and Venezuela and 53 sales and service operations in 28 countries. The major products manufactured and supplied by Camco include gas lift equipment, subsurface safety systems, packers, well completion equipment, and wireline tools and service units. Camco also represents internationally a select group of companies whose products complement Camco's own product lines.

Camco's record is remarkable. When oil prices began to soften in 1981, the oil field service industry was devastated. For example, one competitor, Smith International, *lost* $94 million in 1983 and $68 million in 1984, and for a time Smith's future seemed in doubt. Hughes Tool did even worse, losing well over $200 million in 1983 and 1984.

CARLISLE CORPORATION

Corporate Headquarters: 1600 Columbia Plaza
                          250 East Fifth Street
                          Cincinnati, OH 45202
Telephone: (513) 241-2500
Incorporated in Delaware
New York Stock Exchange—CSL

Business: Manufactures single ply rubber roofing, brake linings, specialty wire and cable, magnetic tapes and magnetically coated plastics.

Officers:

George F. Dixon, Jr., Chairman

Malcolm C. Myers, Vice Chairman and Chief Executive Officer

Robert J. Deffeyes, President and Chief Operating Officer

Jerome H. Eichert, Executive Vice President, Treasurer and Chief Financial Officer

Vice Presidents: Roger A. Brown, Gerald L. Doerger, John W. Guffey, Jr., Robert J. Royle, William H. Unger

Edwin M. North, Secretary and General Counsel

Robert J. Westerkamp, Controller

Statement of Income (Year ends 12/31—$ figures in 000's)

	1984	1983
Net Sales	$527,177	$411,848
Costs and Expenses		
Cost of Goods Sold	$388,525	$312,010
Selling and Administrative Expenses	73,707	55,709
	$462,232	$367,719
Operating Profit	$ 64,946	$ 44,129
Other Deductions (Income)		
Interest Expense	$ 5,198	$ 4,466
Interest Income	(1,637)	(1,782)
Other, Net	(40)	(186)
	$ 3,521	$ 2,498
Earnings before Income Taxes	$ 61,424	$41,631
Income Taxes	28,906	18,961
Net Earnings	$ 32,518	$ 22,670

Stockholder's Equity, Jobs, and Labor Productivity ($ figures in 000's)

Year	Stockholder's Equity	Net Sales	Number of Employees	Index of Labor Productivity
1975	$ 38,133	$115,006	3,228	35.628
1976	41,844	146,047	3,661	39.893
1977	55,289	185,762	4,345	42.753
1978	66,647	242,487	4,758	50.964
1979	82,618	324,422	5,500	58.986
1980	104,299	380,800	4,874	78.129
1981	132,433	406,313	4,828	84.158
1982	147,826	377,917	4,324	87.400
1983	162,017	411,848	4,863	84.690
Change, 1983/1975	+325 %	+258 %	+51 %	+138 %

Capital Productivity ($ figures in 000's)

Year	Total Invested Capital	Net Income	Index of Capital Productivity
1975	$ 69,569	$ 2,199	.032
1976	71,727	5,558	.077
1977	78,297	8,878	.113
1978	87,965	13,394	.152
1979	119,388	18,700	.157
1980	146,319	25,776	.176
1981	172,877	35,317	.204
1982	178,644	26,857	.150
1983	208,339	22,670	.109
Change, 1983/1975	+200 %	+931 %	+244 %

Stock Prices and Earnings per Share[*]

	Stock Prices			Earnings[**]
Year	High	Low	Close	Per Share
1975	$ 3.594	$ 2.406	$ 2.750	$ .253
1976	4.125	2.688	3.781	.638
1977	6.250	3.781	5.625	1.003
1978	7.313	4.813	5.969	1.493
1979	14.813	6.000	12.125	2.040
1980	42.875	9.375	42.000	2.780
1981	54.750	24.250	28.750	3.760
1982	34.750	18.500	32.250	2.900
1983	39.500	22.875	27.750	2.450
1984	36.500	24.125	33.875	3.510

Change, 1975–84 +1,132%; change, S&P 500 Index, 1975–84 +82%

[*]Adjusted for stock splits and stock dividends   [**]Includes extraordinary items

This company produces and sells a diverse line of products for industry, primarily made of rubber, plastics, or metal. Its products are sold to both original equipment manufacturers and the aftermarket; more than half of its current volume serves aftermarket areas. Sales of the company's products are primarily to six markets: construction materials, data communications, aerospace/electronics, automotive, recreational tire, and general industry. Carlisle has a threefold profitability objective, around which both corporate and division planning and executive compensation incentive programs are designed. They set as minimum targets: 20 percent annual earnings growth rate; 7 percent return on net sales; and 20 percent return on capital invested in the business.

Carlisle gives real meaning to decentralization. This $500 million sales company is run with a headquarters staff 20 executives, who share just 6 secretaries.

CHARTER MEDICAL CORP.

Corporate Headquarters: 577 Mulberry Street, PO Box 209
Macon, GA 31298

Telephone: (912) 742-1161
Incorporated in Delaware
American Stock Exchange—CMDA

Business: Owns and operates 60 psychiatric, addictive disease and general acute care hospitals in the United States and the United Kingdom.
Officers:

William A. Fickling, Jr. Chairman and Chief Executive Officer
Ray Stevenson, President
James T. McAfee, Jr., Exec. Vice President, Hospital Operations
J. Rodney Laughlin, Senior Vice President
C. Michael Ford, Vice President, Finance
W. Lamar Chesney, Vice President and Controller
William F. Cummings, Ph.D., Vice President, Corporate Planning
Fred C. Follmer, Vice President, Hospital Financial Operations
Ben G. Porter, Vice President, Corporate, Government & Industry Relations
Robert P. Porter, Vice President, Health Care Services
Vice Presidents, Hospital Operations: James D Daher, G. Wayne McAlister, George D. Shaunnessy, David K. Watson, Wm. Bradley Weber

Statement of Income (Year ends 9/30—$ figures in 000's)

	1984	1983
Operating Revenues	$493,273	$422,081
Less Provision for Contractual Allowances	50,051	49,127
Less Provisions for Doubtful Accounts	18,167	14,258
	$425,055	$358,696
Costs and Expenses		
Operating Expenses	$318,308	$276,351
Depreciation	14,335	10,895
Interest	28,949	23,414
Income before Taxes	$ 63,463	$ 48,036
Provision for Income Taxes	28,304	21,174
Net Income	$ 35,159	$ 26,862

Stockholder's Equity, Jobs, and Labor Productivity ($ figures in 000's)

Year	Stockholder's Equity	Net Sales	Number of Employees	Index of Labor Productivity
1975	$16,147	$ 50,692	3,189	15.896
1976	17,578	64,457	3,539	18.213
1977	16,180	75,044	3,872	19.381
1978	17,174	93,527	4,000	23.382
1979	18,507	123,172	4,200	29.327
1980	24,733	161,896	5,500	29.436
1981	36,386	228,027	5,700	40.005
1982	72,935	294,784	7,300	40.381
1983	89,054	358,696	8,400	42.702
Change, 1983/1975	+452 %	+608 %	+163 %	+169 %

Capital Productivity ($ figures in 000's)

Year	Total Invested Capital	Net Income	Index of Capital Productivity
1975	$ 48,724	$ 1,450	.030
1976	60,689	1,646	.027
1977	60,028	2,214	.037
1978	73,871	4,759	.064
1979	103,270	5,484	.053
1980	111,944	7,439	.066
1981	155,006	11,570	.075
1982	244,798	18,381	.075
1983	304,519	26,862	.088
Change, 1983/1975	+525 %	+1,753 %	+196 %

Stock Prices and Earnings per Share[*]

Year	Stock Prices			Earnings[**] Per Share
	High	Low	Close	
1975	$ .274	$ .082	$ .154	$ .036
1976	.307	.154	.302	.041
1977	.444	.176	.395	.059
1978	1.339	.390	.867	.168
1979	1.630	.864	1.547	.196
1980	5.333	1.333	4.778	.270
1981	9.148	4.593	6.296	.436
1982	15.741	4.519	14.630	.643
1983	20.083	11.667	12.083	.887
1984	22.667	12.333	22.000	1.173

Change, 1975–84 +14,220%; change, S&P 500 Index, 1975–84 +82%

[*]Adjusted for stock splits and stock dividends   [**]Includes extraordinary items

111

CORPORATE PROFILE—CHARTER MEDICAL CORPORATION

This is an international health care company whose principal business is providing medical treatment services to hospital patients. Charter Medical owns and operates or has under development nearly 60 psychiatric, addictive disease, and general acute care hospitals throughout the United States and in London. Under agreement with a Saudi Arabian company, Charter Medical also provides full community health and hospital management services for King Khalid Military City in the Kingdom of Saudi Arabia. The company uses acquisitions as a principal means of achieving growth. Fiscal 1985 should show continued growth in both operating revenues and net income.

Charter Medical's niche markets in psychiatric health care and substance abuse programs seem to be shielding the company from much of the slowdown in demand and squeezed margins that are affecting larger, broader-based health care providers.

CHILTON CORP.

Corporate Headquarters: 12606 Greenville Avenue
                          Dallas, TX 75243
Telephone: (214) 699-6111
Incorporated in Texas
American Stock Exchange—CHN

Business: Provides credit reporting services, collects delinquent accounts, prepares mortgage reports and writes credit insurance.
Officers:
  J.E.R. Chilton, Chairman of the Board
  Ross G. Cummings, Vice President of Finance and Treasurer
  Douglas Howell, Vice President, Corporate Development
  John C. Robuck, Vice President, Accounts Receivable Management
  Larry L. Smith, Vice President, Bureau Operations and Marketing
  Van A. Smith, President
  James E. Sutton, Vice President, Public Affairs, Secretary, and General Counsel
  Ronald L. Woodall, Vice President, Data Processing

Statement of Income (Year ends 3/31—$ figures in 000's)

	1985	1984
Net Sales	$86,479	$68,459
Cost of Sales	32,440	29,831
Gross Profit	54,039	26,080
Selling, General and Administrative Expenses	35,486	26,080
Operating Income	18,553	12,548
Depreciation and Amortization	5,945	3,371
Interest Expense	125	105
Income before Provision for Income Taxes	12,483	9,073
Income Taxes	4,642	3,735
Net Income	$ 7,841	$ 5,338

Stockholder's Equity, Jobs, and Labor Productivity ($ figures in 000's)

Year	Stockholder's Equity	Net Sales	Number of Employees	Index of Labor Productivity
1975	$ 18	$21,833	1,241	17.593
1976	1,586	23,158	1,288	17.980
1977	3,316	27,704	1,356	20.431
1978	5,220	32,907	1,399	23.522
1979	4,061	37,071	1,435	25.833
1980	5,646	39,459	1,444	27.326
1981	6,901	44,960	1,366	32.914
1982	9,457	54,029	1,531	35.290
1983	23,707	68,459	1,663	41.166
Change, 1983/1975	+ 131,606 %	+ 214 %	+ 34 %	+ 134 %

Capital Productivity ($ figures in 000's)

Year	Total Invested Capital	Net Income	Index of Capital Productivity
1975	$11,630	$1,164	11.630
1976	12,231	1,541	12.231
1977	15,253	1,828	15.253
1978	17,392	1,972	17.392
1979	18,920	1,238	18.920
1980	18,060	1,255	19.060
1981	17,255	1,529	17.255
1982	21,658	3,230	21.658
1983	33,606	5,338	33.606
Change, 1983/1975	+ 189 %	+ 359 %	+ 189 %

Stock Prices and Earnings per Share*

Year	Stock Prices			Earnings** Per Share
	High	Low	Close	
1975	$ 1.083	$ .333	$ .778	$ .203
1976	1.500	.806	1.389	.273
1977	1.806	1.250	1.583	.322
1978	2.750	1.333	1.750	.344
1979	1.833	1.333	1.417	.211
1980	1.944	.972	1.666	.213
1981	2.306	1.528	1.833	.256
1982	6.222	1.722	5.389	.511
1983	17.417	4.917	13.917	.747
1984	20.625	9.125	18.750	1.060

Change, 1975–84 + 2,311%; change, S&P 500 Index, 1975–84 + 82%

*Adjusted for stock splits and stock dividends   **Includes extraordinary items

Note: The fiscal year financial results in the tables above are shown in the year in which most of the results were achieved.

114

Chilton is the oldest independent company in the United States that offers information management services to the nation's credit grantors. The company is well-known to financial institutions and retailers by virtue of its credit reporting, collection, and check authorization services. The company processes credit data in a highly efficient, accurate, economic manner maintaining in excess of 80 million credit records. It has grown through both internal expansion and acquisition. It recently entered the medical services area providing in-house accounts receivable support to hospitals. The company is strategically driven with a primary focus on its core market. Chilton directs its organizational efforts to enhance its technological advantages over competitors and follows an aggressive market expansion program to meet the product and service requirements of its clients. The company has set its revenue and profit objectives to maintain an average annual growth rate of 15 percent per year.

COMMUNICATIONS INDUSTRIES, INC.

Corporate Headquarters: 1100 Frito-Lay Tower
Exchange Park
Dallas TX 75235
Telephone: (214) 357-4001
Incorporated in Texas
Over the Counter—COMM

Business: Provides paging, mobile telephone and telephone answering services and manufactures peripheral equipment used in mobile communication.

Officers:
Clayton E. Niles, Chairman and Chief Executive Officer
Roger D. Linquist, President and Chief Operating Officer
Raymond T. Adams, Director, Investor Relations
Michael H. Barnes, Vice President, Finance and Administration and Chief Financial Officer
Thomas J. Bolger, Director, Human Resources
Louis E. Brown, Vice President, Research and Development
Neil J. O'Brien, Secretary
Vice Presidents: Charlie E. Jackson, Albert S. Loverde, Peter Mailandt, Ph.D., Lloyd M. Smith

Statement of Income (Year ends 12/31—$ figures in 000's)

	1984	1983
Net Sales		
Manufactured Products	$38,657	$33,574
Radio Common Carrier	59,524	41,275
Total Net Sales	$98,181	$74,849
Cost of Sales		
Manufactured Products	$22,249	$18,435
Radio Common Carrier	22,491	15,784
	$44,739	$34,219
Gross Profit	$53,442	$40,630
Selling, General and Administrative Expense	$32,950	$24,088
Other Expense (Income)		
Gains on Sales of Assets (Net)	$ (2,069)	$ (1,995)
Interest and Dividend Income	(2,274)	(2,735)
Interest Expense	1,508	465
Unrealized Loss (Gain) on Securities	96	69
Amortization of Intangibles	362	352
Write Off of Cellular License Applications	1,250	—
Equity in Losses of Cellular Joint Ventures	159	—
	$ (968)	$ (3,844)
Income before Taxes	$21,460	$20,386
Income Taxes	7,350	8,138
Net Income	$14,110	$12,248

Note: The above data has been restated to reflect recent merger and acquisition activity and pooling of income from subsidiary companies. These changes are not reflected in the tables on the following pages.

116

Stockholder's Equity, Jobs, and Labor Productivity ($ figures in 000's)

Year	Stockholder's Equity	Net Sales	Number of Employees	Index of Labor Productivity
1975	$ 7,939	$18,816	691	27.230
1976	11,877	22,819	769	29.674
1977	12,925	27,693	782	35.413
1978	14,308	32,472	888	36.568
1979	17,801	35,953	928	38.742
1980	23,850	45,802	1,030	44.468
1981	32,188	52,367	930	56.309
1982	55,683	61,465	935	65.738
1983	59,095	64,215	979	65.592
Change, 1983/1975	+644 %	+241 %	+42 %	+141 %

Capital Productivity ($ figures in 000's)

Year	Total Invested Capital	Net Income	Index of Capital Productivity
1975	$ 9,866	$ 1,494	.151
1976	12,946	1,931	.149
1977	14,965	2,428	.162
1978	17,272	2,933	.170
1979	20,273	3,584	.177
1980	26,134	4,990	.191
1981	34,259	7,756	.226
1982	59,118	9,001	.152
1983	67,965	10,790	.159
Change, 1983/1975	+589 %	+622 %	+5 %

Stock Prices and Earnings per Share[*]

Year	Stock Prices			Earnings[**] Per Share
	High	Low	Close	
1975	$ 3.309	$ 1.531	$ 3.012	$ .308
1976	3.778	2.790	3.309	.356
1977	4.000	2.864	3.506	.411
1978	7.148	3.259	5.407	.492
1979	8.222	5.185	7.185	.587
1980	18.444	6.667	16.667	7.33
1981	26.333	13.667	22.000	.973
1982	32.750	17.000	32.250	1.050
1983	40.500	20.000	26.500	1.180
1984	27.250	16.500	17.500	1.290

Change, 1975–84 +481%; change, S&P 500 Index, 1975–84 +82%

[*]Adjusted for stock splits and stock dividends [**]Includes extraordinary items

CORPORATE PROFILE—COMMUNICATIONS INDUSTRIES, INC.

The company is a recognized leader in the field of mobile communications and provides paging, mobile telephone, and telephone answering services. It manufactures peripheral equipment used in mobile communications and voice store-and-forward systems, as well. The company currently serves approximately 250,000 personal paging units, 10,000 conventional mobile telephone units, and 10,700 voice messaging and telephone answering service subscribers throughout the country. As a participant in 7 of the top 30 celular markets, celular telephone service will soon be an added CI offering. Manufactured products include antennas, duplexers, combiners, filters, radio telephone and paging terminals, voice store-and-forward systems, and other related electronic equipment. The company has been able to grow consistently in both net sales and net income and has turned in a strong performance with regard to improving labor productivity. The company's 1985 results are expected to fall below those of 1984. At press time, the company is awaiting regulatory approval for its merger with Pacific Telesis.

COMMUNITY PSYCHIATRIC CENTERS

Corporate Headquarters: 517 Washington Street
San Francisco, CA 94111

Telephone: (415) 397-6151
Incorporated in Nevada
New York Stock Exchange—CMA

Business: Operates 22 psychiatric hospitals in the U.S. and the U.K., and 49 centers for hemodialysis for patients with kidney disease.
Officers:

Robert L. Green, Chairman of the Board
James W. Conte, President
Robert F. Derenthal, Vice President
Loren B. Shook, Vice President
Richard L. Conte, Vice President
Robert L. McDonald, Vice President
James P. Smith, Vice President, Treasurer
John C. Hughes, Vice President

Statement of Income (Year ends 11/30—$ figures in 000's)

	1984	1983
Revenues		
Operating Revenues, Net of Contractual Allowances	$173,610	$138,186
Other Income, Including Net Gains and Losses on Security Transactions	9,002	8,523
	$182,612	$146,709
Costs and Expenses		
Operating	$ 74,342	$ 61,047
General and Administrative	34,479	30,021
Depreciation	4,546	3,677
Interest (principally on long-term debt)	1,778	3,326
	$115,145	$ 98,071
Earnings before Income Taxes	$ 67,467	$ 48,638
Income Taxes	31,401	21,779
Net Income	$ 36,066	$ 26,859

119

Stockholder's Equity, Jobs, and Labor Productivity ($ figures in 000's)

Year	Stockholder's Equity	Net Sales	Number of Employees	Index of Labor Productivity
1975	$ 11,214	$ 16,764	850	19.722
1976	12,456	20,165	938	21,498
1977	15,293	27,371	1,000	27.371
1978	18,286	32,920	1,175	28.017
1979	23,009	40,545	1,300	31.188
1980	31,668	59,356	2,200	26.980
1981	49,195	90,026	2,900	31.043
1982	75,375	116,966	2,825	41.404
1983	146,811	138,186	3,478	39.846
Change, 1983/1975	+1,209 %	+724 %	+308 %	+102 %

Capital Productivity ($ figures in 000's)

Year	Total Invested Capital	Net Income	Index of Capital Productivity
1975	$ 23,536	$ 1,800	.076
1976	26,050	2,136	.082
1977	26,370	3,352	.127
1978	30,968	4,881	.158
1979	35,464	6,370	.180
1980	58,251	8,429	.145
1981	97,737	12,703	.130
1982	129,284	18,173	.141
1983	179,973	26,859	.149
Change, 1983/1975	+665 %	+1,392 %	+95 %

Stock Prices and Earnings per Share[*]

Year	Stock Prices			Earnings[**] Per Share
	High	Low	Close	
1975	$ .741	$ .315	$ .491	$ .094
1976	.815	.491	.796	.113
1977	1.556	.676	1.500	.173
1978	3.352	1.222	2.241	.244
1979	4.648	2.185	4.519	.314
1980	7.407	3.704	7.074	.379
1981	10.630	6.519	9.889	.521
1982	17.500	8.000	16.056	.716
1983	30.333	15.417	23.000	.947
1984	30.000	16.875	26.625	1.220

Change, 1975–84 +1,197%; change, S&P 500 Index, 1975–84 +82%

[*]Adjusted for stock splits and stock dividends   [**]Includes extraordinary items

Since going public in 1969 with just two freestanding acute psychiatric hospitals, the company has expanded to 22 of these facilities. Seven hospitals are in California, two in Florida, and one each in Georgia, Idaho, Illinois, Indiana, Louisiana, Mississippi, Missouri, Oregon, Texas and Washington; and three are located overseas in England. The growth of the company's hospital division has been made aided by the development and continuing improvement of tranquilizers and antidepressant medications that are helping reduce the average hospital stay from years to weeks. This development, in turn, has made insurance benefits more practical and shifted primary patient care from state hospitals to community-based facilities, such as those owned by the company. In 1973, Community Psychiatric Centers entered into a second line of business by acquiring three dialysis centers, which provide hemodialysis for patients with kidney disease. The company now owns and operates 49 such outpatient dialysis centers. In 1984 the company's acute psychiatric hospitals accounted for 70 percent of operating revenues and 76 percent of operating profits. Dialysis centers accounted for 24 percent of operating revenues and 22 percent of operating profits. The balance of operating revenues and profits were accounted for by a home health care business, acquired in May 1983, which operates 13 offices on the West Coast.

Community Psychiatric Centers is a premier growth company having turned in a remarkable record of consistency in performance.

COOPER TIRE & RUBBER COMPANY

Corporate Headquarters: Lima and Western Avenues
Findlay, OH 45840

Telephone: (419) 423-1321
Incorporated in Delaware
New York Stock Exchange—CTB

Business: Produces a wide variety of carbon black and fabric reinforced parts, manufactures tires, tubes, reinforced hose, molded and extruded rubber products.

Officers:

Edward E. Brewer, Chairman and Chief Executive Officer

Ivan W. Gorr, President and Chief Operating Officer

William T. Fitzgerald, Executive Vice President

Vice Presidents: Frank A. Bartos, Charles H. Bernhardt, John Fahl, William S. Klein, Karl W. Klose, Frank P. Millham

J. Alec Reinhardt, Vice President—Finance, Chief Financial Officer, and Secretary

Julein A. Faisant, Controller

William C. Hattendorf, Treasurer

Richard D. Teeple, General Counsel

Statement of Income (Year ends 12/31—$ figures in 000's)

	1984	1983
Revenues		
Net Sales	$555,388	$457,780
Other Income	1,162	1,902
	$556,549	$459,681
Costs and Expenses		
Cost of Products Sold	$482,358	$390,114
Selling, General and Administrative	29,582	26,657
Interest and Debt Expense	2,631	3,115
	$514,571	$419,886
Income before Income Taxes	$ 41,978	$ 39,796
Provision for Income Taxes	17,400	18,390
Net Income	$ 24,578	$ 21,406

Stockholder's Equity, Jobs, and Labor Productivity ($ figures in 000's)

Year	Stockholder's Equity	Net Sales	Number of Employees	Index of Labor Productivity
1975	$ 32,369	$165,248	3,627	45.561
1976	39,309	240,114	3,929	61.113
1977	45,330	246,542	4,040	61.025
1978	49,328	260,657	3,993	65.278
1979	48,704	283,236	3,687	76.820
1980	60,438	323,953	3,885	83.386
1981	81,806	393,945	3,869	101.821
1982	121,451	430,354	4,169	103.227
1983	139,601	457,780	4,455	102.756
Change, 1983/1975	+331 %	+177 %	+23 %	+126 %

Capital Productivity ($ figures in 000's)

Year	Total Invested Capital	Net Income	Index of Capital Productivity
1975	$ 65,865	$ 4,392	.067
1976	70,994	9,544	.134
1977	81,831	7,658	.094
1978	83,198	5,565	.067
1979	106,274	5,162	.049
1980	117,245	12,825	.109
1981	125,268	17,266	.138
1982	159,931	19,008	.119
1983	173,015	21,406	.124
Change, 1983/1975	+163 %	+387 %	+86 %

Stock Prices and Earnings per Share[*]

Year	Stock Prices			Earnings[**] Per Share
	High	Low	Close	
1975	$ 2.469	$ 1.313	$ 2.219	$ .538
1976	4.188	2.281	3.844	1.228
1977	4.594	2.969	3.406	.978
1978	3.594	2.531	2.531	.700
1979	4.250	2.531	2.969	.650
1980	6.938	2.406	6.875	1.680
1981	10.500	6.125	7.250	2.060
1982	18.875	6.938	18.375	2.210
1983	22.750	12.375	15.875	2.150
1984	19.000	12.625	17.375	2.460

Change, 1975–84 +683%; change, S&P 500 Index, 1975–84 +82%

[*]Adjusted for stock splits and stock dividends   [**]Includes extraordinary items

This company is a highly productive and cost efficient specialist in the rubber industry. It produces a wide variety of carbon black and fabric reinforced parts for consumers and industry. It manufactures and markets automobile and truck tires, inner tubes, reinforced hose, high-technology rubber-to-metal bonded parts, and complex molded and extruded rubber products. In many ways this organization might resemble many of the companies considered a part of the slow growth "smoke-stack America" segment of the economy, if it were not for its impressive performance over the last decade. While the company's performance has been affected by the business cycle, there is no question that it is one of the best performing firms in the entire U.S. economy.

COX COMMUNICATIONS, INC.

Corporate Headquarters: 1400 Lake Hearn Drive
Atlanta, GA 30319

Telephone: (404) 843-5000
Incorporated in Georgia
New York Stock Exchange—COX

Business: Operates TV stations, radio stations, cable TV systems and runs automobile auctions.

Officers:
  William A. Schwartz, President and Chief Executive Officer
  John R. Dillion, Vice President, Finance
  Timothy W. Hughes, Vice President, Human Resources
  Raymond J. Tucker, Vice President and Secretary
  John G. Boyette, Treasurer
  Jimmy W. Hayes, Controller

Broadcasting Div.
  Walter C. Liss, Jr. President
  Michael S. Kievman, Senior Executive Vice President
  Stanley G. Mouse, Senior Vice President

Cable Television Div.
  David R. Van Valkenburg, President
  G. Lewis Davenport, Senior Vice President, Operations
  Arthur A. Dwyer, Senior Vice President, Operations—Marketing & Programming
  Barry R. Elson, Senior Vice President, Operations
  Geoffrey W. Gates, Senior Vice President, Engineering & Technology

Statement of Income (Year ends 12/31—$ figures in 000's)

	1984	1983
Net Revenues	$742,855	$614,623
Expenses		
Operating	238,663	187,669
Selling, General and Administrative	241,210	209,321
Depreciation and Amortization	93,337	76,551
Total	$573,210	$473,541
Operating Income	169,645	141,082
Interest Expense	29,486	17,422
Net Gain (loss) on Dispositions	9,724	3,101
Other Income (Expense)—Net	3,277	(181)
Income before Taxes	$153,160	$126,580
Federal and State Income Taxes	65,868	48,630
Net Income	$ 87,292	$ 77,950

125

Stockholder's Equity, Jobs, and Labor Productivity ($ figures in 000's)

Year	Stockholder's Equity	Net Sales	Number of Employees	Index of Labor Productivity
1975	$ 33,160	$110,246	2,500	44.098
1976	58,132	130,090	2,600	50.035
1977	50,344	186,430	3,870	48.173
1978	71,074	230,444	4,070	56.620
1979	104,463	271,187	4,600	58.954
1980	162,265	309,232	4,854	63.707
1981	236,478	403,497	5,842	69.068
1982	286,434	514,746	6,800	75.698
1983	339,137	614,623	7,200	85.364
Change, 1983/1975	+923 %	+458 %	+188 %	+94 %

Capital Productivity ($ figures in 000's)

Year	Total Invested Capital	Net Income	Index of Capital Productivity
1975	$132,603	$14,304	.108
1976	147,012	19,759	.134
1977	233,826	25,456	.109
1978	254,124	33,847	.133
1979	286,590	43,767	.153
1980	361,268	56,399	.156
1981	474,128	55,490	.117
1982	620,132	65,421	.105
1983	682,111	77,950	.114
Change, 1983/1975	+414 %	+445 %	+6 %

Stock Prices and Earnings per Share*

Year	Stock Prices			Earnings** Per Share
	High	Low	Close	
1975	$ 7.375	$ 2.563	$ 7.250	$ .613
1976	9.469	6.875	8.313	.840
1977	9.188	6.375	9.125	1.028
1978	14.969	8.000	13.938	1.268
1979	16.156	13.750	16.063	1.625
1980	30.625	15.000	27.375	2.085
1981	39.125	27.125	36.000	2.040
1982	48.000	23.875	42.750	2.310
1983	55.250	40.500	45.125	2.750
1984	54.875	39.125	49.375	3.090

Change, 1975–84 +405%; change, S&P 500 Index, 1975–84 +82%

*Adjusted for stock splits and stock dividends   **Includes extraordinary items

The company is organized into four major operating divisions: broadcasting; cable television; automobile auctions; and most recently, CyberTel, a paging and mobile telephone operation in St. Louis. Cox entered the automobile auction industry in 1968 to diversify due to the then-established FCC regulations, which limited the number of broadcasting stations a company could own. This company has maintained a strong record of growth in revenues and net income, and in light of recent changes in FCC regulations, the company is expected to become more active in pursuing acquisition opportunities in the broadcasting area as its principal means of achieving continuing growth.

Late in 1985, Cox Communications, Inc. was acquired by the privately owned Atlanta based Cox Enterprises, Inc. newspaper chain. Cox Communications was then removed from Standard & Poor's index of 500 stocks.

DATAPRODUCTS CORP.

Corporate Headquarters: 6200 Canoga Avenue
Woodland Hills, CA 91365

Telephone: (818) 887-8000
Incorporated in Delaware
American Stock Exchange—DPC

Business: Designs, manufactures and markets a full range of computer printers, components and supplies.

Officers:

Graham Tyson, Chairman of the Board, President and Chief Executive Officer
Gary D. Bernard, Vice President, Human Resources
Norman A. Fletcher, Vice President, Components Operations
Clifford J. Helms, Vice President, Technical Programs
Clifford M. Jones, Vice President, Development
John T. Laws, Vice President, Finance and Administration
John W. Leggat, III, Vice President, Marketing
Paul J. McIntire, Vice President, New Business Development
Frank J. McQuaid, Vice President
Paul J. Smith, Vice President, Operations
Paul D. Weiser, Vice President, Secretary and Corporate Counsel
Cliff O. Bickell, Treasurer

Statement of Income (Year ends 3/30/85 and 3/31/84—$ figures in 000's)

	1985	1984
Net Sales	$471,828	$398,636
Cost of Goods	324,792	271,013
Gross Profit	$147,036	$127,623
Selling, General and Administrative Expenses	$ 83,877	$ 69,279
Research and Development Expenses	30,803	29,816
Operating Income	$ 32,356	$ 29,528
Interest Expense	$ 3,508	$ 88
Income before Provision for Income Taxes	$ 28,848	$ 29,440
Income Taxes	1,155	3,400
Net Income	$ 27,693	$ 26,040

Stockholder's Equity, Jobs, and Labor Productivity ($ figures in 000's)

Year	Stockholder's Equity	Net Sales	Number of Employees	Index of Labor Productivity
1975	$ 28,837	$ 85,085	3,000	28.362
1976	41,774	115,298	3,300	34.939
1977	57,302	138,748	3,650	37.986
1978	70,773	163,569	3,950	41.410
1979	76,707	180,319	4,450	40.521
1980	135,854	270,125	4,900	55.128
1981	140,409	268,956	4,500	59.768
1982	151,970	295,101	4,300	68.628
1983	203,718	398,636	5,651	70.543
Change, 1983/1975	+606%	+364%	+88%	+149%

Capital Productivity ($ figures in 000's)

Year	Total Invested Capital	Funds from Operations	Index of Capital Productivity
1975	$ 62,031	$ 8,782	.142
1976	74,389	13,953	.188
1977	89,330	19,801	.222
1978	101,525	21,274	.210
1979	116,190	6,757	.058
1980	184,733	27,485	.149
1981	189,373	20,007	.106
1982	194,398	25,408	.131
1983	232,872	35,277	.151
Change, 1983/1975	+275%	+302%	+7%

Stock Prices and Earnings per Share*

| Year | Stock Prices | | | Earnings** Per Share |
	High	Low	Close	
1975	$ 3.250	$ 1.063	$ 2.313	$ .515
1976	7.313	2.313	5.876	.855
1977	9.563	4.688	8.875	1.075
1978	12.688	6.688	7.813	.975
1979	10.688	6.313	10.438	.505
1980	19.313	5.438	18.438	1.135
1981	22.250	9.125	10.438	.370
1982	18.000	8.000	18.000	.770
1983	31.500	16.750	28.500	1.260
1984	31.500	13.375	15.250	1.320

Change, 1975–84 +156%; change, S&P 500 Index, 1975–84 +82%

*Adjusted for stock splits and stock dividends   **Includes extraordinary items

Note: The fiscal year financial results in the tables above are shown in the year in which most of the results were achieved.

DataProducts was established in 1962 to provide a full range of peripheral products for the computer industry, concentrating on volume sales to original equipment manufacturers that sell computer systems to the actual user.

Today, 23 years later, DataProducts is a leading manufacturer specializing in the design, production and marketing of computer printers, components and supplies. The company markets its broad line of printers worldwide and has manufacturing facilities in the United States, Ireland, and Puerto Rico.

DataProducts, like many companies involved in supplying the computer industry, has experienced its share of ups and downs. The increasing maturity of the industry will provide continuous challenges to management.

DIGITAL EQUIPMENT CORPORATION

Corporate Headquarters: 146 Main Street
                           Maynard, MA 01754

Telephone: (617) 493-5350
Incorporated in Massachusetts
New York Stock Exchange—DEC

Business: Designs, manufactures, sells and services computers and associated peripheral equipment, and related software and supplies.

Officers:
Kenneth H. Olsen, President
John K. Alexanderson, Vice President, Peripherals and Supplies Group
Alfred M. Bertocchi, Vice President, Finance and Administration
Don K. Busiek, Vice President, Corporate Software Services
George A. Chamberlain, 3d., Vice President, Engineering and Mfg.
Samuel H. Fuller, Vice President, Research and Architecture
Rose Ann Giordano, Vice President, Large Systems Marketing
William C. Hanson, Vice President, Systems Manufacturing
G. William Helm, Jr., Treasurer
Winston R. Hindle, Jr., Vice President, Corporate Operations
Robert C. Hughes, Vice President, Business and Office Systems Marketing
Edward A. Kramer, Vice President, Technical Marketing
William H. Long, Vice President, Corporate Projects
Albert E. Mullin, Jr., Vice President, Corporate Relations
Edward A. Schwartz, Vice President, General Counsel and Secretary
Joel Schwartz, Vice President, Educational Marketing
John L. Sims, Vice President, Corporate Personnel
John F. Smith, Vice President, Manufacturing and Engineering
William G. Witmore, Vice President, General International Area

Statement of Income (Year ends 6/29/85 and 6/30/84—$ figures in 000's)

	1985	1984
Revenues		
Equipment Sales	$4,534,165	$3,831,073
Service and Other Revenues	2,152,151	1,753,353
Total Operating Revenues	$6,686,316	$5,584,426
Costs and Expenses		
Cost of Equipment Sales and Service	$4,087,475	$3,379,632
Research and Engineering Expenses	717,273	630,696
Selling, General and Administrative	1,431,769	1,179,529
Operating Income	$ 449,799	$ 394,569
Interest Expense	82,003	35,096
Interest Income	(63,026)	(41,477)
Income before Income Taxes	$ 430,822	$ 400,950
Income Taxes		
Provision for Income Taxes	$ 47,390	$ 72,171
Reversal of DISC Taxes	(63,250)	—
Total Income Taxes	$ (15,860)	$ 72,171
Net Income	$ 446,682	$ 382,779

Stockholder's Equity, Jobs, and Labor Productivity ($ figures in 000's)

Year	Stockholder's Equity	Net Sales	Number of Employees	Index of Labor Productivity
1975	$ 394,385	$ 533,774	19,000	28.093
1976	606,045	736,288	25,000	29.452
1977	735,463	1,058,614	36,000	29.406
1978	904,758	1,436,562	39,000	36.835
1979	1,120,236	1,804,091	44,000	41.002
1980	1,651,749	2,368,045	55,000	43.055
1981	2,679,689	3,198,097	63,000	50.736
1982	3,164,463	3,880,770	67,000	57.836
1983	3,541,281	4,271,851	73,000	58.519
Change, 1983/1975	+798 %	+700 %	+284 %	+108 %

Capital Productivity ($ figures in 000's)

Year	Total Invested Capital	Funds from Operations	Index of Capital Productivity
1975	$ 479,600	$ 70,353	.147
1976	697,402	103,974	.149
1977	826,018	148,863	.180
1978	1,246,380	207,976	.167
1979	1,460,949	246,589	.169
1980	2,141,470	357,285	.167
1981	2,768,120	456,096	.165
1982	3,256,863	570,713	.175
1983	3,634,091	555,497	.153
Change, 1983/1975	+658 %	+690 %	+4 %

Stock Prices and Earnings per Share[*]

Year	Stock Prices			Earnings[**] Per Share
	High	Low	Close	
1975	$ 47.000	$15.125	$45.625	$1.283
1976	60.833	45.167	53.875	1.980
1977	54.000	36.625	46.250	2.780
1978	54.875	38.500	53.625	3.400
1979	69.500	48.625	68.875	4.100
1980	98.750	59.250	95.000	5.450
1981	113.250	80.250	86.500	6.700
1982	115.000	61.750	99.500	7.530
1983	132.125	64.000	72.000	5.000
1984	111.250	70.375	110.750	5.730

Change, 1975–84 +143%; change, S&P 500 Index, 1975–84 +82%

[*]Adjusted for stock splits and stock dividends   [**]Includes extraordinary items

132

CORPORATE PROFILE—DIGITAL EQUIPMENT CORPORATION

Digital Equipment Corporation is one of the world's largest manufacturers of networked computer systems and associated peripheral equipment and the leader in systems integration with its network, communications, and software products. The company's products are used worldwide in a variety of applications: including scientific research, computation, communications, education, data analysis, industrial control, timesharing, commercial data processing, graphic arts, word processing, personal computing, health care, instrumentation, engineering, and simulation. Fiscal 1985 continued to reflect strong growth in both operating revenues and net income and, in fact, the company posted a record in net income surpassing the previous high recorded during fiscal 1982. Aggressive new product development has contributed significantly to the company's outstanding growth record. With revenues now in excess of $6.6 billion, the company has grown more than tenfold since 1975.

D.O.C. OPTICS CORPORATION (formerly Acrylics Optics Corporation)

Corporate Headquarters: 19800 West Eight Mile Road
Southfield, MI 48075

Telephone: (313) 354-7100

Incorporated in Delaware

Over the Counter—DOCO

Business: As of January 1, 1985, the company operated 98 optical centers to provide eye exams, retail eyeglasses, contact lenses, etc.

Officers:

Donald L. Golden, O.D., Chairman and President

Jack L. Posar, Treasurer

Milton Fisher, Vice President

Michael E. Golden, Vice President and Secretary

Richard S. Golden, Vice President

Randal E. Golden, Assistant Secretary and Directory of Laboratory Operations

Anthony H. Stack, Chief Financial Officer

Thomas R. Liegl, Controller

Dennis I. Chaiken, Director of Materials Management

Steven R. Laffey, Director of Real Estate and Construction

Statement of Income (Year ends 12/31—$ figures in 000's)

	1984	1983
Net Sales	$39,174	$33,620
Cost of Sales	24,126	18,742
Gross Margin	$15,048	$14,878
Selling, General and Administrative Expenses	$13,075	$10,957
Operating Income	$ 1,973	$ 3,921
Other Income (Expense)	4	(70)
Operating Income from Joint Venture	228	306
Income before Provision for Income Taxes	$ 2,204	$ 4,157
Provision for Income Taxes	738	1,795
Net Income	$ 1,466	$ 2,362

Stockholder's Equity, Jobs, and Labor Productivity ($ figures in 000's)

Year	Stockholder's Equity	Net Sales	Number of Employees	Index of Labor Productivity
1975	$ 1,761	$ 5,118	232	22.060
1976	2,127	6,678	295	22.637
1977	2,832	9,426	340	27.724
1978	3,115	13,152	350	37.577
1979	3,996	15,849	410	38.656
1980	5,284	19,057	420	45.374
1981	6,037	22,764	490	44.635
1982	7,293	25,796	588	43.871
1983	12,602	33,626	722	46.565
Change, 1983/1975	+616 %	+557 %	+211 %	+111 %

Capital Productivity ($ figures in 000's)

Year	Total Invested Capital	Net Income	Index of Capital Productivity
1975	$ 2,646	$ 332	.125
1976	2,786	366	.131
1977	3,179	705	.222
1978	4,202	904	.215
1979	5,162	1,021	.198
1980	6,770	1,399	.207
1981	7,507	753	.100
1982	8,545	1,256	.147
1983	13,722	2,362	.172
Change, 1983/1975	+419 %	+611 %	+37 %

Stock Prices and Earnings per Share[*]

Year	Stock Prices			Earnings[**] Per Share
	High	Low	Close	
1975	$ .390	$ .140	.140	$ .118
1976	.687	.265	.265	.130
1977	.406	.296	.296	.250
1978	1.469	.781	1.219	.333
1979	1.438	.906	1.000	.418
1980	2.219	.906	2.156	.603
1981	4.250	1.625	2.500	.325
1982	2.500	1.188	1.875	.545
1983	13.375	1.875	12.750	1.010
1984	14.375	6.750	6.750	.560

Change, 1975–84 +4,821%; change, S&P 500 Index, 1975–84 +82%

[*]Adjusted for stock splits and stock dividends   [**]Includes extraordinary items

CORPORATE PROFILE—D.O.C. OPTICS CORPORATION

This company operates approximately 100 retail optical centers, each of which provides eye examinations and sells eyeglasses, contact lenses and related accessories. The company fabricates a large assortment of eyeglasses in its own optical laboratories using purchased lens blanks and frames. During its most recent fiscal year the company derived more than 80 percent of its revenues from the sale of optical merchandise. Although its net sales have consistently increased, its ability to maintain consistent gross margins as it has expanded has not nearly been as steady.

Rapid expansion depressed earnings somewhat in 1984, but those problems seemed to have been solved by 1985. In any case, D.O.C. Optics is another health care provider that is positioned well to serve an increasingly aging population with an indispensable product.

DRANETZ TECHNOLOGIES, INC.

Corporate Headquarters: 1000 New Durham Road
                                             Edison, NJ 08818
Telephone: (201) 287-3680
Incorporated in New Jersey
Over the Counter—DRAN

Business: Designs and manufactures proprietary electronic instruments for the computer, electric utility and telecommunications industries.
Officers:
   Abraham I. Dranetz, President
   Irving Backinoff, Senior Vice President
   Ezra Mintz, Vice President
   Vice Presidents: Anthony W. Orlacchio, Robert O. Wilson, David A.
      Fuhrman, Joseph Martins, B. C. Biega
   Joseph P. Lowrey, Treasurer
   Richard W. Dite, Controller
   Benjamin Weiner, Secretary

Statement of Income (Year ends 12/31/—$ figures in 000's)

	1984	1983
Net Sales	$26,891	$24,827
Investment Income	1,131	672
Total Income	$28,022	$25,499
Costs and Expenses:		
Cost of Goods Sold	$11,299	$11,274
Research and Development	1,553	1,383
Selling, General and Administrative	7,620	5,837
Total Costs and Expenses	$20,472	$18,493
Income before Income Taxes	$ 7,550	$ 7,005
Income Taxes	2,866	3,636
Net Income	$ 4,684	$ 3,636

137

Stockholder's Equity, Jobs, and Labor Productivity ($ figures in 000's)

Year	Stockholder's Equity	Net Sales	Number of Employees	Index of Labor Productivity
1975	$ 631	$ 1,618	55	29.418
1976	837	3,111	122	25.500
1977	1,647	6,467	155	41.723
1978	2,703	8,396	182	46.132
1979	4,306	11,895	219	54.315
1980	6,300	15,326	234	65.496
1981	8,121	16,013	244	65.627
1982	10,116	18,577	216	86.005
1983	13,629	24,827	234	106.098
Change, 1983/1975	+ 2,060 %	+ 1,434 %	+ 326 %	+ 261 %

Capital Productivity ($ figures in 000's)

Year	Total Invested Capital	Net Income	Index of Capital Productivity
1975	$ 631	$ 13	.021
1976	907	205	.226
1977	1,647	795	.483
1978	2,703	1,110	.411
1979	4,488	1,663	.371
1980	6,519	2,082	.319
1981	8,307	1,943	.234
1982	10,265	2,141	.209
1983	13,629	3,636	.267
Change, 1983/1975	+ 2,060 %	+ 27,869 %	+ 1,195 %

Stock Prices and Earnings per Share[*]

Year	Stock Prices			Earnings[**] Per Share
	High	Low	Close	
1975	$ .296	$ .018	$ .018	$ .003
1976	.277	.111	.111	.047
1977	.740	.185	.185	.181
1978	3.630	.350	2.519	.246
1979	4.148	2.296	3.852	.364
1980	11.333	3.500	8.444	.453
1981	10.778	6.222	6.222	.418
1982	8.556	4.778	7.889	.458
1983	18.375	8.125	15.500	.780
1984	16.000	9.500	10.125	1.000

Change, 1975–84 + 56,250%; change, S&P 500 Index, 1975–84 + 82%

[*]Adjusted for stock splits and stock dividends   [**]Includes extraordinary items

CORPORATE PROFILE—DRANETZ TECHNOLOGIES, INC.

Dranetz Technologies designs, manufactures, and sells proprietary electronic instruments for the computer, electric utility, telecommunications, industrial process control, and energy management industries. The company's products are marketed worldwide to end users through independent sales representatives. The company achieved steady annual growth through fiscal 1985 and experienced volume softness and pressure on earnings during fiscal year 1986. The company has a strong balance sheet and has historically enjoyed high margins.

This small company does everything nearly to perfection. It could well serve as a model of the best in American business.

DREYFUS CORP.

Corporate Headquarters: 767 Fifth Avenue
New York, NY 10153

Telephone: (212) 715-6000
Incorporated in New York
New York Stock Exchange—DRY

Business: Manages a variety of mutual funds.
Officers:
  Howard Stein, Chairman and Chief Executive Officer
  Julian M. Smerling, Vice Chairman
  Joseph S. DiMartino, President and Chief Operating Officer
  Alan M. Eisner, Vice President and Chief Financial Officer
  Daniel C. Maclean III, Vice President and General Counsel
  Rodger A. Lawson, Vice President, Marketing
  Robert F. Dubuss, Vice President
  Monte J. Gordon, Vice President, Research
  Peter A. Santoriello, Vice President
  John J. Pyburn, Assistant Vice President

Statement of Income (Year ends 12/31—$ figures in 000's)

	1984	1983
Revenues		
Mgmt., Investment Advisory and Administrative Fees	$111,378	$103,910
Interest and Dividends	28,731	17,777
Other (Net)	3,525	5,375
Total Revenue	$143,634	$127,063
Expenses		
Salaries	$ 18,240	$ 17,202
Advertising and Other Direct Selling Exp.	13,895	12,976
Other Selling, General and Administrative Expenses	17,994	17,415
Interest	17,677	11,166
Total Expenses	$ 67,805	$ 58,759
Income before Taxes	$ 75,829	$ 68,304
Provision for Income Taxes		
Federal	29,500	25,501
State and Local	7,700	8,000
Net Income	$ 38,629	$ 34,004

Stockholder's Equity, Jobs, and Labor Productivity ($ figures in 000's)

Year	Stockholder's Equity	Net Sales	Number of Employees	Index of Labor Productivity
1975	$16,837	$ 17,425	210	82.976
1976	18,959	18,374	208	88.337
1977	12,773	19,988	200	99.940
1978	15,063	25,062	221	113.403
1979	20,150	34,202	312	109.622
1980	28,557	58,730	400	146.825
1981	44,131	86,996	500	173.992
1982	70,040	122,316	600	203.860
1983	92,519	127,063	650	195.482
Change, 1983/1975	+450 %	+629 %	+210 %	+136%

Capital Productivity ($ figures in 000's)

Year	Total Invested Capital	Net Income	Index of Capital Productivity
1975	$ 16,837	$ 3,244	.193
1976	18,959	3,287	.173
1977	13,210	3,577	.271
1978	15,408	3,835	.249
1979	20,381	5,840	.287
1980	29,725	11,936	.402
1981	44,131	21,470	.487
1982	70,040	33,984	.485
1983	167,519	34,004	.203
Change, 1983/1975	+895 %	+948 %	+5 %

Stock Prices and Earnings per Share*

Year	Stock Prices			Earnings** Per Share
	High	Low	Close	
1975	$ 1.396	$ .625	$ 1.021	$ .208
1976	1.583	1.042	1.376	.217
1977	1.729	1.229	1.667	.263
1978	2.958	1.667	1.875	.383
1979	3.479	1.917	3.167	.585
1980	8.875	2.792	7.479	1.175
1981	18.875	7.063	16.750	2.065
1982	27.875	12.125	18.875	3.250
1983	35.000	18.500	23.500	3.270
1984	40.000	23.250	37.750	3.720

Change, 1975–84 +1,686%; change, S&P 500 Index, 1975–84 +82%

*Adjusted for stock splits and stock dividends **Includes extraordinary items

This well-known firm manages and markets a variety of mutual funds using direct marketing techniques that basically combine advertising, direct mail, and telephone support. The company also provides services to banks that prefer to manage their own portfolios. In addition, Dreyfus has its own Gold Mastercard product. At yearend 1984 the company's net assets were approximately $22 billion with a little more than one-third of the total made up of the Dreyfus Liquid Asset Fund. The company's net income has grown more than tenfold in the last decade, and 1985 showed the company achieving all-time record highs in revenues and net income.

DYNATECH CORPORATION

Corporate Headquarters: 3 New England Executive Park
Burlington, MA 01803
Telephone: (617) 272-3304
Incorporated in Massachusetts
Over the Counter—DYTC

Business: Manufactures electronics-based test and measurement instruments in the fields of data, microwave and video communications.
Officers:
Warren M. Rohsenow, Chairman
J. P. Barger, President
Kenneth D. Roberts, Senior Vice President and Treasurer
Group Vice Presidents: James R. Turner, William W. Welsh, Jr., Ronald H. Weatherhogg, John F. Reno
Vice Presidents: Dwight W. Harvie, R. Claude Olier, Dorothy G. Cooley, John A. Powers, David S. Howell
Robert H. Hertz, Corporate Controller
Edward T. O'Dell, Jr., Secretary
Vera B. Durling, Assistant Secretary
Donald E. Worfolk, Assistant Secretary

Statement of Income (Year ends 3/31—$ figures in 000's)

	1985	1984
Sales	$204,626	$149,424
Cost of Sales	89,012	63,679
Gross Profit	$115,614	$ 85,745
Selling, General and Administrative Expense	$ 69,692	$ 52,563
Product Development Expense	14,651	12,111
Interest Expense	2,813	1,082
Other Income	(150)	(316)
Income before Gain on Sale of Subsidiaries and Provision for Income Taxes	$ 28,608	$ 20,305
Gain on Sale of Subsidiaries	4,001	—
Income before Provision for Income Taxes	$ 32,609	$ 20,305
Provision for Federal, Foreign and State Income Taxes	$ 13,427	$ 9,929
Net Income	$ 19,182	$ 11,013

Stockholder's Equity, Jobs, and Labor Productivity ($ figures in 000's)

Year	Stockholder's Equity	Net Sales	Number of Employees	Index of Labor Productivity
1975	$ 3,046	$ 12,857	300	42.857
1976	4,210	14,991	300	49.970
1977	5,761	19,246	400	48.115
1978	8,325	27,527	600	45.878
1979	11,543	37,974	800	47.468
1980	14,192	51,772	1,000	51.772
1981	21,973	69,822	1,250	55.858
1982	29,638	99,096	1,606	61.704
1983	48,346	146,965	2,000	73.483
Change, 1983/1975	+ 1,487 %	+ 1,043 %	+ 567 %	+ 72 %

Capital Productivity ($ figures in 000's)

Year	Total Invested Capital	Funds from Operations	Index of Capital Productivity
1975	$ 4,871	$ 1,128	.232
1976	5,768	1,428	.248
1977	8,804	1,940	.220
1978	12,207	3,016	.247
1979	16,132	3,933	.244
1980	25,229	5,058	.200
1981	31,583	7,295	.231
1982	42,763	10,101	.236
1983	59,457	15,257	.257
Change, 1983/1975	+ 1,121 %	+ 1,253 %	+ 11 %

Stock Prices and Earnings per Share[*]

Year	Stock Prices			Earnings[**] Per Share
	High	Low	Close	
1975	$ 1.417	$ .444	$ .559	$ .202
1976	2.083	.583	1.722	.247
1977	2.278	1.444	2.111	.324
1978	8.000	1.778	6.444	.476
1979	11.333	6.222	7.556	.600
1980	13.667	6.111	11.778	.622
1981	15.444	8.000	12.000	.760
1982	18.333	7.833	16.167	.947
1983	26.375	16.500	18.500	1.140
1984	20.250	11.000	18.500	1.960

Change, 1975–84 + 3,230%; change, S&P 500 Index, 1975–84 + 82%

[*]Adjusted for stock splits and stock dividends   [**]Includes extraordinary items

Dynatech is a diversified, rapidly growing high-technology company that manufactures and sells electronics-based test and measurement instruments. Its products are concentrated in niches of dynamic markets, primarily in the fields of data, microwave, and video communications. This company, which has shown continuous gains in sales and funds from operations, prides itself on a well-developed set of corporate strategies and philosophies. Among the most important of these is the commitment to highly decentralized operations, coupled with the company's recognition that product life cycles, especially in high-technology markets, are extremely short. As a result, the company attempts to exploit a niche strategy in which it can achieve a number one or number two market position. The company's stated objective is to grow 25 percent a year internally in sales and earnings and to maintain a return on shareholders' equity after taxes in the range of 30 percent.

E.G & G INC.

Corporate Headquarters: 45 Williams Street
Wellesley, MA 02181

Telephone: (617) 237-5100
Incorporated in Massachusetts
New York Stock Exchange—EGG

Business: Businesses are grouped into five major market segments: Instruments, Components, Environmental and Biomedical Services, Custom Services and Systems and Dept. of Energy Support.

Officers:

Bernard J. O'Keefe, Chairman

Dean W. Freed, President and Chief Executive Officer

John K. Buckner, Senior Vice President, Finance

Senior Vice Presidents: David J. Beaubien, Charles C. Francisco, George H. Gage, Joseph Giuffrida, John M. Kucharski

Leo M. Kelly, Vice President, General Counsel and Clerk

Vice Presidents: William T. Barrett, Arthur Bisberg, Harold D. Cunningham, Jean R. Erkelbout, Samuel Rubinovitz, Louis P. Valente, Charles M. Williams

John R. Dolan, Corporate Controller

Peter A. Broadbent, Treasurer

Statement of Income (Year ends 12/30—$ figures in 000's)

	1984	1983
Net Sales and Contract Revenues	$1,071,653	$904,237
Costs and Expenses		
Cost of Sales	878,269	739,823
Selling, General and Administrative	120,825	105,753
Total Costs and Expenses	$ 999,094	$845,576
Net Revenue	$ 72,559	$ 58,661
Net Fees from Nontechnical Support Activities	$ 8,160	$ 5,900
Income from Operations	$ 80,719	$ 64,561
Other Income	4,263	13,149
Income before Income Taxes	$ 84,982	$ 77,710
Income Taxes	31,443	31,065
Net Income	$ 53,539	$ 46,645

Stockholder's Equity, Jobs, and Labor Productivity ($ figures in 000's)

Year	Stockholder's Equity	Net Sales	Number of Employees	Index of Labor Productivity
1975	$ 48,709	$176,056	9,500	18.532
1976	60,869	251,007	12,500	20.081
1977	78,586	375,915	13,600	27.641
1978	63,515	440,526	14,760	29.846
1979	81,614	522,183	15,500	33.689
1980	109,083	613,093	17,000	36.064
1981	137,738	704,161	18,000	39.120
1982	175,201	800,843	18,000	44.491
1983	215,208	904,237	20,000	45.212
Change, 1983/1975	+342 %	+414 %	+111 %	+144 %

Capital Productivity ($ figures in 000's)

Year	Total Invested Capital	Net Income	Index of Capital Productivity
1975	$ 60,348	$ 6,881	.114
1976	75,457	9,603	.127
1977	90,828	13,068	.144
1978	75,104	16,721	.223
1979	92,656	20,634	.223
1980	121,522	26,310	.217
1981	148,536	34,119	.230
1982	187,355	40,157	.214
1983	226,508	46,645	.206
Change, 1983/1975	+275 %	+578 %	+81 %

Stock Prices and Earnings per Share*

Year	Stock Prices			Earnings** Per Share
	High	Low	Close	
1975	$ 4.969	$ 2.500	$ 3.531	$ .283
1976	4.875	3.375	4.250	.338
1977	5.375	3.969	4.438	.415
1978	8.250	4.125	7.250	.613
1979	12.313	6.375	12.219	.785
1980	24.313	11.250	21.813	.965
1981	22.000	16.188	19.750	1.210
1982	30.625	14.500	28.250	1.380
1983	38.125	26.000	32.500	1.560
1984	36.125	26.125	31.625	1.880

Change, 1975–84 +796%; change, S&P 500 Index, 1975–84 +82%

*Adjusted for stock splits and stock dividends   **Includes extraordinary items

147

E.G&G, Inc. is a diversified, technology-oriented company employing approximately 22,000 people. The company manufactures and markets electronic instruments and electronic and mechanical components concentrated in biomedical and energy-related research, services, and equipment. With its government contracts, E.G&G participates in long-term engineering and site-management programs that support the national defense and security; the nation's manned space program; and nuclear, fossil, and alternative energy research and development. During 1984 the major portion of the company's revenues came from components, custom services and systems, and Department of Energy projects. These three segments taken together represented nearly 90 percent of the company's sales and approximately three-fourths of the company's earnings. Under an effective strategic planning and control system, E.G&G is home for some 175 distinct businesses. The businesses provide advanced technical and scientific products and services to commercial, industrial, and governmental customers throughout the world. E.G&G represents an outstanding, well-recognized growth organization. Its achievements were noted in last year's Forbes ranking of electronic companies, in which it placed first among companies surveyed in profitability, second in earnings per share growth, and fifth in sales growth. Earnings per share have risen steadily since 1975.

To truly understand this company, it is necessary to know that it was founded by Harold "Doc" Edgerton, one of science's legends. This is a company about science and inquiry, run by scientists and engineers who have learned that profits are necessary to support their inquiries. E.G&G seems to have only upward growth and profits in its future.

ELECTROSPACE SYSTEMS, INC.

Corporate Headquarters: 1601 North Plano Road
                                           Richardson, TX 75083
Telephone: (214) 231-9303
Incorporated in Texas
New York Stock Exchange—ELE

Business: Designs, manufactures and installs telecommunications and navigation systems and equipment for military and industrial customers.

Officers:

James R. Lightner, Chairman, President and Treasurer
Dr. Robert L. Carrel, Executive Vice President and Secretary
Milton W. Holcombe, Vice President and Assistant Treasurer
Richard C. Fenwick, Vice President and Assistant Secretary
Donald E. Heitzman, Vice President, Marketing
Lonnie B. Roberts, Corporate Controller
Cecil C. Harvell, Assistant Vice President, Marketing

Statement of Income (Year ends 3/29/85 and 3/30/84—$ figures in 000's)

	1985	1984
Revenues	$107,839	$79,503
Cost of Revenues	90,755	65,962
Gross Profit on Revenues	$ 17,084	$13,541
General and Administrative Costs Not Allocated to Contract Costs	$ 1,031	$ 828
Interest Expense	230	174
Operating Profit	$ 15,823	$12,539
Other Income		
Interest	$ 2,466	$ 1,511
Miscellaneous	302	334
	$ 2,768	$ 1,845
Income before Provision for Income Tax	$ 18,591	$14,384
Provision for Income Tax	8,180	6,396
Net Income	$ 10,411	$ 7,988

Stockholder's Equity, Jobs, and Labor Productivity ($ figures in 000's)

Year	Stockholder's Equity	Net Sales	Number of Employees	Index of Labor Productivity
1975	$ 1,710	$ 8,525	275	31.000
1976	2,345	11,275	327	34.480
1977	3,000	14,535	434	33.491
1978	4,464	21,270	575	36.991
1979	6,353	33,561	975	34.422
1980	8,922	45,578	910	50.086
1981	13,105	55,088	952	57.866
1982	19,432	62,105	922	67.359
1983	26,908	79,503	1,148	69.253
Change, 1983/1975	+ 1,474 %	+ 833 %	+ 318 %	+ 123 %

Capital Productivity ($ figures in 000's)

Year	Total Invested Capital	Funds from Operations	Index of Capital Productivity
1975	$ 2,422	$ 645	.266
1976	2,920	752	.258
1977	3,460	1,193	.345
1978	6,588	2,207	.335
1979	8,853	3,469	.392
1980	11,102	2,888	.260
1981	14,959	5,717	.382
1982	21,247	6,000	.282
1983	34,832	10,541	.303
Change, 1983/1975	+ 1,338 %	+ 1,534 %	+ 14 %

Stock Prices and Earnings per Share[*]

Y r	Stock Prices			Earnings[**] Per Share
	High	Low	Close	
1975	n.a.	n.a.	n.a.	$.052
1976	n.a.	n.a.	n.a.	.057
1977	$ .667	$ .250	$ .250	.083
1978	1.500	.667	.667	.158
1979	1.653	1.653	1.653	.203
1980	6.528	1.664	5.760	.271
1981	6.880	4.160	6.800	.435
1982	15.900	6.300	14.000	.600
1983	28.400	13.700	18.400	.760
1984	24.625	13.250	21.000	.970

Change, 1977–84 + 8,400%; change, S&P 500 Index, 1975–84 + 73%

[*]Adjusted for stock splits and stock dividends   [**]Includes extraordinary items

Note: The fiscal year financial results in the tables above are shown in the year in which most of the results were achieved.

The company designs, manufactures, and installs telecommunications and navigation systems and equipment for military and industrial customers worldwide. The company's major product areas are: command, control, communications, aircraft modification, electronic warfare, military test ranges, and commercial telecommunications. Approximately 95 percent of the company's business in the past year was as a prime contractor or subcontractor to the U.S. government. During the last decade, Electrospace stock has split seven times, and the company's success as a government contractor has increasingly been recognized by the investment community.

Over one-third of its employees are scientists and engineers. Most of Electrospace's government business is won by competitive bid. The company has virtually no debt. In short, this is a defense contractor American business and government can be proud of.

EL PASO ELECTRIC COMPANY

Corporate Headquarters: 303 North Oregon Street
El Paso, TX 79901

Telephone: (915) 543-5711

Incorporated in Texas

Over the Counter—ELPA

Business: Generates and distributes electric power in the Rio Grande Valley.

Officers:

Evern R. Wall, President and Chairman of the Board

Billye E. Bostic, Executive Vice President

Statement of Income (Year ends 12/31—$ figures in 000's)

	1984	1983
Operating Revenues	$329,015	$302,443
Operating Expenses		
Operations		
Fuel	85,206	80,883
Purchased and Interchanged Power	43,329	34,679
Other	41,791	42,466
Maintenance	8,234	11,736
Depreciation and Amortization	12,445	11,740
Taxes		
Federal Income, Current	11,474	11,251
Federal Income, Deferred	23,912	12,313
Charge Equivalent to Investment Tax Credit, Net		
of Amortization	6,317	14,445
Other	17,364	16,724
Operating Income	78,943	66,206
Allowance for Equity Funds Used		
during Construction	54,663	41,660
Interest and Net Investment Income	7,249	4,028
Other Net	(309)	(267)
Federal Income Taxes Applicable to Other Income	(1,355)	593
Income before Interest Charges	139,191	112,220
Interest Charges (Credits)		
Interest on Long-Term Obligations	68,300	49,272
Other Interest	9,266	8,845
Interest Capitalized	(1,960)	(723)
Allowance for Borrowed Funds Used during		
Construction	(44,701)	(32,435)
Net Income	$108,286	$ 87,261

Stockholder's Equity, Jobs, and Labor Productivity ($ figures in 000's)

Year	Stockholder's Equity	Net Sales	Number of Employees	Index of Labor Productivity
1975	$ 64,313	$ 91,460	760	210.342
1976	77,729	111,188	798	139.333
1977	79,624	112,339	827	135.839
1978	112,022	136,556	851	160.465
1979	151,426	159,712	903	176.868
1980	221,686	210,513	979	215.029
1981	289,750	250,379	1,016	246.436
1982	385,417	270,090	1,083	249.391
1983	437,894	302,443	1,107	273.210
Change, 1983/1975	+581 %	+231 %	+46 %	+127 %

Capital Productivity ($ figures in 000's)

Year	Total Invested Capital	Net Income	Index of Capital Productivity
1975	$ 176,458	$10,098	.057
1976	189,059	11,517	.061
1977	237,268	11,422	.048
1978	288,210	16,024	.056
1979	392,020	23,190	.059
1980	507,422	41,177	.081
1981	625,238	56,697	.091
1982	874,218	70,888	.081
1983	1,048,330	87,261	.083
Change, 1983/1975	+494 %	+764 %	+46 %

Stock Prices and Earnings per Share[*]

Year	Stock Prices			Earnings[**] Per Share
	High	Low	Close	
1975	$11.250	$ 8.500	$10.125	$1.300
1976	11.625	9.750	11.625	1.290
1977	12.625	11.000	11.625	1.110
1978	11.875	9.875	10.500	1.300
1979	11.000	9.000	9.000	1.450
1980	10.125	7.875	9.375	2.050
1981	11.625	9.000	10.750	2.230
1982	12.750	10.000	12.250	2.480
1983	15.875	12.000	13.375	2.480
1984	14.500	10.000	13.000	2.880

Change, 1975–84 +28%; change, S&P 500 Index, 1975–84 +82%

[*]Adjusted for stock splits and stock dividends   [**]Includes extraordinary items

153

The company distributes electricity through an interconnected system to approximately 206,000 customers in El Paso, Texas and in an area in the Rio Grande Valley across Texas and New Mexico. In total, the service area has an estimated population of 660,000, including approximately 500,000 people in the metropolitan area of El Paso. Copper smelting and refining, oil refining, garment manufacturing, cattle raising, and agriculture are important industries in El Paso, which is also an important transportation and distribution center. During 1984, approximately 77 percent of the company's operating revenues were derived from Texas, 18 percent from New Mexico, and 5 percent from Federal Energy Regulatory Commission (FERC) jurisdictional customers. Also in 1984, no single customer of the company accounted for more than 4 percent of operating revenues. The projected annual peak load growth rate for the company's Texas and New Mexico service area during the 1984-1994 period is 4 percent.

ENTEX INC.

Corporate Headquarters: 1200 Milam
                          Houston, TX 77002
Telephone: (713) 654-5100
Incorporated in Texas
New York Stock Exchange—ETX

Business: Primarily engaged in the distribution of natural gas, but also owns a savings & loan association.

Officers:

Jackson C. Hinds, Chairman of the Board & Chief Executive Officer

Kenneth E. Montague, Vice Chairman of the Board

Wayne D. Johnson, President

John C. Capshaw, Exec. Vice President, Energy Resource Group & President, Entex Coal Co.

W. F. "Bill" Hinds, Exec. Vice President, General Manager of Distribution Operations

Howard E. Bell, Senior Vice President & Manager, Houston Division

Thomas L. Bourdreaux, Senior Vice President, Corporate Planning and Rates

E. M. DeMouche, Senior Vice President, Gas Supply, & President, Unit Gas Transmission Co.

Hubert Gentry, Jr., Senior Vice President & General Counsel

Sam J. Jeffrey, Senior Vice President & Chief Financial Officer

L. P. Jones, Senior Vice President, Marketing & Public Relations

Thomas J. Lee, Jr., Senior Vice President, Public Affairs

Patrick W. Lenahan, Senior Vice President, Mfg., & President & Chief Executive Officer, Datotek, Inc.

R. P. McCants, Senior Vice President, Technical Services

Statement of Income (Year ends 6/30—$ figures in 000's)

	1985	1984
Net Sales	$967,089	$1,092,852
Cost of Sales	670,805	789,816
Gross Profit	$296,284	$ 303,036
Selling, General and Administrative Expenses	$201,665	$ 208,018
Operating Income	$ 94,619	$ 95,018
Depreciation and Amortization Allowances	$ 25,997	$ 22,960
Income before Provision for Income Taxes	$ 68,622	$ 72,058
Income Taxes	24,065	22,058
Other Income (Losses)	$ (17,475)	$ 12,884
Net Income before Extraordinary Items	$ 27,082	$ 62,054
Income (Losses) from Extraordinary Items	$ 12,380	$ (1,539)
Net Income	$ 39,462	$ 60,515

Stockholder's Equity, Jobs, and Labor Productivity ($ figures in 000's)

Year	Stockholder's Equity	Net Sales	Number of Employees	Index of Labor Productivity
1975	$ 55,409	$ 190,875	2,361	80.845
1976	68,117	292,016	3,200	91.255
1977	92,736	554,219	3,180	174.283
1978	126,324	630,774	3,290	191.725
1979	153,992	682,718	4,574	149.261
1980	177,074	824,068	5,016	164.288
1981	202,019	981,647	4,969	197.554
1982	229,905	1,194,423	5,000	238.885
1983	270,136	1,317,898	5,000	263.580
Change, 1983/1975	+388 %	+591 %	+112 %	+226 %

Capital Productivity ($ figures in 000's)

Year	Total Invested Capital	Net Income	Index of Capital Productivity
1975	$118,049	$12,458	.106
1976	224,605	17,560	.078
1977	229,263	31,706	.138
1978	267,101	37,876	.142
1979	335,225	41,660	.124
1980	439,254	39,335	.090
1981	440,433	42,858	.097
1982	460,413	47,657	.104
1983	529,635	57,118	.108
Change, 1983/1975	+344 %	+359 %	+2 %

Stock Prices and Earnings per Share[*]

Year	Stock Prices			Earnings[**] Per Share
	High	Low	Close	
1975	$ 5.000	$ 2.417	$ 4.604	$ .618
1976	8.000	4.300	7.975	.838
1977	10.400	7.200	9.800	1.445
1978	14.400	8.350	12.900	1.808
1979	19.100	11.300	18.000	1.984
1980	18.625	11.750	15.375	1.870
1981	15.750	10.125	13.000	2.030
1982	20.125	10.125	18.750	2.250
1983	24.250	17.250	20.625	2.650
1984	21.750	16.000	20.250	2.760

Change, 1975–84 +346%; change, S&P 500 Index, 1975–84 +82%

[*]Adjusted for stock splits and stock dividends   [**]Includes extraordinary items

This company is primarily a public utility that purchases and distributes natural gas to approximately 1.25 million retail residential, commercial, and industrial customers in Texas, Louisiana, and Mississippi. It operates through natural gas distribution systems in 504 communities in those states. Either directly or through wholly owned subsidiaries, Entex also engages in contract drilling and selected manufacturing operations. The company also owns all of the outstanding stock of University Savings Association, a Texas-chartered savings and loan association. During fiscal 1985 natural gas operations represented more than 90 percent of the company's revenues and more than 100 percent of its operating income, since the company suffered losses in its other operations. The company's net income peaked in fiscal 1983, and in fiscal 1985 it adopted a plan to dispose of its refinery and roofing divisions, which were operated by its Allied Materials Corporation subsidiary. This plan caused the company to reflect a significant extraordinary item, further depressing fiscal 1985 net income.

E SYSTEMS, INC.

Corporate Headquarters: 6250 LBJ Freeway, P.O. Box 226030
                        Dallas, TX 75266
Telephone: (214) 661-1000
Incorporated in Delaware
New York Stock Exchange—ESY

Business: Develops one-of-a-kind electronic defense systems.
Officers:
  John W. Dixon, Chairman and Chief Executive Officer
  David R. Tacke, President and Chief Operating Officer
  E. Gene Keiffer, Vice President, Electronics Systems Group
  A. Lowell Lawson, Vice President, Aircraft Systems Group
  Eaton Adams, Jr., Vice President, Customer Relations
  Eugene E. Berg, Vice President, Corporate Planning
  James W. Crowley, Vice President, Secretary, and General Counsel
  Lee M. Crutchfield, Vice President, Corporate Administration
  Charles R. Farmer, Jr., Vice President, General Manager, Garland Div.
  T. Brice Johnson, Jr., Vice President, General Manager, Greenville Div.
  Thomas D. Kelly, Vice President, Finance and Chief Financial Officer
  James W. Pope, Vice President and Controller
  Joe W. Russell, Vice President, Corporate Relations
  Harry L. Thurmon, Vice President, New Business Development

Statement of Income (Year ends 12/31—$ figures in 000's)

	1984	1983
Net Sales	$819,353	$826,819
Other Income	6,605	10,686
Costs and Expenses		
Contract and Manufacturing Costs	646,090	667,928
Selling, General and Administrative Expenses	76,481	75,112
Interest Expense	2,121	1,712
Income before Taxes	101,266	92,752
Federal Income Taxes		
Current	34,624	33,833
Deferred	4,157	3,674
Net Income	$ 61,109	$ 55,246

Stockholder's Equity, Jobs, and Labor Productivity ($ figures in 000's)

Year	Stockholder's Equity	Net Sales	Number of Employees	Index of Labor Productivity
1975	$ 42,308	$254,202	9,067	28.036
1976	52,108	319,900	10,540	30.351
1977	67,917	347,353	9,816	35.386
1978	89,371	340,399	10,765	31.631
1979	105,865	393,728	10,734	36.680
1980	137,951	422,229	10,624	41.625
1981	157,140	572,045	11,771	48.598
1982	188,733	754,385	12,142	62.130
1983	238,333	826,819	11,941	69.242
Change, 1983/1975	+ 463 %	+ 225 %	+ 32 %	+ 147%

Capital Productivity ($ figures in 000's)

Year	Total Invested Capital	Net Income	Index of Capital Productivity
1975	$ 59,304	$ 7,163	.121
1976	68,836	14,528	.211
1977	83,430	18,980	.227
1978	116,894	12,650	.108
1979	146,666	18,617	.127
1980	158,320	12,759	.081
1981	187,160	23,837	.127
1982	214,809	35,779	.167
1983	246,242	55,246	.224
Change, 1983/1975	+ 315 %	+ 671 %	+ 86 %

Stock Prices and Earnings per Share*

Year	Stock Prices			Earnings** Per Share
	High	Low	Close	
1975	$ 3.729	$ .866	$ 2.237	$ .352
1976	5.464	2.256	5.464	.680
1977	6.188	4.266	4.922	.908
1978	6.633	3.656	4.641	.572
1979	8.750	3.938	8.219	.780
1980	13.500	6.750	12.500	.468
1981	13.906	9.656	12.531	.835
1982	25.375	10.875	24.125	1.210
1983	44.750	23.000	31.500	1.820
1984	33.875	21.750	24.000	2.020

Change, 1975–84 + 475%; change, S&P 500 Index, 1975–84 + 82%

*Adjusted for stock splits and stock dividends   **Includes extraordinary items

This company is a major provider to the U.S. government of sophisticated strategic and tactical products and services that can best be typified as one-of-a-kind electronic defense systems. The company's operations can be grouped into three basic product categories. The Electronic Warfare category includes strategic systems for intelligence, reconnaissance, and surveillance applications and tactical systems relating to electronic countermeasures and jamming and deception devices. The Command Control and Communications category includes communications equipment and command and control systems that process data for ready analysis and decision making. In the Guidance, Controls, and Navigation category, automatic control products for aircraft, missile steering and tracking systems, and aircraft navigation aids are developed and manufactured. This high-technology government supplier has achieved a prominent position in the area of electronic defense systems.

This is another defense contractor to be proud of. E-Systems operates at the absolute leading edge of technology. It invests heavily in research and development to keep the company and the country strong. Almost half of all of the employees have technical and scientific backgrounds. And, finally, E-Systems has achieved its current leading position virtually debt free.

FAMILY DOLLAR STORES, INC.

Corporate Headquarters: 10401 Old Monroe Road
Charlotte, NC 28212

Telephone: (704) 847-6961
Incorporated in Delaware
New York Stock Exchange—FDO

Business: Operates small, self-service, retail, discount stores throughout the Southeast and Mid-Atlantic.

Officers:

Leon Levine, Chairman and Treasurer
Lewis E. Levine, President
Howard R. Levine, Senior Vice President, Merchandising and Advertising
George R. Mahoney, Jr., Senior Vice President, General Counsel
William Oddy, Senior Vice President, Finance and Administration
James A. Seagraves, Senior Vice President, Store Operations
Stephen G. Simms, Senior Vice President, Real Estate and Construction
Thomas L. DeSensi, Vice President, Store Operations
Daniel Jenkins, Vice President, Advertising and Sales Promotion
Albert S. Rorie, Vice President, Data Processing
Daniel M. Smith, Vice President, General Merchandise Manager
Douglas B. Sullivan, Vice President, Real Estate
Norman B. Weizer, Vice President, Store Operations
Donald D. Jensen, Controller
Daylon W. Powell, Assistant Treasurer
Janice B. Burris, Assistant Secretary

Statement of Income (Year ends 8/31—$ figures in 000's)

	1985	1984
Revenues		
Net Sales	$410,088	$340,919
Other	5,385	5,578
	$415,474	$346,497
Costs and Expenses		
Cost of Sales	$252,247	$211,530
Selling, General and Administrative	111,222	90,491
	$363,469	$302,021
Income before Income Taxes	$ 52,005	$ 44,476
Income Taxes	23,998	20,919
Net Income	$ 28,007	$ 23,557

161

Stockholder's Equity, Jobs, and Labor Productivity ($ figures in 000's)

Year	Stockholder's Equity	Net Sales	Number of Employees	Index of Labor Productivity
1975	$12,773	$ 53,188	2,060	25.819
1976	15,949	71,709	1,930	37.155
1977	19,905	90,586	2,805	32.294
1978	25,109	117,521	3,100	37.910
1979	31,535	151,834	4,250	35.726
1980	38,594	166,854	3,500	47.673
1981	46,368	181,713	3,800	47.819
1982	54,979	207,419	4,200	49.385
1983	69,957	264,440	4,400	60.100
Change, 1983/1975	+ 448 %	+ 397 %	+ 114 %	+ 133 %

Capital Productivity ($ figures in 000's)

Year	Total Invested Capital	Net Income	Index of Capital Productivity
1975	$12,798	$ 1,348	.105
1976	15,949	3,833	.240
1977	19,905	4,689	.236
1978	25,109	6,151	.245
1979	31,535	7,737	.245
1980	38,594	8,337	.216
1981	46,368	9,117	.197
1982	54,979	10,695	.195
1983	69,957	15,727	.225
Change, 1983/1975	+ 447 %	+ 1,067 %	+ 113 %

Stock Prices and Earnings per Share[*]

Year	Stock Prices			Earnings[**] Per Share
	High	Low	Close	
1975	$ .778	$ .222	$ .741	$.050
1976	1.241	.667	.944	.144
1977	1.093	.796	1.056	.175
1978	2.444	1.037	1.444	.228
1979	2.333	1.426	1.889	.284
1980	2.667	1.444	2.296	.304
1981	3.333	2.259	3.333	.326
1982	8.694	2.972	7.861	.380
1983	18.000	7.667	13.833	.553
1984	19.500	10.833	16.250	.827

Change, 1975–84 + 2,094%; change, S&P 500 Index, 1975–84 + 82%

[*]Adjusted for stock splits and stock dividends   [**]Includes extraordinary items

This company is one of the fastest growing discount store chains in the United States. During the fiscal year ended August 31, 1985, 155 new stores were added to the chain to bring the number of stores in operation to 920. The company plans to open approximately 180 new stores during fiscal year 1986. The stores are located in a contiguous 20 state area ranging as far north as Pennsylvania and Ohio, south to Florida and west to Texas. The stores' relatively small size—generally from 6,000 to 8,000 square feet—gives the company great flexibility to open outlets in all markets, from small rural towns to large urban centers. The merchandise is sold in a no-frills, low-overhead, self-service environment on a cash-and-carry basis. Substantially all merchandise is priced at $17.99 or less. This outstanding retailer has compiled 25 years of consistent growth in sales and earnings. The company has no long-term debt and is expected to continue to grow significantly through the addition of new stores and continued emphasis on its "low- to middle-income" market niche.

FARMERS GROUP, INC.

Corporate Headquarters: 4680 Wilshire Blvd.
Los Angeles, CA 90010

Telephone: (213) 932-3200
Incorporated in Nevada
Over the Counter—FGRP

Business: A management and holding company for a group of insurance companies.

Officers:

Richard G. Lindsley, Chairman of the Board and Chief Executive Officer
Leo E. Denlea, Jr., President and Chief Operating Officer

Statement of Income (Year ends 12/31—$ figures in 000's)

	1984	1983
Consolidated Revenues	$893,828	$789,869
Management of Property and Casualty Insurance Companies and Other		
Gross Operating Revenues	451,723	407,241
Agent's New Business Commissions	26,844	24,959
Net Operating Revenues	424,879	382,282
Salaries and Employee Benefits	149,137	137,127
Buildings and Equipment	32,842	30,862
General and Administrative Expenses	85,593	73,993
Total Operating Expenses	$266,572	$241,982
Operating Income	157,307	140,300
Interest and Dividends	13,110	11,842
Real Estate Investment Income, Principally Gains on Sales	3,287	2,883
Income before Provision for Income Taxes	173,704	155,025
Provision for Income Taxes	80,812	71,375
Net Income	92,892	83,650
Life Insurance Subsidiaries		
Life and Annuity Premiums	183,274	160,088
Accident and Health Premiums	177,893	151,738
Total Premium Income	361,167	311,826
Investment Income, Net of Expenses	107,782	95,761
Total Revenues	468,949	407,587
Life and Annuity Benefits	99,772	90,107
Accident and Health Benefits	138,568	128,574
Increase in Liability for Future Policy Benefits	25,321	23,175
Amortization of Deferred Policy Acquisition Costs	42,061	37,089
Commission	24,839	21,787
Total Operating Expenses	$364,823	$330,652
Income before Provision for Income Taxes	104,117	76,935
Provision for Income Taxes	11,148	22,900
Net Income	$ 92,969	$ 54,035
Consolidated Net Income	$185,861	$137,685

Stockholder's Equity, Jobs, and Labor Productivity ($ figures in 000's)

Year	Stockholder's Equity	Net Sales	Number of Employees	Index of Labor Productivity
1975	$186,982	$108,271	6,507	16.369
1976	224,897	138,593	7,610	18.212
1977	405,117	327,140	8,873	36.869
1978	465,447	377,814	9,562	39.930
1979	539,116	434,507	10,496	41.755
1980	618,760	480,448	11,181	42.970
1981	696,438	554,890	11,620	47.753
1982	793,988	633,100	12,140	52.150
1983	894,388	789,869	12,431	63.526
Change, 1983/1975	+378 %	+629 %	+91 %	+282 %

Capital Productivity ($ figures in 000's)

Year	Total Invested Capital	Funds from Operations	Index of Capital Productivity
1975	$196,742	$ 25,014	.127
1976	234,672	32,931	.140
1977	441,263	125,361	.284
1978	501,774	138,396	.276
1979	572,498	159,343	.278
1980	651,947	172,250	.264
1981	728,956	201,057	.276
1982	826,922	212,387	.257
1983	929,996	238,419	.256
Change, 1983/1975	+373 %	+853 %	+102 %

Stock Prices and Earnings per Share[*]

Year	Stock Prices			Earnings[**] Per Share
	High	Low	Close	
1975	$21.333	$13.750	$19.000	$1.303
1976	23.750	17.875	22.750	1.600
1977	23.000	18.750	22.625	2.080
1978	30.500	20.500	23.875	2.500
1979	29.625	21.125	27.000	3.000
1980	32.125	23.000	27.875	3.150
1981	36.250	25.250	32.000	3.530
1982	40.125	29.250	35.250	3.770
1983	49.125	32.000	41.750	4.060
1984	52.500	34.250	49.625	5.480

Change, 1975–84 +161%; change, S&P 500 Index, 1975–84 +82%

[*]Adjusted for stock splits and stock dividends   [**]Includes extraordinary items

Farmers Group is a management company and insurance holding company. Member companies of the Farmers Insurance Group include: Farmers Insurance Exchange, Truck Insurance Exchange, Fire Insurance Exchange, Mid-Century Insurance Company, Farmers New World Life Insurance Company, The Ohio State Life Insurance Company, and Investors Guaranty Life Insurance Company. Ohio State Life and Investors Guaranty Life offer their policies to the public through separate agency organizations, while the policies of the other companies within the group are sold exclusively through the Farmers Insurance Group Agency Force, composed of almost 13,000 direct-writing agents.

Despite the depressed state of the casualty insurance business, lately because of high awards, Farmers' attention to this important area has generated profits from operations every year.

GELMAN SCIENCES INC.

Corporate Headquarters: 600 South Wagner Road, Box 1448
Ann Arbor, MI 48106
Telephone: (313) 665-0651
Incorporated in Michigan
American Stock Exchange—GSC

Business: Manufactures microporous polymeric membranes and filtration devices and systems using those membranes.

Officers:

Charles Gelman, Chairman & President

William Emhiser, Vice President & General Manager, Laboratory Division

Santosh Mehra, Senior Vice President, Finance & Corp. Staff & Chief Financial Officer

James C. Marshall, Senior Vice President, Operations

Paul Seliskar, Vice President & General Manager, Industrial Division

Monty E. Vincent, Senior Vice President & President, Medical Device Division

Anthony Bernard, Vice President, International Operations

Statement of Income (Year ends 7/31—$ figures in 000's)

	1985	1984
Net Sales	$46,896	$42,611
Other Income-Net	165	524
	$47,062	$43,135
Costs and Expenses		
Costs of Products Sold	$26,767	$43,135
Selling and Administrative	15,240	13,729
Research and Development	2,885	2,899
Interest and Finance Charges	1,233	1,055
Litigation Settlement	—	756
	$46,126	$40,834
Earnings before Income Taxes and Extraordinary Credit	$ 936	$ 2,301
Income Taxes	214	664
Extraordinary Item	—	175
Net Earnings	$ 722	$ 1,812

Stockholder's Equity, Jobs, and Labor Productivity ($ figures in 000's)

Year	Stockholder's Equity	Net Sales	Number of Employees	Index of Labor Productivity
1975	$ 3,241	$12,284	382	32.157
1976	4,948	17,768	525	33.844
1977	5,846	20,730	550	37.691
1978	7,250	26,576	590	45.044
1979	9,372	34,015	710	47.908
1980	9,986	43,394	770	56.356
1981	15,727	38,314	650	58.945
1982	14,242	37,092	605	61.309
1983	15,682	40,331	657	61.387
Change, 1983/1975	+384 %	+228 %	+72 %	+91 %

Capital Productivity ($ figures in 000's)

Year	Total Invested Capital	Net Income	Index of Capital Productivity
1975	$ 6,413	$ 918	.143
1976	7,474	1,472	.197
1977	8,878	1,229	.138
1978	12,469	2,040	.164
1979	15,691	2,800	.178
1980	20,253	1,478	.073
1981	22,817	1,506	.066
1982	25,817	1,247	.050
1983	23,474	3,827	.163
Change, 1983/1975	+266 %	+317 %	+14 %

Stock Prices and Earnings per Share[*]

Year	Stock Prices			Earnings[**] Per Share
	High	Low	Close	
1975	$ 6.167	$ 1.667	$ 5.417	$ .247
1976	10.167	5.500	8.500	.493
1977	11.000	5.333	10.667	.273
1978	16.667	7.333	10.167	.560
1979	19.250	10.000	17.583	.760
1980	19.479	9.688	15.208	.183
1981	20.000	12.000	13.875	2.780
1982	14.250	8.000	10.375	.010
1983	18.375	10.125	14.250	.700
1984	16.250	9.750	10.500	.730

Change, 1975–84 +94%; change, S&P 500 Index, 1975–84 +82%

[*]Adjusted for stock splits and stock dividends   [**]Includes extraordinary items

This company's major area of business is the servicing of the industrial, scientific, and medical communities with its expertise in polymeric membranes. The company provides the means of separation and purification through the utilization of these membranes. These separation technologies are applied to various types of filtration, fluid analysis, clinical diagnosis, and medical Product engineering support of this technology is the second area of business for the company. This includes the development and manufacture of membranes, filtration equipment and hardware, electrophoretic diagnostic procedures, and disposable filtration devices. The company's 1985 net earnings did not show an increase over the 1984 level, partially reflecting a litigation settlement charge. The company has assembled an impressive array of technology, and now the issue of translating this resource into sales and earnings growth is of paramount importance.

GENERAL MICROWAVE CORPORATION

Corporate Headquarters: 155 Marine Street
Farmingdale, NY 11735

Telephone: (516) 694-3600
Incorporated in New York
American Stock Exchange—GMIC

Business: Manufactures instruments and components for measuring and controlling microwaves.

Officers:

Sherman A. Rinkel, President
Moe Wind, Senior Vice President, Treasurer and Assistant Secretary
Bernard Grand, Vice President, Engineering
Leonard Trugman, Vice President, Manufacturing
Bernard Smilowitz, Vice President, Research and Development
Howard Cohen, Vice President, Administration
Michael Stolzar, Secretary and Assistant Treasurer

Statement of Income (Year ends 2/28/85 and 2/29/84—$ figures in 000's)

	1985	1984
Net Sales	$13,481	$11,876
Expenses		
Cost of Sales	$ 8,254	$ 7,177
Selling and Advertising	1,675	1,464
Research and Development	453	388
General and Administrative	1,157	968
	$11,539	$ 9,997
Other Deductions (Income)		
Interest Expense	$ 13	$ 33
License and Royalty Income	(12)	(17)
Dividends on Investments	(598)	(309)
Sundry	124	14
	$ (473)	$ (279)
Income before Taxes	$ 2,416	$ 2,158
Income Taxes	795	817
Net Income	$ 1,621	$ 1,341

Stockholder's Equity, Jobs, and Labor Productivity ($ figures in 000's)

Year	Stockholder's Equity	Net Sales	Number of Employees	Index of Labor Productivity
1975	$ 2,118	$ 3,996	125	31.968
1976	2,204	3,597	120	29.975
1977	2,401	4,548	131	34.718
1978	2,408	5,159	138	37.384
1979	2,603	5,790	150	38.600
1980	2,731	7,553	150	50.353
1981	3,155	8,701	160	54.381
1982	3,411	9,468	175	54.103
1983	10,430	11,876	212	56.019
Change, 1983/1975	+ 392 %	+ 197 %	+ 70 %	+ 75 %

Capital Productivity ($ figures in 000's)

Year	Total Invested Capital	Net Income	Index of Capital Productivity
1975	$ 2,161	$ 388	.180
1976	2,235	261	.117
1977	2,429	394	.162
1978	2,508	308	.123
1979	2,715	382	.141
1980	2,833	373	.132
1981	3,245	696	.214
1982	3,492	890	.255
1983	10,491	2,130	.203
Change, 1983/1975	+ 386 %	+ 449 %	13 %

Stock Prices and Earnings per Share*

Year	Stock Prices			Earnings** Per Share
	High	Low	Close	
1975	$ 1.750	$ .500	$ .500	$ .330
1976	2.000	1.500	1.500	.180
1977	2.125	1.750	1.750	.320
1978	2.750	1.500	1.500	.190
1979	2.750	1.250	2.125	.260
1980	7.750	2.000	5.250	.210
1981	8.250	4.250	6.500	.540
1982	9.500	4.000	8.500	.730
1983	18.250	8.750	15.500	1.120
1984	17.750	11.500	14.000	1.210

Change, 1975–84 + 2,800%; change, S&P 500 Index, 1975–84 + 82%

*Adjusted for stock splits and stock dividends **Includes extraordinary items

CORPORATE PROFILE—GENERAL MICROWAVE CORPORATION

The business of this company is the design, development, manufacture, and marketing of microwave components and subsystems and related electronic test and measurement equipment. A substantial portion of the company's products is sold to manufacturers and users of microwave systems and equipment for applications in the defense electronics industry. The company also sells components and equipment for use in the industrial test equipment and commercial telecommunications industries. A substantial portion of the company's revenues is derived from military sources, as the company manufactures components and instruments for a number of ongoing military programs. The company has traditionally developed new products for sale as standard catalog items as well as products designed to customer specifications under fixed price contracts. The company markets its microwave products in the United States and Canada through 12 sales engineers and marketing support personnel and through 8 independent sales organizations. Foreign sales accounted for approximately 23 percent of the company's net sales in fiscal 1985. This company, while among the smallest of the firms profiled in this book, has achieved consistent growth in its market niche.

GERBER SCIENTIFIC INC.

Corporate Headquarters: 83 Gerber Road West
                         South Windsor, CT 06074

Telephone: (203) 644-1551
Incorporated in Connecticut
New York Stock Exchange—GBR

Business: Develops computer-aided design and computer-aided manufacturing (CAD/CAM) technologies and systems for factory automation.

Officers:

H. Joseph Gerber, President
Stanley Leven, Senior Vice President, Secretary and General Counsel
David J. Logan, Senior Vice President, Engineering
Robert J. Maerz, Senior Vice President, Operations and Marketing
George M. Gentile, Senior Vice President, Finance and Treasurer

Statement of Income (Year ends 4/30—$ figures in 000's)

	1985	1984
Net Sales	$224,158	$173,593
Cost of Goods	105,371	87,418
Gross Profit	118,787	86,175
Selling, General and Administrative Expenses	60,340	49,629
Research and Development Expense	16,893	10,594
Operating Income	41,554	25,952
Non-Operating Income	5,486	2,563
Interest Expense	3,333	3,506
Income before Provision for Taxes	43,707	25,009
Income Taxes	18,800	10,600
Income from Minority Interests	152	268
Net Income	$ 25,059	$ 14,677

Stockholder's Equity, Jobs, and Labor Productivity ($ figures in 000's)

Year	Stockholder's Equity	Net Sales	Number of Employees	Index of Labor Productivity
1975	$ 7,219	$ 14,480	380	38.105
1976	8,280	20,778	460	45.170
1977	10,037	27,232	629	43.294
1978	13,841	45,049	900	50.054
1979	19,517	74,400	1,300	57.231
1980	33,589	93,105	1,300	71.619
1981	36,690	114,756	1,400	81.969
1982	36,336	117,247	1,500	78.165
1983	92,914	173,593	1,650	105.208
Change, 1983/1975	+ 1,187 %	+ 1,099 %	+ 334 %	+ 176 %

Capital Productivity ($ figures in 000's)

Year	Total Invested Capital	Net Income	Index of Capital Productivity
1975	$ 12,259	$ 17	.001
1976	12,880	1,024	.080
1977	16,545	1,707	.103
1978	24,299	3,877	.160
1979	43,523	5,854	.135
1980	60,765	8,881	.146
1981	63,942	3,261	.051
1982	77,501	4,517	.058
1983	125,303	14,677	.117
Change, 1983/1975	+ 922 %	+ 86,253 %	+ 8,347 %

Stock Prices and Earnings per Share[*]

Year	Stock Prices			Earnings[**] Per Share
	High	Low	Close	
1975	$ .361	$ .111	$ .194	$ .001
1976	.444	.185	.361	.078
1977	.694	.343	.620	.127
1978	2.542	.500	1.792	.280
1979	6.417	1.806	6.417	.420
1980	12.667	4.778	11.000	.627
1981	12.056	4.222	5.222	.231
1982	6.722	2.889	5.667	.316
1983	19.500	5.500	17.833	.947
1984	21.000	12.000	15.875	1.450

Change, 1975–84 + 97,750%; change, S&P 500 Index, 1975–84 + 82%

[*]Adjusted for stock splits and stock dividends   [**]Includes extraordinary items

Note: The fiscal year financial results in the tables above are shown in the year in which most of the results were achieved.

174

Gerber's family of high-technology companies are international leaders in applying computer-aided design and computer-aided manufacturing (CAD/CAM) technologies to factory automation. Gerber factory automation systems are positioned to be key elements in increasing productivity by reducing costs, shortening development and manufacturing cycles, and improving quality. The Gerber companies use their respective technologies to develop CAD/CAM products in computer controlled drafting and photoplotting; low-cost interactive design; computerized marker making, material cutting, and material handling; sophisticated turnkey interactive graphic production systems that integrate several design and manufacturing processes; and microprocessor-controlled production systems. Gerber automation systems are used by a wide range of industries including aerospace, apparel, automotive, electronics, tool and die, printing, graphic arts, and sign making. This company has achieved major status in the factory automation industry and refers to itself as the "productivity company." There seems to be a significant market potential for applying computer technology to automatic manufacturing processes, and this company, through an aggressive new product development group, technological and engineering strengths, and aggressive marketing, stands an excellent chance to be a major participant in this major industry.

GRAY COMMUNICATIONS SYSTEMS, INC.

Corporate Headquarters: P.O. Box 3909
Albany, GA 31706

Telephone: (912) 436-1556
Incorporated in Georgia
Over the Counter—GCOM

Business: Publishes newspapers; television broadcasting, car rental and other services.

Officers:

James H. Gray, Chairman and President
Raymond E. Carow, Executive Vice President
Vice Presidents: Hugh V. Roche, Ray H. Holloway, Perley E. Eppley, Sr.
Barbara Jones, Treasurer
Dorothy A. Zimmerman, Secretary
Richard D. Carson, Controller

Statement of Income (Year ends 6/30—$ figures in 000's)

	1985	1984
Net Sales	$43,465	$41,522
Cost of Sales	27,453	26,493
Gross Profit	$16,012	$15,028
Selling, General and Administrative Expenses	$11,154	$10,473
Operating Income	$ 4,857	$ 4,555
Non-Operating Income	$ 220	$ 202
Interest Expense	168	78
Income before Provision for Income Taxes	$ 4,909	$ 4,680
Income Taxes	2,300	2,130
Net Income	$ 2,609	$ 2,550

Stockholder's Equity, Jobs, and Labor Productivity ($ figures in 000's)

Year	Stockholder's Equity	Net Sales	Number of Employees	Index of Labor Productivity
1975	$ 2,588	$10,025	350	28.643
1976	3,394	12,786	350	36.531
1977	4,335	14,607	376	38.848
1978	5,540	18,044	358	50.402
1979	7,297	23,752	437	54.352
1980	9,368	35,806	450	79.568
1981	11,642	36,979	463	79.868
1982	12,949	39,371	482	81.683
1983	15,027	38,951	488	79.818
Change, 1983/1975	+ 481 %	+ 289 %	+ 39 %	+ 179 %

Capital Productivity ($ figures in 000's)

Year	Total Invested Capital	Net Income	Index of Capital Productivity
1975	$ 7,169	$ 645	.090
1976	8,032	1,022	.127
1977	9,311	1,115	.120
1978	9,845	1,342	.136
1979	11,193	1,753	.157
1980	13,419	2,500	.186
1981	15,390	2,447	.159
1982	16,753	2,059	.123
1983	18,459	2,282	.124
Change, 1983/1975	+ 158 %	+ 254 %	+ 37 %

Stock Prices and Earnings per Share[*]

Year	Stock Prices			Earnings[**] Per Share
	High	Low	Close	
1975	$ 7.000	$ 6.000	$ 6.500	$1.360
1976	7.500	6.000	7.500	2.150
1977	12.750	8.000	12.000	2.350
1978	24.000	11.500	21.000	2.810
1979	42.500	21.000	42.500	3.520
1980	65.500	32.000	59.500	4.950
1981	59.500	38.500	40.500	4.790
1982	44.500	34.000	44.000	4.080
1983	60.500	42.000	60.500	4.590
1984	69.000	55.000	69.000	5.100

Change, 1975–84 + 962%; change, S&P 500 Index, 1975–84 + 82%

[*]Adjusted for stock splits and stock dividends   [**]Includes extraordinary items

177

CORPORATE PROFILE—GRAY COMMUNICATIONS SYSTEMS, INC.

The company operates through four segments: broadcasting, publishing, transportation, and video systems sales. Broadcasting operates three VHF television stations: WALB-TV in Albany, Georgia; WJHG-TV in Panama City, Florida; and KTVE in El Dorado, Arkansas and Monroe, Louisiana. The publishing group operates a daily newspaper, the Albany Herald. Transportation services operates two warehouse-distribution centers, an air service fixed-based operation, and several retail tire stores. Video system sales, which sells and services electronic equipment and designs video and audio systems, serves the broadcasting industry with sales offices located in Alabama, Arkansas, Florida, Georgia, Louisiana, and Tennessee. The majority of the company's operating profits comes from its broadcasting and publishing activities. The company's net income in fiscal 1985 just marginally exceeded 1980's. The company has a strong balance sheet, with cash almost equal to total current liabilities. A return to stronger growth is expected.

GROW GROUP INC.

Corporate Headquarters: Pan Am Building
200 Park Avenue
New York, NY 10166

Telephone: (212) 599-4400
Incorporated in New York
New York Stock Exchange—GRO

Business: Manufactures and markets a broad mix of high technology paints, coatings and products for industrial and consumer markets worldwide.

Officers:

Russell Banks, President and Chief Executive Officer
John F. Gleason, Executive Vice President
Leslie D. Stott, Vice President, Automotive
J. Robert Desjardins, Group Vice President, Trade Sales
Joseph M. Quinn, Vice President, Marine and Corrosion Control
David J. Magid, Group Vice President, Consumer
Bernard T. Hanley, Vice President, Finance
Edward A. Smolinski, Vice President and Treasurer
Grant McLennan, Vice President, Consumer Marketing
W. Horton Russell, Vice President, Manufacturing, Safety, Health and Environment

Statement of Income (Year ends 6/30—$ figures in 000's)

	1984	1983
Revenues	$276,130	$237,592
Costs and Expenses		
Cost of Products Sold	$170,124	$148,031
Research, Development and Quality Control	6,872	5,597
Storage and Delivery	11,997	11,196
Selling and Administrative	67,786	58,592
Interest, Principally on Long-Term Debt	4,096	4,195
Total Costs and Expenses	$260,875	$227,611
Income from Continuing Operations before Income Taxes	$ 15,255	$ 9,981
Income Taxes		
Federal—Current	4,672	1,881
Federal—Deferred	1,052	1,211
State and Local	1,300	1,037
Foreign	151	328
Total Income Taxes	$ 7,175	$ 4,457
Net Income	$ 8,080	$ 5,524

Stockholder's Equity, Jobs, and Labor Productivity ($ figures in 000's)

Year	Stockholder's Equity	Net Sales	Number of Employees	Index of Labor Productivity
1975	$ 9,982	$ 92,538	1,300	71.183
1976	10,370	99,425	2,000	49.713
1977	18,539	176,943	2,200	80.429
1978	21,311	189,418	2,177	87.009
1979	25,672	214,555	2,250	95.358
1980	37,903	227,599	2,250	101.155
1981	42,225	232,483	2,100	110.706
1982	44,715	228,669	1,920	119.098
1983	48,523	235,617	1,930	122.081
Change, 1983/1975	+ 386 %	+ 155 %	+ 49 %	+ 72 %

Capital Productivity ($ figures in 000's)

Year	Total Invested Capital	Net Income	Index of Capital Productivity
1975	$29,423	$1,389	.047
1976	50,906	2,045	.040
1977	59,275	3,805	.064
1978	66,592	4,089	.061
1979	70,586	4,577	.065
1980	79,700	4,612	.058
1981	77,533	5,227	.067
1982	89,976	5,704	.063
1983	91,254	5,524	.061
Change, 1983/1975	+ 210 %	+ 298 %	+ 28 %

Stock Prices and Earnings per Share[*]

Year	Stock Prices			Earnings[**] Per Share
	High	Low	Close	
1975	$ 2.888	$1.534	$ 2.393	$.278
1976	3.932	2.322	3.885	.421
1977	4.278	3.234	3.980	.597
1978	4.962	3.239	3.970	.627
1979	4.607	3.565	3.949	.684
1980	8.293	3.974	7.314	.608
1981	7.775	3.383	4.391	.524
1982	7.407	3.704	7.332	.587
1983	11.825	7.222	11.270	.559
1984	13.333	8.583	12.500	.807

Change, 1975–84 + 423%; change, S&P 500 Index, 1975–84 + 82%

[*]Adjusted for stock splits and stock dividends   [**]Includes extraordinary items

180

This diversified specialty chemical firm is organized into five major groups.

Automotive and Industrial Group: The Automotive and Industrial Group continues to be a major supplier of solvents and high-technology thinners, high-performance coatings, adhesives and plastisols for automotive, aircraft, transportation, sign, marine pleasure craft and industrial finishing fields.

Trade Sales Group: Trade Sales is responsible for the technical development, production and marketing of state-of-the-art paints, epoxies, and varnishes. These products are sold by company-operated facilities and independent dealers to consumers and painting contractors.

Marine and Corrosion Control Group: This group of companies supplies high-technology marine coatings for new ship construction, maintenance and repair, and manufactures corrosion control coatings.

Consumer Group: These companies manufacture and market a wide variety of high-quality household and industrial products, including cleaning, commercial maintenance and chemical products, laundry and dish products, polymers for printing and floor care, and aerosol products.

Grow Ventures Corporation: This is a wholly-owned subsidiary formed to provide management and support services for two subsidiaries, Enviro-Spray Systems, Inc. and Thermaljet, Ltd.

Sales and income from continuing operations have grown steadily for over a decade. However, the loss from discontinuing a wall covering distribution business required a one-time adjustment to net income in 1985 that reduced net income below 1984's record levels. All in all, the Grow Group has weathered the recession very nicely and is once again on an upward track.

JOHN H. HARLAND COMPANY

Corporate Headquarters: 2939 Miller Road
                          Decatur, GA 30035

Telephone: (404) 981-9460
Incorporated in Georgia
New York Stock Exchange—JH

Business: Prints checks and related financial items.
Officers:
  J. William Robinson, Chairman
  Robert R. Woodson, President
  I. Ward Lang, Senior Vice President and Secretary
  Larry F. Williams, Treasurer
  Senior Vice Presidents: A. Clyde Baxter, John A. Conant, C. Frazier
      Hollis, Jr., James E. Hooper
  Vice Presidents: Hugh B. Burns, Charles T. Dawson, Donald K.
      Voshall, Victoria P. Weyand

Statement of Income (Year ends 12/31—$ figures in 000's)

	1984	1983
Net Sales	$217,400	$188,970
Cost and Expenses		
Cost of Sales	$127,556	$110,559
Selling, General and Administrative	43,948	40,472
Employees Profit Sharing	4,266	3,555
	$175,770	$154,586
Income from Operations	$ 41,630	$ 34,384
Interest and Other Income—Net	3,000	2,728
Income before Income Taxes	$ 44,630	$ 37,112
Income Taxes	19,466	16,335
Net Income	$ 25,163	$ 20,776

Stockholder's Equity, Jobs, and Labor Productivity ($ figures in 000's)

Year	Stockholder's Equity	Net Sales	Number of Employees	Index of Labor Productivity
1975	$21,923	$ 44,000	2,030	21.675
1976	26,364	55,761	2,208	25.254
1977	31,189	64,483	2,523	25.558
1978	36,853	75,274	3,068	24.535
1979	43,725	93,693	3,466	27.032
1980	52,377	113,724	3,361	33.836
1981	63,296	143,242	3,791	37.785
1982	76,601	160,239	3,944	40.629
1983	92,778	188,970	4,190	45.100
Change, 1983/1975	+ 323 %	+ 330 %	+ 106 %	+ 108 %

Capital Productivity ($ figures in 000's)

Year	Total Invested Capital	Net Income	Index of Capital Productivity
1975	$21,923	$ 4,225	.193
1976	26,364	5,128	.195
1977	31,189	6,139	.197
1978	36,853	7,374	.200
1979	43,725	9,007	.206
1980	52,377	11,131	.213
1981	63,296	13,929	.220
1982	76,601	17,075	.223
1983	92,778	20,776	.224
Change, 1983/1975	+ 323 %	+ 392 %	+ 16 %

Stock Prices and Earnings per Share[*]

	Stock Prices			Earnings[**]
Year	High	Low	Close	Per Share
1975	$ 4.875	$ 2.667	$ 2.896	$ .267
1976	3.604	2.667	3.104	.322
1977	4.021	3.063	3.917	.382
1978	5.188	3.250	4.000	.455
1979	6.330	3.917	6.167	.550
1980	10.438	5.813	9.906	.675
1981	13.188	8.625	12.250	.840
1982	18.875	7.813	18.625	1.020
1983	23.938	17.500	18.500	1.230
1984	24.500	16.250	23.813	1.480

Change, 1975–84 + 722%; change, S&P 500 Index, 1975–84 + 82%

[*]Adjusted for stock splits and stock dividends   [**]Includes extraordinary items

CORPORATE PROFILE—JOHN H. HARLAND COMPANY

This company has compiled a growth record that exceeds that of any firm on the New York or American stock exchanges based on consecutive sales, earnings and dividend increases. The basic business of this company is the production and sale of checks and related products sold to financial institutions in all 50 states. The company has nearly 400 sales reps and 40 plants dedicated to this product line. In addition, the company operates the J. William Company, a direct mail organization that at this time contributes only modestly to Harland's overall sales. The company has one of the most consistent records of sales and net income growth of any of the 101 companies and from all indications is expected to continue its impressive performance.

G. HEILEMAN BREWING CO. INC.

Corporate Headquarters: 100 Harborview Plaza
La Crosse, WI 54601

Telephone: (608) 785-1000
Incorporated in Wisconsin
New York Stock Exchange—GHB

Business: Produces and distributes malt beverages in all 50 states under labels such as Old Style, Blatz, Ranier, Schmidt, Wiedemann, Black Label, etc.

Officers:

Russell G. Cleary, Chairman, President, and Chief Executive Officer
John S. Pedance, Executive Vice President, Marketing
Robert J. Korkowski, Executive Vice President, Finance and Assistant Secretary
John S. Isherwood, Senior Vice President of Operations
John D. Glenn, Executive Vice President, Operations
Peter F. O'Sullivan, Vice President, Purchasing and Production Coordination
John B. Barrett, Vice President, Commodities
Ralph E. Horn, Vice President, Administration
Ronald J. Drout, Vice President, Brand Management, Central Sales Division
Thomas J. Myers, Vice President, Brand Management, Eastern Sales Division
Daniel J. Schmid, Jr., Vice President and Controller
George E. Smith, Treasurer

Statement of Income (Year ends 12/31—$ figures in 000's)

	1984	1983
Sales	$1,341,549	$1,325,632
Less Excise Taxes	170,188	174,677
Costs and Expenses		
Costs of Goods Sold	$ 851,697	$ 822,100
Marketing, General and Administrative	234,516	220,599
Income from Operations	$ 85,148	$ 108,226
Other Income (Expenses)		
Investment Income	$ 2,156	$ 4,350
Interest Expense	(7,121)	(9,821)
Other, Net	4,629	3,540
Income before Taxes	$ 84,812	$ 106,335
Provision for Income Taxes	39,014	49,336
Net Income	$ 45,798	$ 56,969

Stockholder's Equity, Jobs, and Labor Productivity ($ figures in 000's)

Year	Stockholder's Equity	Net Sales	Number of Employees	Index of Labor Productivity
1975	$ 33,282	$ 171,172	2,500	68.469
1976	42,841	211,405	3,000	70.468
1977	54,907	265,232	3,300	80.373
1978	69,599	329,958	4,000	82.490
1979	91,599	556,994	5,300	105.093
1980	119,424	722,021	5,600	128.932
1981	151,749	807,041	5,400	149.452
1982	194,073	870,841	5,400	161.267
1983	239,315	1,150,955	6,315	182.259
Change, 1983/1975	+619 %	+572 %	+153 %	+166 %

Capital Productivity ($ figures in 000's)

Year	Total Invested Capital	Net Income	Index of Capital Productivity
1975	$ 60,285	$ 5,710	.095
1976	67,310	11,295	.168
1977	77,909	14,501	.186
1978	94,327	18,038	.191
1979	131,181	27,329	.208
1980	172,545	34,683	.201
1981	212,724	40,230	.189
1982	364,603	45,654	.125
1983	335,034	56,969	.170
Change, 1983/1975	+456 %	+898 %	+80 %

Stock Prices and Earnings per Share[*]

	Stock Prices			Earnings[**]
Year	High	Low	Close	Per Share
1975	$ 1.981	$ .981	$ 1.333	$ .224
1976	2.444	1.333	2.407	.441
1977	3.759	2.315	3.259	.564
1978	4.648	2.926	3.926	.698
1979	9.792	3.875	9.208	1.050
1980	12.667	7.083	11.125	1.327
1981	16.313	9.563	12.125	1.525
1982	19.938	10.500	19.875	1.725
1983	44.000	18.625	29.750	2.150
1984	30.500	14.375	17.125	1.730

Change, 1975–84 +1,184%; change, S&P 500 Index, 1975–84 +82%

[*]Adjusted for stock splits and stock dividends   [**]Includes extraordinary items

CORPORATE PROFILE—G. HEILEMAN BREWING COMPANY, INC.

The company is engaged in the manufacture and sale of malt beverages through approximately 2,200 independent wholesalers in all fifty states. Principal brands are Old Style, Blatz, Rainier, Schmidt, Wiedemann, Black Label, Red White & Blue, Lone Star, Colt 45, and Mickey's Malt Liquor, which together with super-premium Special Export and Henry Weinhard's account for over 80 percent of its total beer sales. The company's annual brewing capacity approximates 26 million barrels. For the year 1984, it ranked as the fourth largest brewer in the nation according to published trade reports. Through subsidiaries that represent about 10 percent of sales the company is also engaged in the wholesale bakery business and in the production and sale of snack foods. 1984 saw net income fall, thus breaking the company's record of growth during the previous decade. The brewing industry continued "in turmoil" in 1985.

The conventional wisdom in the brewing industry is that a company must have national distribution so it can profit from the cost efficiencies of national advertising. Anheuser-Busch and Miller operate at the national level, and Coors and Stroh are making major efforts to join them. Meanwhile, Heileman has pursued a completely different strategy. It has elected to collect a group of very strong regional brands that can do well in their local markets with lower advertising costs.

As many brewers attempt to expand distribution and others seek to fight off incursions, extreme price pressure has built up at the local market level. Heileman will have to survive this intense price competition. Its past record indicates that it will survive.

HEWLETT PACKARD COMPANY

Corporate Headquarters: 3000 Hanover Street
Palo Alto, CA 94304

Telephone: (415) 857-1501
Incorporated in California
New York Stock Exchange—HWP

Business: Designs and manufactures a wide range of measuring and computer products and systems.

Officers:

David Packard, Chairman

William R. Hewlett, Vice Chairman

John A. Young, President and Chief Executive Officer

Dean O. Morton, Executive Vice President and Chief Operating Officer

Executive Vice Presidents: Richard C. Alberding, Robert L. Boniface, John L. Doyle, Paul C. Ely, Jr., William E. Terry

Alfred P. Oliverio, Senior Vice President

Vice Presidents: James L. Arthur, Alan D. Bickell, Joel S. Birnbaum, Johan F. Blokker, Douglas C. Chance, Jean C. Chognard, Harold E. Edmondson, Richard A. Hackborn, Franco Mariotti, William G. Parzybok, Jr., Lewis E. Platt, Cyril J. Yansouni

S. T. Jack Brigham III, Vice President, General Counsel and Secretary

Robert P. Wayman, Vice President, Chief Financial Officer and Controller

George F. Newman, Jr., Treasurer

Statement of Income (Year ends 10/31—$ figures in 000,000's)

	1984	1983
Net Sales	$6,044	$4,710
Costs and Expenses		
Cost of Goods Sold	$2,865	$2,195
Research and Development	592	493
Marketing	1,066	771
Administrative and General	661	523
	$5,184	$3,982
Earnings before Taxes	$ 860	$ 728
Provision for Taxes (Net)	195	296
Net Earnings	$ 665	$ 432

Stockholder's Equity, Jobs, and Labor Productivity ($ figures in 000's)

Year	Stockholder's Equity	Net Sales	Number of Employees	Index of Labor Productivity
1975	$ 559,103	$ 981,167	20,300	32.489
1976	674,146	1,111,648	32,200	34.523
1977	822,000	1,360,000	34,100	38.746
1978	1,002,000	1,728,000	42,400	40.755
1979	1,235,000	2,361,000	52,000	45.404
1980	1,547,000	3,099,000	57,000	54.368
1981	1,920,000	3,578,000	64,000	55.906
1982	2,349,000	4,254,000	68,000	62.559
1983	2,887,000	4,710,000	72,000	65.417
Change, 1983/1975	+416 %	+380 %	+138 %	+101 %

Capital Productivity ($ figures in 000's)

Year	Total Invested Capital	Funds from Operations	Index of Capital Productivity
1975	$ 565,890	$133,924	.237
1976	684,404	143,093	.209
1977	836,500	180,000	.215
1978	1,012,000	220,000	.217
1979	1,250,000	302,000	.242
1980	1,576,000	389,000	.247
1981	1,946,000	485,000	.249
1982	2,388,000	640,000	.268
1983	2,958,000	728,000	.246
Change, 1983/1975	+423 %	+444 %	+4 %

Stock Prices and Earnings per Share[*]

| Year | Stock Prices | | | Earnings[**] Per Share |
	High	Low	Close	
1975	$15.063	$ 7.047	$11.813	$ .378
1976	14.719	10.000	10.906	.405
1977	10.938	8.516	9.156	.534
1978	11.594	7.719	11.234	.659
1979	15.719	10.500	14.781	.858
1980	24.250	12.813	22.375	1.118
1981	26.938	19.188	19.813	1.275
1982	41.250	18.000	36.500	1.525
1983	48.250	34.250	42.375	1.690
1984	45.500	31.125	33.875	2.590

Change, 1975–84 +187%; change, S&P 500 Index, 1975–84 +82%

[*]Adjusted for stock splits and stock dividends   [**]Includes extraordinary items

189

CORPORATE PROFILE—HEWLETT-PACKARD COMPANY

This company is engaged worldwide in the design, manufacture, marketing, and servicing of a broad array of precision electronic instruments and systems for measurement, analysis, and computation. Its products, which number more than 7,000, are used in industry, business, engineering, science, education, and medicine. In July 1984, the company began to implement a major reorganization that will more closely align its organizational structure with the customers and markets it serves. This business sector concept is market-based and has replaced the product group-based organizational structure historically used by the company. As part of this new structure effort, the company has consolidated worldwide marketing and field sales activities of the former Computer Marketing and Instrument Marketing groups into a single organizational unit. Hewlett-Packard has been well recognized in both the investment and business communities as a prime example of an outstanding well-managed, high-growth, innovative, and entrepreneurial organization.

HOLLY CORPORATION

Corporate Headquarters: 2600 Diamond Shamrock Tower
717 North Harwood Street
Dallas, TX 75201
Telephone: (214) 979-0210
Incorporated in Delaware
American Stock Exchange—HOC

Business: Refines and markets petroleum products.
Officers:
  Lamar Norsworthy, Chairman and Chief Executive Officer
  E. I. Parsons, President
  Jack P. Reid, Executive Vice President, Refining
  William J. Gray, Senior Vice President, Marketing and Supply
  Gordon R. Bussey, Vice President, Marketing
  W. Truett Loyd, Vice President, Supply and Transportation
  Mike Mirbagheri, Vice President, International Crude Oil and Refined
    Products
  Dewie O. Stevenson, Vice President, Manufacturing
  Henry L. Stern, Senior Vice President, General Counsel and Secretary
  James W. Robertson, Vice President and Treasurer
  Henry A. Teichholz, Controller

Statement of Income (Year ends 7/31—$ figures in 000's)

	1985	1984
Revenues	$407,786	$401,614
Costs and Expenses		
Cost of Sales	$380,420	$387,075
General and Administrative	6,648	7,455
Depreciation and Amortization	5,819	5,663
	$392,887	$400,193
Operating Income	$ 14,899	$ 1,421
Non-Operating Income	5,025	4,349
Gain from Discontinued Operations	—	25,173
Income before Provision for Income Taxes	$ 19,924	$ 30,943
Income Tax Provision	9,426	2,474
Net Income	$ 10,498	$ 28,469

Stockholder's Equity, Jobs, and Labor Productivity ($ figures in 000's)

Year	Stockholder's Equity	Net Sales	Number of Employees	Index of Labor Productivity
1975	$15,092	$115,981	275	421.749
1976	19,508	128,968	277	465.588
1977	26,315	154,666	316	489.449
1978	33,591	207,060	328	631.280
1979	40,743	268,730	343	783.469
1980	50,055	409,221	351	1,165.872
1981	56,421	415,974	355	1,171.758
1982	65,804	538,622	394	1,367.061
1983	68,999	444,058	362	1,226.680
Change, 1983/1975	+357 %	+283 %	+32 %	+191%

Capital Productivity ($ figures in 000's)

Year	Total Invested Capital	Funds from Operations	Index of Capital Productivity
1975	$21,960	$ 5,547	.253
1976	24,202	8,759	.362
1977	35,595	11,245	.316
1978	35,338	13,032	.369
1979	43,532	13,008	.299
1980	65,839	18,774	.285
1981	74,042	17,369	.235
1982	70,185	26,481	.377
1983	70,789	22,652	.320
Change, 1983/1975	+222 %	+308 %	+27 %

Stock Prices and Earnings per Share[*]

	Stock Prices			Earnings[**]
Year	High	Low	Close	Per Share
1975	$ 3.375	$1.375	$ 2.125	$ .440
1976	5.250	2.000	4.875	.620
1977	8.750	4.625	7.500	.820
1978	9.250	5.500	7.375	.860
1979	14.625	6.375	14.500	.840
1980	19.375	7.375	15.250	1.100
1981	16.375	8.000	10.750	.670
1982	10.750	4.875	8.500	1.250
1983	14.000	7.250	10.875	.800
1984	13.375	6.500	8.000	3.570

Change, 1975–84 +277%; change, S&P 500 Index, 1975–84 +82%

[*]Adjusted for stock splits and stock dividends   [**]Includes extraordinary items

192

The basic business of Holly Corporation is the refining and marketing of petroleum products. Prior to July 1984, the company was also engaged in domestic exploration, development, and production of oil and gas, but these properties were sold during June 1984. The company's principal subsidiary is Navajo Refining Company, which owns and operates a high-conversion petroleum refinery in New Mexico. This refinery has been in operation for more than 30 years. During the last several years, the company's earnings have shown an erratic pattern, even though net income for 1984 showed a dramatic improvement over the earlier period of the 1980s. An interesting aspect of this company is that its chairman and president has been an executive of the firm since 1971, when he was only 25 years old.

HOSPITAL CORP. OF AMERICA

Corporate Headquarters: One Park Plaza
                          Nashville, TN 37203

Telephone: (615) 327-9551
Incorporated in Tennessee
New York Stock Exchange—HCA

Business: Owns and/or operates over 400 hospitals throughout the world.
Officers:

  Donald S. MacNaughton, Chairman of the Board and Chairman of the
     Executive Committee
  Thomas F. First, Jr., President and Chief Executive Officer
  Thomas F. First, Sr., M.D., Chief Medical Director
  R. Clayton McWhorter, Executive Vice President, Operations
  David G. Williamson, Jr., Executive Vice President, Development
  H. E. Adams, III, Vice President and President, HCA Int'l Co.
  Sam A. Brooks, Jr., Vice President, Finance
  Winfield Dunn, D.D.S., Vice President, Public Affairs
  Donald W. Fish, Vice President, Secretary and General Counsel
  C. Richard Gaston, Vice President, Human Resources
  Joseph C. Hutts, Jr., Vice President, Business Development
  James W. Main, Vice President and President HCA Management
     Company
  Charles N. Martin, Jr., Vice President, Acquisitions & Development
  John H. Tobin, Jr., Vice President, Division Operations
  L. Stanton Tuttle, Vice President and President, HCA Psychiatric
     Company

Statement of Income (Year ends 12/31—$ figures in 000's)

	1984	1983
Operating Revenues	$4,177,971	$3,917,057
Less Provisions for Contractual		
Allowances and Doubtful Accounts	679,327	714,069
Net Operating Revenues	3,498,644	3,202,988
Operating Costs and Expenses		
Operating Expenses	2,663,055	2,535,343
Depreciation and Amortization	192,165	155,965
Interest	187,821	162,476
Income from Operations	455,603	349,204
Investment Earnings and Other Income—Net	50,356	42,514
Income before Taxes	505,959	391,718
Provision for Income Taxes	209,200	148,500
Net Income	$ 296,759	$ 243,218

Stockholder's Equity, Jobs, and Labor Productivity ($ figures in 000's)

Year	Stockholder's Equity	Net Sales	Number of Employees	Index of Labor Productivity
1975	$ 142,069	$ 356,304	23,000	15.491
1976	186,803	455,283	28,000	16.260
1977	216,275	550,671	32,000	17.208
1978	250,714	697,148	40,000	17.429
1979	381,734	900,004	35,500	25.352
1980	440,277	1,231,548	46,000	26.773
1981	576,812	2,063,637	75,000	27.515
1982	1,021,157	2,976,912	76,000	39.170
1983	1,344,718	3,202,987	71,000	45.112
Change, 1983/1975	+847 %	+799 %	+209 %	+191 %

Capital Productivity ($ figures in 000's)

Year	Total Invested Capital	Net Income	Index of Capital Productivity
1975	$ 432,455	$ 20,947	.048
1976	497,256	27,324	.055
1977	560,862	33,687	.060
1978	658,618	42,043	.064
1979	817,273	55,000	.067
1980	1,243,809	80,995	.065
1981	2,416,435	111,131	.046
1982	2,859,684	171,935	.060
1983	3,277,330	243,218	.074
Change, 1983/1975	+658 %	+1,061 %	+53 %

Stock Prices and Earnings per Share[*]

Year	Stock Prices			Earnings[**] Per Share
	High	Low	Close	
1975	$ 5.350	$ 1.725	$ 4.100	$ .450
1976	5.700	4.040	5.200	.542
1977	6.782	4.344	6.719	.650
1978	11.500	5.625	10.167	.797
1979	14.917	13.438	27.126	1.017
1980	27.751	13.438	27.126	1.300
1981	37.970	23.719	25.688	1.673
1982	44.814	18.563	41.626	2.250
1983	56.625	35.375	39.500	2.800
1984	48.750	35.750	37.750	3.350

Change, 1975–84 +821%; change, S&P 500 Index, 1975–84 +82%

[*]Adjusted for stock splits and stock dividends   [**]Includes extraordinary items

CORPORATE PROFILE—HOSPITAL CORPORATION OF AMERICA

This company is a major health care company, which together with its subsidiaries is engaged in the operation of hospitals and other medical facilities in the United States and in foreign countries. At the end of 1984 the company owned or managed in excess of 400 hospitals with a bed capacity of nearly 60,000. It has achieved phenomenal growth during the last decade and has turned in an impressive record of improving labor productivity. However, like the others serving the changing health care market, it is facing increasing competition and a changing market environment that will test management's ability to continue to grow in a more difficult external environment.

As the largest of the for-profit health care suppliers, HCA has a lot at stake as the U.S. health care industry continues its restructuring. With all its financial muscle, HCA also is in the position to gain a lot. For example, as poorly managed nonprofit hospitals go under, HCA is able to add high-quality physical plant and equipment at attractive prices.

HCA is also making a major effort in Great Britian. That country's National Health Service is a continuing failure that is creating a market for private health care.

However the U.S. health care industry develops, Hospital Corporation of America will be a major figure.

196

HUMANA INC.

Corporate Headquarters: 1800 First National Tower
                         Louisville, KY 40202
Telephone: (502) 561-2000
Incorporated in Delaware
New York Stock Exchange—HUM

Business: Owns and operates general care medical hospitals and provides integrated health care services including prepaid health plans.
Officers:
   David A. Jones, Chairman of the Board and Chief Executive Officer
   Wendell Cherry, President and Chief Operating Officer
   William C. Ballard, Jr., Executive Vice President, Finance and Administration
   Thomas J. Flynn, Executive Vice President and General Counsel
   William H. Lomicka, Senior Vice President, Finance
   H. Linden McLellan, Senior Vice President, Facility Management
   H. Herbert Phillips, Senior Vice President, Administration
   Fred Pirman, Jr., Senior Vice President, Information Systems
Operating Management:
   Carl F. Pollard, Senior Executive Vice President
Hospital Division:
   Paul A. Gross, Executive Vice President, Division President
   Jack Clark, Executive Vice President, Mid-South Region
   George M. Lansdell, Executive Vice President, Western Region
   Lee R. Ledbetter, Executive Vice President, Florida Region
   Wayne T. Smith, Executive Vice President, Central Region

Statement of Income (Year ends 8/31—$ figures in 000's)

	1985	1984
Revenues	$2,875,140	$2,606,415
Provision for Contractual Allowances and Doubtful Accounts	686,750	645,226
Net Revenues	$2,188,390	$1,961,189
Operating Expenses	$1,546,128	$1,420,429
Depreciation and Amortization	147,337	120,560
Interest	118,825	87,950
	$1,812,290	$1,628,939
Income before Income Taxes	$ 376,100	$ 332,250
Income Taxes	159,880	138,909
Net Income	$ 216,220	$ 193,341

Stockholder's Equity, Jobs, and Labor Productivity ($ figures in 000's)

Year	Stockholder's Equity	Net Sales	Number of Employees	Index of Labor Productivity
1975	$ 59,673	$ 195,405	13,800	14.160
1976	67,815	260,648	14,800	17.611
1977	78,714	315,959	15,700	20.125
1978	62,049	642,238	36,000	17.840
1979	109,010	926,654	35,900	25.812
1980	158,267	1,116,824	39,100	28.563
1981	297,314	1,342,906	40,400	33.240
1982	385,212	1,516,311	39,100	38.780
1983	608,633	1,765,122	42,000	42.027
Change, 1983/1975	+920 %	+803 %	+204 %	+197%

Capital Productivity ($ figures in 000's)

Year	Total Invested Capital	Net Income	Index of Capital Productivity
1975	$ 261,223	$ 6,828	.026
1976	279,585	8,845	.032
1977	308,291	11,773	.038
1978	765,212	22,097	.029
1979	934,739	40,887	.044
1980	1,004,649	64,602	.064
1981	1,094,298	93,177	.085
1982	1,310,150	127,146	.097
1983	1,736,919	160,649	.092
Change, 1983/1975	+565 %	+2,253 %	+254 %

Stock Prices and Earnings per Share[*]

Year	Stock Prices			Earnings[**] Per Share
	High	Low	Close	
1975	$ .990	$ .286	$ .842	$ .097
1976	1.207	.790	1.189	.123
1977	1.684	.998	1.589	.160
1978	4.258	1.380	3.932	.236
1979	6.621	3.789	6.543	.411
1980	15.209	5.833	14.870	.640
1981	19.323	12.084	14.584	.971
1982	28.751	12.578	28.126	1.338
1983	33.333	19.583	21.875	1.633
1984	33.000	21.500	23.500	1.960

Change, 1975–84 +2,691%; change, S&P 500 Index, 1975–84 +82%

[*]Adjusted for stock splits and stock dividends   [**]Includes extraordinary items

198

Humana company is in the health care business, which it conducts through three operating divisions: Hospital Division, Group Health Division and Health Services Division. The principal source of the company's revenues (approximately 96 percent in fiscal 1985) is provided by the Hospital Division, which, at August 31, 1985, operated 87 hospitals containing 17,706 licensed beds. The Group Health Division was formed in fiscal 1984, when it began offering indemnity type health insurance and prepaid health care products under the trade name of Humana Care Plus primarily in those markets where company hospitals are located. These products generally permit individuals freedom to choose any physician or hospital facility, but provide added incentives if the company's hospitals are chosen. The Health Services Division was formed in fiscal 1981. It operates 148 medical care centers that maintain extended hours, including evenings and weekends, in which independent physicians provide medical care to their ambulatory patients. It is well known that admissions and occupancy rates for hospital operators have been declining because of pressure to cut costs by employers and the federal government. To counter this trend, Humana is moving into different facets of health care, with an eye to becoming a full-service medical company. Its past growth and performance have been spectacular, and its bright prospects for the future are only clouded by the overall dynamics of our rational health care delivery system.

JAMES RIVER CORP. OF VIRGINIA

Corporate Headquarters: Tredegar Street
Richmond, VA 23219

Telephone: (804) 644-5411
Incorporated in Virginia
New York Stock Exchange—JR

Business: An integrated producer of pulp, paper and converted paper, and plastic products.

Officers:

Brenton S. Halsey, Chairman, Chief Executive Officer

Robert C. Williams, President, Chief Operating Officer

Judd H. Alexander, Executive Vice President

Ronald B. Estridge, Vice President, Group Exec. Specialty Papers Business

Charles M. Foster, Vice President, Group Exec. Dixie Products Business

Richard S. Longnecker, Vice President, Group Exec. Paperboard Packaging Business

E. Lee Showalter, Vice President, Group Exec. Communication Papers Business

Ronald L. Singer, Vice President, Group Exec. Towel & Tissue Business

Leon Katz, Senior Vice President, Corporate Research & Development

David J. McKittrick, Senior Vice President, Chief Financial Officer

Lawrence S. Morrow, Senior Vice President, Corporate Services & Operations Technology

James E. Rogers, Senior Vice President, Corporate Development

Robert J. Sherry, Senior Vice President, Human Resource Development

Statement of Income (Year ends 4/28/85 and 4/29/84—$ figures in 000's)

	1985	1984
Net Sales	$2,492,009	$2,301,076
Cost of Goods	1,895,647	1,728,243
Gross Profit	596,362	572,833
Selling, General and Administrative Expenses	385,816	355,620
Operating Income	210,546	217,213
Non-Operating Income	12,687	11,652
Interest Expense	52,310	55,796
Income before Provision for Income Taxes	170,923	173,069
Income Taxes	69,572	72,592
Net Income	101,351	97,995

Stockholder's Equity, Jobs, and Labor Productivity ($ figures in 000's)

Year	Stockholder's Equity	Net Sales	Number of Employees	Index of Labor Productivity
1975	$ 10,884	$ 70,576	1,230	57.379
1976	19,738	98,607	1,461	67.493
1977	25,145	181,922	2,827	64.352
1978	48,077	297,940	3,802	78.364
1979	61,844	373,946	3,700	101.066
1980	96,155	561,318	8,200	68.453
1981	110,003	772,682	7,900	97.808
1982	344,294	1,656,112	18,500	89.520
1983	462,209	2,301,076	21,000	109.575
Change, 1983/1975	+4,146 %	+3,160 %	+1,607 %	+91 %

Capital Productivity ($ figures in 000's)

Year	Total Invested Capital	Net Income	Index of Capital Productivity
1975	$ 32,289	$ 2,388	.074
1976	48,752	3,477	.071
1977	75,128	6,219	.083
1978	119,906	14,709	.123
1979	127,318	16,659	.131
1980	293,871	17,881	.061
1981	317,338	22,353	.070
1982	822,981	55,148	.067
1983	1,016,809	97,995	.096
Change, 1983/1975	+3,049 %	+4,004 %	+30 %

Stock Prices and Earnings per Share*

Year	Stock Prices			Earnings** Per Share
	High	Low	Close	
1975	$ 2.519	$ 1.580	$ 2.222	$ .431
1976	4.642	2.222	3.407	.484
1977	3.951	2.568	3.852	.770
1978	8.444	3.593	6.889	1.446
1979	11.667	6.389	8.556	1.440
1980	11.333	6.389	10.389	1.240
1981	15.583	9.833	13.167	1.300
1982	25.417	8.833	25.250	2.687
1983	42.250	23.125	35.375	3.400
1984	35.875	23.500	28.750	3.180

Change, 1975–84 +1,194%; change, S&P 500 Index, 1975–84 +82%

*Adjusted for stock splits and stock dividends **Includes extraordinary items

Note: The fiscal year financial results in the tables above are shown in the year in which most of the results were achieved.

The company is an integrated producer of pulp, paper, and converted paper and plastic products. Through its subsidiaries, the company processes basic raw materials—wood, woodpulp, synthetic fibers, and plastic resins—into finished products such as towel and tissue papers, disposable food and beverage service items, and folding cartons. The company also produces a wide array of communications papers and specialty industrial and packaging papers. During its 16-year history, James River has pursued an aggressive acquisition and operating strategy that has significantly expanded its business and the diversity of its products. Just before yearend 1985, the company announced an agreement to purchase a controlling interest in Crown Zellerbach as part of a two-tier sale of that company. If this transaction is completed, it would add nearly $2 billion to James River's net sales.

JOHNSON CONTROLS INC.

Corporate Headquarters: 5757 North Green Bay Ave., P.O. Box 591
Milwaukee, WI 53201

Telephone: (414) 228-1200
Incorporated in Wisconsin
New York Stock Exchange—JCI

Business: Designs, installs, and services control systems for commercial buildings, and manufactures automotive batteries.

Officers:

Fred L. Brengel, President and Chief Executive Officer
Vice Presidents: William P. Chapman, George T. Jacobi, James H. Keyes, Frank M. Sterner, Richard D. Wilson, Milton C. Zilis
William L. Rootham, Vice President and Chief Financial Officer
James M. Wade, Treasurer
Kenneth J. Kammeraad, Secretary
Florence R. Klatt, Assistant Secretary

Statement of Income (Year ends 9/30—$ figures in 000's)

	1984	1983
Net Sales	$1,425,271	$1,323,424
Cost of Sales	1,066,078	988,381
Gross Margin	359,193	335,043
Selling, General and Administrative Expenses	246,325	227,571
Operating Income	112,868	107,472
Other Income (Expense)		
Interest Income	16,495	14,217
Interest Expense	(9,524)	(10,884)
Miscellaneous—(Net)	261	(3,832)
	7,232	(499)
Income before Taxes	120,100	106,973
Provision for Income Taxes	53,377	47,932
Net Income	$ 66,723	$ 59,041

Stockholder's Equity, Jobs, and Labor Productivity ($ figures in 000's)

Year	Stockholder's Equity	Net Sales	Number of Employees	Index of Labor Productivity
1975	$ 68,984	$ 284,243	10,000	28.424
1976	81,197	323,007	10,600	30.472
1977	117,727	372,782	11,750	31.726
1978	223,938	599,925	22,800	26.313
1979	241,984	1,024,448	24,300	42.158
1980	230,524	964,854	18,500	52.154
1981	266,193	1,128,386	20,000	56.419
1982	292,981	1,251,522	20,500	61.050
1983	344,706	1,323,424	20,700	63.934
Change, 1983/1975	+385 %	+355 %	+107 %	+125 %

Capital Productivity ($ figures in 000's)

Year	Total Invested Capital	Net Income	Index of Capital Productivity
1975	$122,419	$ 9,318	.079
1976	131,880	16,483	.125
1977	148,669	23,961	.161
1978	413,456	37,200	.090
1979	426,689	49,920	.117
1980	435,751	33,693	.077
1981	462,336	48,132	.104
1982	486,853	53,839	.111
1983	523,707	59,041	.113
Change, 1983/1975	+328 %	+534 %	+48 %

Stock Prices and Earnings per Share[*]

Year	Stock Prices			Earnings[**] Per Share
	High	Low	Close	
1975	$ 7.750	$ 4.000	$ 6.500	$1.085
1976	13.563	6.313	13.188	1.915
1977	30.875	13.375	30.625	2.760
1978	34.500	21.750	25.250	3.750
1979	31.875	24.125	31.625	3.580
1980	33.000	18.000	30.000	2.410
1981	34.250	22.250	24.500	3.430
1982	38.750	17.500	25.376	3.830
1983	48.750	34.000	48.375	4.170
1984	49.375	37.500	41.375	4.710

Change, 1975–84 +537%; change, S&P 500 Index, 1975–84 +82%

[*]Adjusted for stock splits and stock dividends   [**]Includes extraordinary items

The major businesses of the company are the design, installation, and service of control systems for commercial buildings and the manufacture of automotive batteries. In addition, Johnson Controls supplies industrial markets with control systems and engineered piping systems. This firm is the leading manufacturer of automotive batteries, as well as a leader in providing building control and energy management systems and services. It has enjoyed significant growth during the last decade even though it is not immune to the impact of the business cycle. The company, which celebrated its 100th anniversary during 1985, is solidly positioned in its core businesses.

As the market for "smart buildings" (those that rely on high-technology devices for security, energy conservation, and the like) grows, Johnson Controls will be one of the major players. Sales and service of systems for smart buildings is creating a whole new industry.

KANSAS GAS & ELECTRIC CO.

Corporate Headquarters: 201 North Market Street
Wichita, KA 67202

Telephone: (316) 261-6611
Incorporated in Kansas
New York Stock Exchange—KGE

Business: Generates and distributes electric power in Kansas.
Officers:
Wilson K. Cadman, Chairman of the Board and President
Kent R. Brown, Vice President, Technical Services
Richard M. Haden, Vice President, Administration
Howard J. Hansen, Vice President, Finance
Robert L. Rives, Corporate Relations

Statement of Income (Year ends 12/31—$ figures in 000's)

	1984	1983
Operating Revenues	$410,753	$393,053
Operating Expenses		
Fuel	148,959	139,339
Purchased Power—Net	18,221	24,541
Other Operation	48,573	43,050
Maintenance	26,108	27,871
Depreciation	32,433	29,919
Taxes Other than Income Taxes	16,063	15,078
Income Taxes	41,024	39,903
Total Operating Expenses	331,381	319,701
Operating Income	79,372	73,352
Other Income and Deductions		
Allowance for Other Funds Used during Construction	78,345	63,068
Equity in Earnings of Subsidiary Companies	1,603	1,400
Miscellaneous—Net	2,299	659
Income Taxes	(1,993)	(1,061)
Total Other Income and Deductions	80,254	64,066
Income before Interest Charges	159,626	137,418
Interest Charges		
Interest on Long-Term Debt	87,508	65,948
Other Interest	5,372	3,031
Amortization of Debt Premium, Discount and Expense—Net	729	768
Allowance for Borrowed Funds Used during Construction	(55,841)	(39,867)
Total Interest Charges—Net	37,768	29,880
Net Income	$121,858	$107,538

Stockholder's Equity, Jobs, and Labor Productivity ($ figures in 000's)

Year	Stockholder's Equity	Net Sales	Number of Employees	Index of Labor Productivity
1975	$122,382	$126,166	1,287	98.031
1976	150,840	142,773	1,311	108.904
1977	209,172	196,236	1,337	146.773
1978	242,643	238,460	1,370	174.058
1979	274,096	244,970	1,421	172.393
1980	341,559	293,808	1,514	194.061
1981	391,652	313,098	1,660	188.610
1982	519,182	350,937	1,828	191.979
1983	643,174	393,053	1,928	203.866
Change, 1983/1975	+ 426 %	+ 212 %	+ 50 %	+ 108 %

Capital Productivity ($ figures in 000's)

Year	Total Invested Capital	Net Income	Index of Capital Productivity
1975	$ 406,135	$ 18,446	.045
1976	497,395	23,273	.047
1977	588,265	24,650	.042
1978	710,415	28,964	.041
1979	˙778,316	29,220	.038
1980	909,868	52,895	.058
1981	1,144,609	65,975	.058
1982	1,292,519	84,663	.066
1983	1,555,117	107,588	.069
Change, 1983/1975	+ 283 %	+ 483 %	+ 52 %

Stock Prices and Earnings per Share[*]

Year	Stock Prices			Earnings[**] Per Share
	High	Low	Close	
1975	$19.250	$11.750	$18.750	$2.910
1976	21.875	18.000	21.500	2.880
1977	22.375	19.750	20.250	2.280
1978	21.000	17.750	18.125	2.280
1979	19.750	15.000	15.250	1.840
1980	16.750	13.000	14.625	2.970
1981	16.500	13.750	14.875	2.850
1982	18.500	14.625	18.375	3.000
1983	21.375	16.500	17.250	3.080
1984	19.000	12.500	17.250	3.070

Change, 1975–84 + 848%; change, S&P 500 Index, 1975–84 − 8%

˙Adjusted for stock splits and stock dividends   ˙˙Includes extraordinary items

CORPORATE PROFILE—KANSAS GAS AND ELECTRIC COMPANY

For 75 years this utility company has been a vital factor in the development of southcentral and southeastern Kansas. The company was founded in 1909, when three small energy companies merged to provide the financial, engineering, and management strength to offer adequate and reliable service to the Kansas communities of Wichita, Pittsburg, and Frontenac. This gas and electric utility has achieved an outstanding record in its industry and is expected to grow at historical levels during the coming years.

In 1924, the management of Kansas Gas and Electric made this statement to KG & E employees:

> The continuous, adequate supply of light and power to its customers is an obligation in the fulfillment of which Kansas Gas and Electric Company must not fail, and for the fulfillment of which it must mass such forces as shall make even the meeting of crises paradoxically commonplace. The service of any electric light and power company is too vitally essential to the normal life of every individual in the communities served to be operated by men other than those whose managing genius and farsighted capacity for anticipating public needs have made that service possible.

Now, over 60 years later, this quiet utility continues to accomplish its goal of providing truly excellent performance.

LEAR PETROLEUM CORP.

Corporate Headquarters: 4925 Greenville Avenue
950 One Energy Square
Dallas, TX 75206

Telephone: (214) 363-6085
Incorporated in Delaware
New York Stock Exchange—LPT

Business: Engaged in the exploration for and development and production of oil and natural gas, and in the purchase, transmission and sale of natural gas.

Officers:

Max W. Woodard, Chairman of the Board
Joseph T. Williams, President and Chief Executive Officer
Jack M. Lafield, Senior Vice President, Gas Transmission
Gordon D. Mowl, Senior Vice President, Finance and Administration
H. Monroe Helm, III, Vice President, Investor Relations
Donald L. Peoples, Vice President, Information Services
William K. White, Vice President and Treasurer
Randall B. Wilson, Vice President, Secretary and General Counsel
Lonnie T. Samford, Controller

Statement of Income (Year ends 12/31—$ figures in 000's)

	1984	1983
Revenues		
Gas Transmission	$398,747	$188,866
Oil and Gas	70,615	61,003
Less Intercompany Sales of Gas	(39,037)	(15,834)
Other	10,470	2,693
	440,796	236,729
Costs and Expenses		
Gas Transmission Purchases and Expenses	316,722	129,678
Less Intercompany Purchases of Gas	(39,037)	(15,834)
Oil and Gas Operations	9,741	7,834
Provision for Inventory Price Declines		2,865
General and Administrative	20,149	14,968
Depreciation, Depletion and Amortization	52,049	45,962
Interest	41,642	24,306
Total Costs and Expenses	401,266	209,780
Income before Taxes and Extraordinary Items	39,530	26,949
Income before Extraordinary Items	23,525	19,008
Extraordinary Items—Gain on Extinguishment of Debt, Less Applicable Income Taxes of $1,025,000	1,191	—
Net Income	24,716	19,008
Less Preferred Dividend Requirements	6,325	3,448
Net Income	$ 18,391	$ 15,560

Stockholder's Equity, Jobs, and Labor Productivity ($ figures in 000's)

Year	Stockholder's Equity	Net Sales	Number of Employees	Index of Labor Productivity
1975	$ 3,372	$ 12,298	90	136.644
1976	3,621	21,027	51	412.294
1977	6,578	48,054	95	505.832
1978	15,196	58,724	103	570.136
1979	19,559	78,171	161	485.534
1980	67,346	88,774	209	424.756
1981	77,765	147,889	287	515.293
1982	83,317	203,429	333	610.898
1983	96,851	234,035	386	606.308
Change, 1983/1975	+ 2,772 %	+ 1,803 %	+ 329 %	+ 344 %

Capital Productivity ($ figures in 000's)

Year	Total Invested Capital	Funds from Operations	Index of Capital Productivity
1975	$ 10,235	$ 1,253	.122
1976	11,978	1,230	.103
1977	24,194	4,997	.207
1978	39,681	6,693	.169
1979	79,072	12,279	.155
1980	120,229	21,769	.181
1981	252,092	31,182	.124
1982	344,317	56,451	.164
1983	564,734	73,755	.131
Change, 1983/1975	+ 5,418 %	+ 5,786 %	+ 7 %

Stock Prices and Earnings per Share[*]

| Year | Stock Prices | | | Earnings[**] Per Share |
	High	Low	Close	
1975	$ 1.296	$ .582	$ .714	$ .112
1976	2.269	.756	2.153	.042
1977	6.280	2.160	5.560	.682
1978	6.850	4.300	6.250	.624
1979	24.250	6.167	22.333	.887
1980	35.500	14.500	28.000	.910
1981	30.000	16.125	18.250	.630
1982	19.375	9.750	11.375	.760
1983	31.250	11.000	25.500	1.980
1984	26.250	13.500	21.250	1.940

Change, 1975–84 + 2,876%; change, S&P 500 Index, 1975–84 + 82%

[*]Adjusted for stock splits and stock dividends   [**]Includes extraordinary items

CORPORATE PROFILE—LEAR PETROLEUM CORPORATION

Lear Petroleum Corporation operates two basic businesses—natural gas transmission and oil and gas exploration and production. One business, Producer's Gas Company, purchases, gathers, compresses, transports and sells natural gas into the intrastate market. It also transports and sells gas into the interstate market, both directly and through exchanges, and operates natural gas processing plants. The other business, Lear Petroleum Exploration, Inc., explores for reserve deposits in proven productive trends in domestic onshore basins. By emphasizing drilling on proven producing structures in multipay areas, Lear hopes to achieve a good balance between high-risk, high-potential prospects and moderate-risk, moderate-potential prospects.

LEAR SIEGLER, INC.

Corporate Headquarters:　2850 Ocean Park Boulevard
　　　　　　　　　　　　Santa Monica, CA 90405

Telephone: (213) 452-6000
Incorporated in Delaware
New York Stock Exchange—LSI

Business: A diversified company with interests in aerospace, high techogy, automotive, general aviation, materials handling, recreation, commercial aviation and agriculture.

Officers:
　Robert T. Campion, Chairman and President
　K. Robert Hahn, Vice Chairman
　Norman A. Barkeley, Executive Vice President
　Charles F. Pitts, Senior Vice President, Administration
　James N. Thayer, Senior Vice President, Finance
　Larry R. DeJarnett, Vice President, Information Systems
　Robert U. Grant, Vice President, Management Services
　Elmar Klotz, Vice President, Aerospace Group
　Walter J. Kruel, Vice President, Corporate Planning and Development
　Donald A. Long, Vice President, Automotive Group
　David J. Louks, Vice President and Controller
　Albert F. Myers, Vice President, Purchasing
　Stephen D. Natcher, Vice President, Secretary & General Counsel
　William M. O'Hern, Vice President, Public Relations and Advertising
　Ronald V. Paolucci, Vice President, Industrial Relations
　Kenneth A. Ruck, Vice President, Commercial Products Group
　Donald R. Schort, Jr., Vice President & Treasurer
　Laurence A. Thompson, Vice President, Materials Handling Group
　Robert J. Wyma, Vice President, Aircraft Group

Statement of Income (Year ends 6/30—$ figures in 000's)

	1985	1984
Net Sales	$2,370,715	$1,941,665
Cost of Goods Sold	1,835,166	1,480,628
Gross Profit	$ 535,549	$ 461,037
Selling, General and Administrative Expenses	$ 317,062	$ 276,085
Interest Expense	47,494	32,977
Other (Income) Expense	(12,590)	(6,328)
Earnings before Income Taxes	$ 183,052	$ 158,303
Income Taxes	82,317	73,158
Net Earnings	$ 100,735	$ 85,145

Stockholder's Equity, Jobs, and Labor Productivity ($ figures in 000's)

Year	Stockholder's Equity	Net Sales	Number of Employees	Index of Labor Productivity
1975	$ 86,858	$ 643,755	17,123	37.596
1976	99,571	694,307	16,838	41.235
1977	112,029	920,285	24,400	37.717
1978	158,000	1,155,167	24,921	46.353
1979	238,404	1,327,271	25,066	52.951
1980	289,212	1,423,397	24,077	59.119
1981	355,794	1,530,699	23,985	63.819
1982	378,051	1,487,505	21,983	67.666
1983	418,172	1,464,190	20,004	73.195
Change, 1983/1975	+381 %	+127 %	+17 %	+95 %

Capital Productivity ($ figures in 000's)

Year	Total Invested Capital	Net Income	Index of Capital Productivity
1975	$275,044	$20,088	.073
1976	276,750	25,412	.092
1977	388,115	37,055	.095
1978	403,627	48,200	.119
1979	466,963	63,276	.136
1980	555,470	65,722	.118
1981	559,057	76,067	.136
1982	596,818	72,295	.121
1983	590,387	64,122	.109
Change, 1983/1975	+115 %	+219 %	+49 %

Stock Prices and Earnings per Share[*]

Year	Stock Prices High	Stock Prices Low	Stock Prices Close	Earnings[**] Per Share
1975	$ 8.500	$ 3.500	$ 6.000	$1.300
1976	14.250	6.125	14.125	1.750
1977	17.375	13.250	16.750	2.700
1978	24.000	13.000	18.000	3.550
1979	23.875	17.250	23.000	4.500
1980	41.750	18.125	40.125	4.230
1981	42.875	26.625	29.000	4.710
1982	37.000	20.125	34.875	4.360
1983	48.250	31.750	45.375	3.840
1984	49.500	37.500	44.250	4.960

Change, 1975–84 +638%; change, S&P 500 Index, 1975–84 +82%

[*]Adjusted for stock splits and stock dividends [**]Includes extraordinary items

213

This company is a diversified corporation with more than 50 operating divisions that generate sales in excess of $2 billion. The company was formed as the Siegler Corporation and launched its current strategic thrust when it merged with Lear in 1962. Today it is becoming a diversified aerospace/technology, automotive, and commercial/industrial manufacturer as well as a marketer of products and services through the acquisition of the Bangor Punta Corporation, which brought to Lear Siegler such prominent names as Piper Aircraft Corporation and Smith & Wesson. This acquisition, which was culminated in February 1984, has apparently been smoothly integrated, based on the most recent Lear Siegler fiscal year results. The company has grown significantly during the last decade and has maintained a high average rate of growth, particularly in light of its size and the diversity of the end-use markets it serves.

Lear Siegler accomplishes this exceptional management task—creating profitable growth in a widely diversified collection of basically small companies—by practicing sophisticated and effective strategic planning. Corporate headquarters provides the planning format, but each division is responsible for its own plans.

THE LIMITED INC.

Corporate Headquarters: One Limited Parkway
                                   Columbus, OH 43220

Telephone: (614) 475-4000

Incorporated in Delaware

New York Stock Exchange—LTD

Business: Owns and operates + 1,400 women's apparel stores under the names Limited, Limited Express, Pic-A-Dilly, Lerner, and a direct mail business.

Officers:

    Leslie H. Wexner, Chairman of the Board

    Robert H. Morosky, Vice Chairman

    Bella Wexner, Secretary

    Thomas G. Hopkins, Executive Vice President, Organizational Development

    David T. Kollat, Executive Vice President, Marketing

    Jerald Dick, Vice President, Real Estate

    Alfred S. Dietzel, Vice President, Financial and Public Relations

    Kenneth B. Gilman, Vice President, Corporate Controller

    Charles W. Hinson, Vice President, Store Planning

    Timothy B. Lyons, Vice President, Taxes

Statement of Income (Year ends 12/31—$ figures in 000's)

	1984	1983
Net Sales	$1,343,134	$1,086,890
Costs of Goods Sold, Occupancy and Buying Costs	938,813	758,274
Gross Income	404,321	327,616
General, Administrative and Store Operating Expenses	231,219	192,239
Operating Income	173,102	135,377
Interest Expenses	(16,662)	(10,248)
Other Income—Net	1,055	9,810
Income before Taxes	157,495	134,939
Provision for Income Taxes	65,000	64,000
Net Income	$ 92,495	$ 70,939

Stockholder's Equity, Jobs, and Labor Productivity ($ figures in 000's)

Year	Stockholder's Equity	Net Sales	Number of Employees	Index of Labor Productivity
1975	$ 6,460	$ 39,540	1,485	26.626
1976	11,210	68,866	1,867	36.886
1977	19,302	117,026	2,500	46.810
1978	36,727	203,457	3,800	53.541
1979	41,399	237,972	4,500	52.883
1980	49,308	265,333	5,000	53.067
1981	83,150	364,900	6,700	54.463
1982	122,578	721,394	13,500	53.437
1983	192,576	1,086,890	15,300	70.973
Change, 1983/1975	+2,881 %	+2,646 %	+930 %	+167 %

Capital Productivity ($ figures in 000's)

Year	Total Invested Capital	Net Income	Index of Capital Productivity
1975	$ 11,723	$ 2,193	.187
1976	16,320	4,757	.291
1977	30,227	8,320	.275
1978	72,887	11,867	.163
1979	82,005	4,496	.055
1980	83,733	8,361	.100
1981	99,721	22,386	.224
1982	196,989	33,592	.171
1983	214,339	70,939	.331
Change, 1983/1975	+1,728 %	+3,135 %	+77 %

Stock Prices and Earnings per Share[*]

Year	Stock Prices			Earnings[**] Per Share
	High	Low	Close	
1975	$ .451	$ .083	$ .451	$.023
1976	.979	.443	.979	.049
1977	2.271	.833	2.271	.086
1978	2.719	.938	.938	.113
1979	1.281	.500	.813	.043
1980	1.703	.672	1.391	.078
1981	2.109	1.344	1.781	.201
1982	6.125	1.719	6.000	.288
1983	15.500	5.688	12.250	.590
1984	14.000	7.625	13.500	.770

Change, 1975–84 +2,891%; change, S&P 500 Index, 1975–84 +82%

[*]Adjusted for stock splits and stock dividends   [**]Includes extraordinary items

216

This company is widely recognized as one of the outstanding growth companies of the decade. During the last five years its stock appreciated faster than any of the 1,000 companies surveyed by Forbes. Its primary business is to provide contemporary fashion apparel for women through multiple retail formats. The company has primarily grown through major expansion of its retail outlets, but also has made a limited number of acquisitions. The company has a reputation for maintaining a high-growth culture throughout the various levels of its organization. Its nearly 18,000 sales personnel are referred to as associates. The company has attracted and kept performance oriented staff through a strong program of internal development and promotion. The company intends to continue to grow both within its existing businesses and through additional acquisitions and/or joint ventures. The company also is moving aggressively to develop its own brand of sportswear under the Forenza label.

LOCTITE CORPORATION

Corporate Headquarters: 705 North Mountain Road
Newington, CT 06111

Telephone: (203) 278-1280
Incorporated in Connecticut
New York Stock Exchange—LOC

Business: Worldwide producer of proprietary, high performance adhesives, sealants and other specialty chemicals.

Officers:

Robert H. Krieble, Chairman and Chief Executive Officer
Kenneth W. Butterworth, President and Chief Operating Officer
Robert L. Aller, Treasurer
Vice Presidents: David I. Barton, Bernard J. Bolger, John M. Burke, Edward L. Daisey, Theodore F. Patlovich
Anthony J. Haueisen, Secretary
J. Rodney Reck, Vice President and General Counsel
David Freeman, Vice President, Finance/Operations and Controller

Statement of Income (Year ends 6/30—$ figures in 000's)

	1985	1984
Net Sales	$231,479	$241,744
Cost of Sales	91,868	96,731
Gross Margin	$139,611	$145,013
Research and Development Expense	$ 8,761	$ 7,610
Selling, General and Administrative Expense	95,980	94,337
	$104,741	$101,947
Earnings from Operations	$ 34,870	$ 43,066
Non-Operating Income	$ 6,697	$ 8,001
Interest Expense	(10,082)	(8,908)
Earnings before Income Taxes	$ 31,485	$ 42,159
Income Taxes	11,042	15,810
Net Earnings	$ 20,443	$ 26,349

218

Stockholder's Equity, Jobs, and Labor Productivity ($ figures in 000's)

Year	Stockholder's Equity	Net Sales	Number of Employees	Index of Labor Productivity
1975	$ 24,234	$ 67,277	1,400	48.055
1976	34,409	85,882	1,575	54.528
1977	49,105	105,344	1,775	59.349
1978	66,937	127,866	2,027	63.081
1979	88,095	161,471	2,509	64.357
1980	110,211	199,297	2,589	76.978
1981	116,999	213,912	2,572	83.170
1982	119,752	216,450	2,477	87.384
1983	129,419	215,892	2,355	91.674
Change, 1983/1975	+ 434 %	+ 221 %	+ 68 %	+ 91 %

Capital Productivity ($ figures in 000's)

Year	Total Invested Capital	Net Income	Index of Capital Productivity
1975	$ 51,411	$ 4,243	.083
1976	61,689	10,530	.171
1977	73,664	15,536	.211
1978	89,933	20,025	.223
1979	109,032	23,344	.214
1980	130,569	25,893	.198
1981	137,274	10,377	.076
1982	139,845	15,778	.113
1983	149,319	17,128	.115
Change, 1983/1975	+ 190 %	+ 304 %	+ 39 %

Stock Prices and Earnings per Share[*]

Year	Stock Prices			Earnings[**] Per Share
	High	Low	Close	
1975	$16.250	$ 7.000	$14.500	$ .440
1976	22.500	14.750	19.126	1.090
1977	24.375	16.750	23.375	1.600
1978	34.750	18.000	24.500	2.060
1979	45.000	21.000	32.250	2.400
1980	38.000	27.500	30.500	2.650
1981	31.000	18.125	22.750	1.050
1982	30.750	18.125	28.750	1.590
1983	46.500	28.500	41.500	1.720
1984	42.750	30.625	34.000	2.670

Change, 1975–84 + 135%; change, S&P 500 Index, 1975–84 + 82%

[*]Adjusted for stock splits and stock dividends   [**]Includes extraordinary items

Loctite Corporation is a worldwide producer of proprietary, high-performance adhesives, sealants, and other specialty chemicals. The company's principal markets are industrial manufacturing and repair, professional automotive maintenance, and the home and auto do-it-yourself field. Products include threadlocking sealants, structural adhesives, instant adhesives, gasketing compounds, sealants for electronic components, rust treatments, solvents, and many other specialty chemicals. The company's business is approximately equally split between its three major groups: U.S. Industrial Group, Automotive and Consumer Group, and the International Group. The 1980s recession gave the company problems in maintaining sufficient volume growth to avoid pressure on earnings. This has prevented the company from exceeding the earnings level reached during fiscal 1980. Loctite's recovery should follow the economy's.

LOGICON INC.

Corporate Headquarters: 3701 Skypark Drive
                         Torrance, CA 90505
Telephone: (213) 373-0220
Incorporated in Delaware
New York Stock Exchange—LGN

Business: Provides electronic systems and high-technology services to the government and to the defense industry.

Officers:
  John R. Woodhull, President and Chief Executive Officer
  James D. Hogan, Senior Vice President
  Vice Presidents: Hugh E. Beatty, James P. Brown, Frank T. Cummings, Donald L. Farr, Albert L. Latter, Richard J. McGrath, E. Teague Richmond
  James R. Edwards, Secretary and General Counsel
  Robert G. Walden, Senior Vice President and Chief Financial Officer
  Ralph L. Webster, Vice President, Controller

Statement of Income (Year ends 3/31—$ figures in 000's)

	1985	1984
Revenues		
Services and Systems	$165,966	$126,514
Interest	2,290	1,519
	168,256	128,033
Costs and Expenses		
Cost of Services and Systems	140,177	105,898
Selling and Administrative Expenses	11,729	10,416
	115,906	116,314
Income before Taxes on Income	16,350	11,719
Provision for Income Taxes	8,103	5,843
Net Income	$ 8,247	$ 5,876

Stockholder's Equity, Jobs, and Labor Productivity ($ figures in 000's)

Year	Stockholder's Equity	Net Sales	Number of Employees	Index of Labor Productivity
1975	$ 5,389	$ 31,732	858	38.984
1976	6,716	28,472	748	38.064
1977	8,117	33,335	882	27.795
1978	9,652	43,600	1,027	42.454
1979	11,671	48,878	903	54.128
1980	13,624	56,004	1,072	52.243
1981	16,110	61,340	990	61.960
1982	26,541	101,723	1,443	70.494
1983	32,659	126,514	1,812	69.820
Change, 1983/1975	+506 %	+299 %	+111 %	+89 %

Capital Productivity ($ figures in 000's)

Year	Total Invested Capital	Net Income	Index of Capital Productivity
1975	$ 5,526	$ 841	.152
1976	6,716	1,301	.194
1977	8,117	836	.103
1978	9,652	1,462	.151
1979	11,671	1,955	.168
1980	13,911	1,795	.129
1981	16,366	2,479	.151
1982	26,765	4,402	.164
1983	32,659	5,876	.180
Change, 1983/1975	+491 %	+599 %	+18 %

Stock Prices and Earnings per Share[*]

	Stock Prices			Earnings[**]
Year	High	Low	Close	Per Share
1975	$ 1.750	$ 1.000	$ 1.125	$ .327
1976	2.792	1.125	2.500	.500
1977	5.875	2.417	4.458	.307
1978	6.500	3.250	3.958	.533
1979	6.625	3.750	6.542	.707
1980	9.958	4.958	8.833	.613
1981	12.667	7.583	10.417	.820
1982	19.417	7.667	19.333	1.000
1983	32.000	18.750	29.750	1.280
1984	31.000	18.000	25.875	1.790

Change, 1975–84 +2,200%; change, S&P 500 Index, 1975–84 +82%

[*]Adjusted for stock splits and stock dividends   [**]Includes extraordinary items

Note: The fiscal year financial results in the tables above are shown in the year in which most of the results were achieved.

The company provides professional services—including scientific research and the application of computer and systems technology—for industry and government. Ninety-seven percent of revenues is derived from military work performed for the U.S. Department of Defense. One of the major markets the company serves is command, control, communications, and intelligence systems. Another market is strategic and space systems, for which Logicon provides varied services. At the end of the last fiscal year Logicon had 100 proposals outstanding, which if awarded to the company would represent about $125 million in new business. Last year Logicon won more than half of its competitive bids—a positive reflection of the company's ability to compete. The company has maintained an impressive record of growth, both through internal expansion and by acquisition of other professional service firms.

LUBY'S CAFETERIAS INC.

Corporate Headquarters: 2211 Northeast Loop 410, P.O. Box 33069
San Antonio, TX 78265

Telephone: (512) 654-9000
Incorporated in Texas
New York Stock Exchange—LUB

Business: Owns and operates cafeterias in the Southwest.

Officers:

George H. Wenglein, Chairman of the Board
John B. Lahourcade, President and Chief Executive Officer
Ralph Erben, Executive Vice President and Chief Operating Officer
Dawes Bodell, Vice President and Treasurer
Don M. Goudge, Vice President, Equipment
Paul H. Gowen, Vice President, Construction
Herbert D. Knight, Senior Vice President, Unit Operations
Alvin B. Beal, Senior Vice President, Property Development
Vernon C. Schrader, Vice President, Marketing
William E. Robson, Vice President, Food Service
Davis, W. Simpson, Vice President, Management Personnel
John E. Curtis, Jr., Vice President, Finance and Assistant Secretary
Area Vice Presidents: Alfred D. Adair, Wyatt H. Barnett, James I. Dove, Jerry Eldredge, Clyde C. Hays, III, Harold W. Kieke, Arnold C. Larsen, Walter W. Redding, Tom O. Sheeran, Jr., Jimmy W. Woliver
James R. Hale, Secretary

Statement of Income (Year ends 8/31—$ figures in 000's)

	1985	1984
Sales	$195,998	$170,818
Costs and Expenses		
Cost of Sales	104,637	93,272
Operating, General and Administrative	59,682	50,691
Income from Operations	$ 31,679	$ 26,855
Other Income (Expenses)		
Fees from Managed Cafeterias	$ —	$ 435
Interest and Other	3,151	3,599
Interest Expense	(97)	(156)
Income before Federal Income Taxes	$ 34,733	$ 30,733
Federal Income Taxes	15,148	13,379
Net Income	$ 19,585	$ 17,354

Stockholder's Equity, Jobs, and Labor Productivity ($ figures in 000's)

Year	Stockholder's Equity	Net Sales	Number of Employees	Index of Labor Productivity
1975	$ 7,765	$ 37,989	2,650	14.335
1976	10,324	46,161	2,864	16.118
1977	13,308	53,619	3,016	17.778
1978	23,272	65,462	3,400	19.254
1979	27,883	76,623	3,700	20.709
1980	33,582	89,893	4,000	22.473
1981	40,511	108,214	4,400	24.594
1982	61,860	127,331	4,800	26.527
1983	71,104	141,426	5,000	28.285
Change, 1983/1975	+816 %	+273 %	+89 %	+97 %

Capital Productivity ($ figures in 000's)

Year	Total Invested Capital	Net Income	Index of Capital Productivity
1975	$13,769	$ 2,117	.154
1976	15,476	3,094	.200
1977	19,698	3,781	.192
1978	30,275	4,991	.165
1979	34,617	6,506	.188
1980	40,023	8,018	.200
1981	46,641	9,787	.210
1982	67,666	11,589	.171
1983	76,565	13,917	.182
Change, 1983/1975	+456 %	+557 %	+18 %

Stock Prices and Earnings per Share[*]

Year	Stock Prices			Earnings[**] Per Share
	High	Low	Close	
1975	$ 2.010	$ .846	$ 2.010	$ .205
1976	3.026	2.036	3.026	.299
1977	4.992	2.987	4.992	.365
1978	9.120	4.280	6.880	.477
1979	8.000	6.240	6.720	.576
1980	11.400	6.250	11.000	.712
1981	16.950	10.725	16.350	.870
1982	24.451	15.150	21.826	1.014
1983	28.876	21.001	28.407	1.148
1984	31.970	23.626	27.001	1.433

Change, 1975–84 +1,243%; change, S&P 500 Index, 1975–84 +82%

[*]Adjusted for stock splits and stock dividends   [**]Includes extraordinary items

The company owns and operates 85 cafeterias in Texas, New Mexico, and Oklahoma. The cafeterias cater primarily to shoppers, store and office workers at lunchtime, and to families at dinner. Generally from 10,000 to 11,000 square feet in area, a Luby cafeteria can typically accommodate 300 guests in its carpeted dining room. Each facility offers a broad and varied menu, and normally serves 12 to 15 entrees, 12 to 15 vegetable dishes, 22 to 25 salads, and 22 to 25 desserts. Each cafeteria is operated as a separate unit under the control of a manager who has full responsibility for day-to-day operations. Each cafeteria manager is compensated on the basis of his cafeteria's profits. Management believes that granting broad authority to its cafeteria managers and compensating them on the basis of their performance are significant factors in the profitability of its cafeterias. This company, through the combination of new stores and increased volume per store, has achieved an impressive performance record in the highly competitive food-away-from-home market.

M/A COM, INC.

Corporate Headquarters: 7 New England Executive Park
                          Burlington, MA 01803
Telephone: (617) 272-9600
Incorporated in Massachusetts
New York Stock Exchange—MAI

Business: Manufactures sophisticated telecommunications systems and components for defense and commercial applications, and products for the CATV market.

Officers:

  Richard T. DiBona, Chairman of the Board, President and Chief Executive Officer
  Joseph C. Bothwell, Jr., Vice President, Corporate Development
  Hugh E. Bradshaw, Vice President, Secretary and Corporate Counsel
  Dr. Frank A. Brand, Executive Vice President and Chief Operating Officer
  Paul F. Brauneis, Vice President and Comptroller
  Thomas F. Burke, Executive Vice President, Administration and Finance
  Diane D. Calagione, Asst. Secretary and Asst. Corporate Counsel
  Frank M. Drendel, Vice Chairman of the Board, Executive Vice President

Statement of Income (Year ends 9/29/84 and 10/1/83—$ figures in 000's)

	1984	1983
Net Sales	$768,449	$637,279
Costs and Expenses		
Cost of Sales	$536,891	$438,274
Company Sponsored Research and Development	33,598	26,880
Selling, General and Administrative Expenses	133,618	116,550
Interest Expense	13,832	11,741
Interest Income	(6,510)	(6,606)
	$711,429	$586,839
Income from Continuing Operations before Provision for Income Taxes	$ 57,020	$ 50,440
Provision for Income Taxes	18,820	19,010
Income from Continuing Operations	$ 38,200	$ 31,430
Loss from Discontinued Operations, Less Applicable Income Taxes	—	(1,766)
Extraordinary Gain	—	—
Net Income	$ 38,200	$ 29,664

227

Stockholder's Equity, Jobs, and Labor Productivity ($ figures in 000's)

Year	Stockholder's Equity	Net Sales	Number of Employees	Index of Labor Productivity
1975	$ 26,885	$ 54,751	1,894	28.908
1976	30,297	60,645	1,955	31.020
1977	34,210	65,499	2,238	29.267
1978	42,121	99,317	2,907	34.165
1979	51,192	123,981	3,184	38.939
1980	140,552	322,480	6,274	51.399
1981	255,132	514,668	8,096	63.571
1982	308,610	587,646	8,700	67.546
1983	375,347	637,279	9,508	67.026
Change, 1983/1975	+ 1,296 %	+ 1,064 %	+ 402 %	+ 132 %

Capital Productivity ($ figures in 000's)

Year	Total Invested Capital	Funds from Operations	Index of Capital Productivity
1975	$ 28,041	$ 4,240	.151
1976	31,311	5,050	.161
1977	35,068	5,506	.157
1978	44,717	8,957	.200
1979	65,923	12,322	.187
1980	158,299	32,269	.204
1981	403,509	60,405	.150
1982	441,544	64,428	.146
1983	519,833	82,286	.158
Change, 1983/1975	+ 1,754 %	+ 1,841 %	+ 5 %

Stock Prices and Earnings per Share[*]

Year	Stock Prices			Earnings[**] Per Share
	High	Low	Close	
1975	$ 2.986	$ 1.083	$ 1.514	$ .168
1976	2.569	1.538	2.528	.227
1977	3.208	2.250	3.167	.283
1978	6.667	2.813	5.833	.367
1979	11.458	5.458	10.500	.493
1980	33.375	9.813	32.126	.770
1981	35.500	20.750	25.250	1.050
1982	27.000	11.875	23.125	.880
1983	35.125	18.375	19.875	.720
1984	21.750	13.125	19.250	.900

Change, 1975–84 + 1,172%; change, S&P 500 Index, 1975–84 + 82%

[*]Adjusted for stock splits and stock dividends   [**]Includes extraordinary items

M/A-COM is a leading manufacturer of sophisticated telecommunications systems and components for national defense and commercial applications; it also produces cable and other products for the CATV industry. Commercial telecommunications systems include satellite earth stations for television reception and digital data communications equipment for international and domestic common carriers and private business networks, using satellites, fiber optics, and microwave transmission. Equipment and software for defense applications are principally used in satellite systems. In addition M/A-COM supplies mini- and microcomputer systems to both commercial and government customers. M/A-COM also manufactures microwave and millimeter components and integrated assemblies, using advanced microwave and semiconductor technology for defense applications in radar, electronic countermeasures, missile guidance, and communications systems. This outstanding growth company recently was restructured in order to further integrate the various acquisitions made during the 1978-81 period.

M/A-COM's scrambling-unscrambling equipment has set the standard for the cable TV industry. This could provide the company with a long-term, profitable position in cable TV transmission and reception.

MAYFLOWER CORPORATION

Corporate Headquarters: 9998 North Michigan Road
Carmel, IN 46032

Telephone: (317) 875-1000
Incorporated in Indiana
American Stock Exchange—MFL

Business: Provides household goods, electronic products and general commodities moving services, school bus operating services, and distributes home entertainment products.

Officers:

John B. Smith, Chairman, President and Chief Executive Officer
Gary L. Light, Executive Vice President and Chief Financial Officer
Executive Vice Presidents: Richard L. Russell, Michael L. Smith
Senior Vice Presidents: James W. Bryan, Harold R. Elliot, Jr., Ted A. Helkema, Dennis C. Norman, Kenneth R. Richman, Donald K. Sears, Elizabeth O. Stevens, Donald H. Warner, Daniel E. Yates
Patrick F. Carr, Senior Vice President and Treasurer
Robert H. Irvin, Senior Vice President and Secretary
Walter S. Wiseman, Jr., Vice President

Statement of Income (Year ends 12/31—$ figures in 000's)

	1984	1983
Operating Revenues		
Truck Transportation Services	$370,785	$308,181
Other Products and Services	87,472	71,070
Bus Services and Sales	22,466	—
	$480,723	$379,251
Operating Expenses		
Truck Transportation	$243,348	$202,762
Other Products and Services	75,143	61,198
Bus Services and Sales	16,250	—
Selling, General and Administrative	122,760	103,244
	$457,501	$367,204
Operating Profit	$ 23,222	$ 12,047
Other Income (Expense), Net	843	1,216
Income before Income Taxes	$ 24,065	$ 13,263
Income Taxes	10,129	5,627
Net Income	$ 13,936	$ 7,636

Stockholder's Equity, Jobs, and Labor Productivity ($ figures in 000's)

Year	Stockholder's Equity	Net Sales	Number of Employees	Index of Labor Productivity
1975	$11,782	$104,844	887	118.201
1976	16,401	162,141	881	184.042
1977	20,102	189,409	968	195.670
1978	22,147	206,713	1,052	196.500
1979	24,201	256,108	1,294	197.920
1980	24,775	271,380	1,309	207.319
1981	27,741	330,375	1,357	243.460
1982	30,595	341,225	1,236	276.072
1983	53,291	379,251	1,378	275.218
Change, 1983/1975	+352%	+262%	+55%	+133%

Capital Productivity ($ figures in 000's)

Year	Total Invested Capital	Net Income	Index of Capital Productivity
1975	$18,220	$2,039	.112
1976	22,235	4,074	.183
1977	25,662	4,625	.180
1978	27,528	3,134	.114
1979	34,075	3,201	.094
1980	37,076	1,775	.048
1981	42,487	4,243	.100
1982	36,662	4,270	.116
1983	57,012	7,636	.134
Change, 1983/1975	+213%	+275%	+20%

Stock Prices and Earnings per Share*

Year	Stock Prices High	Stock Prices Low	Stock Prices Close	Earnings** Per Share
1975	n.a.	n.a.	n.a.	$ .489
1976	$ 3.241	$2.376	$ 2.765	.906
1977	3.565	2.614	3.280	.996
1978	5.124	3.085	3.085	.673
1979	3.294	2.470	3.129	.690
1980	4.721	1.976	3.843	.382
1981	4.293	2.841	3.662	.909
1982	7.778	3.056	7.778	.917
1983	12.639	7.222	10.139	1.300
1984	17.000	8.750	16.750	2.060

Change, 1976–84 +506%; change, S&P 500 Index, 1976–84 +53%

*Adjusted for stock splits and stock dividends   **Includes extraordinary items

Mayflower Corporation is one of the nation's leading truck transportation companies. In recent years it has become increasingly diversified. The company has earned a solid reputation for the service it provides in moving household goods, and this segment of the company accounted for 46 percent of 1984 revenues. Mayflower also offers a wide range of other services within truck transportation, including shipping and warehousing of electronic products and general commodities. A second segment of Mayflower is R.W. Harmon & Sons, Inc., the company's newly acquired contract school bus transportation and sales business. This new subsidiary should contribute to growth as school districts increasingly turn to professional management for their transportation systems. The third portion of the Mayflower picture is the company's distribution/home entertainment business, ADI Appliances, Inc. This segment derives the major portion of its revenue from the wholesaling of home electronic products and the distribution and rental of popular prerecorded video cassettes.

Mayflower is well along the path to becoming a $1 billion transportation company. It is following a carefully crafted plan to reduce its reliance on household furnishings moving, with its cyclical ups and downs, but still build upon the company's established strengths.

MCORP
(formerly Mercantile Texas Corporation)

Corporate Headquarters: 500 Dallas Building
Dallas, TX 75201

Telephone: (214) 698-5000
Incorporated in Delaware
New York Stock Exchange—MBK

Business: Bank holding company for a number of Texas banks.
Officers:
Gene H. Bishop, Chairman and Chief Executive Officer
John T. Cater, President and Chief Operating Officer
Karl T. Butz, Jr., Vice Chairman—Credit
Charles E. McMahen, Vice Chairman—Administration
William J. Renfro, Managing Director—Austin
John H. Garner, Managing Director—Corpus Christi
George L. Clark, Managing Director—Dallas
James B. Gardner, Managing Director—Dallas
H. M. Daugherty, Jr., Managing Director—El Paso
B. Lamar Ball, Jr., Managing Director—Fort Worth
C. Richard Vermillion, Jr., Managing Director—Houston
J. Thomas Hudgins, Managing Director—Houston
Robert G. Davis, Managing Director—San Antonio

Statement of Income (Year ends 12/31—$ figures in 000's)

	1984	1983
Interest Income	$1,446,517	$1,000,142
Interest Expense	1,047,964	685,506
Net Interest Income	$ 398,553	$ 314,636
Provision for Possible Loan Losses	118,023	65,460
Net Interest Income after Provision for Possible Loan Losses	$ 280,530	$ 249,176
Non-Interest Income	$ 181,199	$ 112,971
Non-Interest Expenses	359,031	271,735
Income before Income Taxes	$ 102,698	$ 90,412
Income Tax (Benefit)	(5,012)	(9,948)
Net Income	$ 107,710	$ 100,360

Stockholder's Equity, Jobs, and Labor Productivity ($ figures in 000's)

Year	Stockholder's Equity	Net Sales	Number of Employees	Index of Labor Productivity
1975	$ 86,428	$ 72,176	980	73.649
1976	109,837	90,306	2,400	37.628
1977	133,611	206,465	2,616	78.924
1978	201,413	298,545	2,955	101.030
1979	241,130	427,179	3,372	126.684
1980	276,915	550,443	3,700	148.768
1981	360,356	823,464	4,429	185.925
1982	549,751	1,138,755	6,313	180.383
1983	659,655	1,113,113	6,933	160.553
Change, 1983/1975	+ 663 %	+ 1,442 %	+ 607 %	+ 118 %

Capital Productivity ($ figures in 000's)

Year	Total Invested Capital	Net Income	Index of Capital Productivity
1975	$100,128	$ 10,483	.105
1976	199,260	12,752	.064
1977	224,561	25,340	.113
1978	289,199	31,103	.108
1979	361,673	39,389	.109
1980	395,770	47,543	.120
1981	475,147	62,974	.133
1982	724,954	101,998	.141
1983	850,592	100,360	.118
Change, 1983/1975	+ 750 %	+ 857 %	+ 13 %

Stock Prices and Earnings per Share[*]

Year	Stock Prices			Earnings[**] Per Share
	High	Low	Close	
1975	$18.083	$15.083	$15.750	$2.667
1976	20.333	16.083	20.333	2.540
1977	21.667	18.083	18.333	2.600
1978	19.750	17.000	17.000	3.040
1979	19.000	16.500	16.583	3.653
1980	19.000	13.667	17.667	4.280
1981	20.333	16.833	18.000	4.807
1982	22.167	16.500	20.583	4.567
1983	28.167	20.417	26.750	4.473
1984	33.000	23.625	33.000	4.700

Change, 1975–84 + 110%; change, S&P 500 Index, 1975–84 + 82%

[*]Adjusted for stock splits and stock dividends   [**]Includes extraordinary items

MCorp was created in October 1984 with the merger of Mercantile Texas Company and Southwest Bancshares, Inc. The company is a major financial service institution, with 64 member banks and three major nonbank service groups. The company's banking activities are concentrated in the State of Texas, with assets of more than $20 billion and a total capitalization in excess of $1.4 billion. At yearend 1984, MCorp ranked 22nd in assets, 15th in total deposits, and 10th in domestic deposits among the country's leading banking organizations. The company's growth in net income has been at a slower rate in recent years following several years of explosive growth during the 1975-1982 period.

MCorp has also chosen to concentrate on the commercial middle market (credit needs in the $1 million to $10 million range) in Texas. To accomplish this basic goal, MCorp is organized into seven banking regions within Texas. Each banking region has a managing director(s) to help member banks within the region be responsive to customer's needs. Mbanks offer customers a wide variety of services, including discount brokerage and 24-hour banking capabilities.

MEI CORPORATION

Corporate Headquarters: 800 F & M Marquette National Bank
Building
90 South 7th Street
Minneapolis, MN 55402

Telephone: (612) 339-8853
Incorporated in Delaware
New York Stock Exchange—MEI

Business: Bottles and distributes Pepsi-Cola, Seven-Up, Dr. Pepper and Orange Crush in 19 states and manufactures private label health and snack foods.

Officers:

Carl R. Pohlad, Chairman of the Board
Paul R. Christen, Vice Chairman of the Board
Donald E. Benson, President
Philip N. Hughes, Senior Vice President
Lyle C. Kasprick, Vice President
James A. Lee, Vice President, Finance
James A. Cesario, Controller
Cynthia L. Bergren, Assistant Controller
James O. Pohlad, Treasurer

Statement of Income (Year ends 12/31—$ figures in 000's)

	1984	1983
Operations		
Sales	$734,262	$616,463
Less Cost of Sales	419,341	341,375
Operating Expense	219,516	190,395
Operating Income	$ 95,405	$ 84,693
Expenses and Other Income		
General and Administrative	$ 6,613	$ 7,045
Interest Expense	17,154	14,294
Interest and Other Income, Net	(8,816)	(7,621)
	$ 14,951	$ 13,718
Income before Income Taxes	$ 80,454	$ 70,975
Provision for Income Taxes	36,662	32,700
Net Income	$ 43,792	$ 38,275

Stockholder's Equity, Jobs, and Labor Productivity ($ figures in 000's)

Year	Stockholder's Equity	Net Sales	Number of Employees	Index of Labor Productivity
1975	$16,159	$ 86,005	1,617	53.188
1976	20,097	92,782	1,746	53.140
1977	30,616	166,534	2,873	57.965
1978	42,200	209,452	2,998	69.364
1979	54,360	240,788	2,992	80.477
1980	60,932	349,720	3,725	93.885
1981	68,810	445,781	4,056	109.907
1982	73,162	502,722	4,301	116.885
1983	76,220	616,463	4,903	125.732
Change, 1983/1975	+ 372 %	+ 617 %	+ 203 %	+ 136 %

Capital Productivity ($ figures in 000's)

Year	Total Invested Capital	Funds from Operations	Index of Capital Productivity
1975	$ 41,098	$ 6,599	.161
1976	49,212	8,387	.170
1977	72,860	14,134	.194
1978	102,199	20,230	.198
1979	128,421	23,932	.186
1980	153,402	29,672	.193
1981	197,491	40,486	.205
1982	261,536	49,055	.188
1983	329,984	61,246	.186
Change, 1983/1975	+ 703 %	+ 828 %	+ 16 %

Stock Prices and Earnings per Share*

Year	Stock Prices			Earnings** Per Share
	High	Low	Close	
1975	$ 1.938	$ .563	$ 1.750	$ .415
1976	2.813	1.750	2.563	.440
1977	4.875	2.000	4.500	.580
1978	6.438	3.813	5.375	.785
1979	7.688	5.188	6.063	.950
1980	9.625	4.875	9.375	1.170
1981	17.125	9.125	15.313	1.595
1982	32.375	14.750	28.375	1.900
1983	39.125	25.000	35.375	2.270
1984	40.000	31.500	37.375	2.600

Change, 1975–84 + 2,036%; change, S&P 500 Index, 1975–84 + 82%

*Adjusted for stock splits and stock dividends **Includes extraordinary items

This company operates principally in two industries: soft drinks and snack and health foods. Through its beverage subsidiaries, MEI is, at press time, the third largest bottler of Pepsi-Cola products in the United States, with 24 production plants and 46 warehouses serving parts of 19 states. In many of its franchised bottling operations MEI also produces and distributes Seven-Up, Dr. Pepper, Orange Crush, and other soft drinks. MEI's snack and health food division produces, manufactures, distributes, and markets snacks, health foods, and candy products for both the private-label market and retail proprietary brands. This company has turned in continuous growth in sales and net income.

MEI is a good example of the dynamic character of America's 101 Best Performing Companies. MEI's strong performance record made the company an attractive takeover candidate. Management spent much of 1984 trying to organize a leveraged buyout. Existing contractual agreements with Pepsi-Cola put serious roadblocks in the LBO plan. This culminated in December 1985 when the management sold the entire soft drink bottling business to Pepsi-Cola. Since beverages accounted for 70 percent of MEI's business and snacks and health foods for only 30 percent, the "new" MEI will be a substantially different company. It will be interesting to see what management makes of the new MEI.

HERMAN MILLER, INC.

Corporate Headquarters:　8500 Byron Road
　　　　　　　　　　　　　Zeeland, MI 49464
Telephone: (616) 772-3300
Incorporated in Michigan
Over the Counter—MLHR

Business: Manufactures furniture, furniture products and office work environments.

Officers:

Max O. DePree, Chairman, President and Chief Executive Officer
David L. Armstrong, Vice President—Marketing
Clarence W. Boeve, Vice President
Robert V. Cooper, Vice President—Manufacturing
Robert A. Harvey, Vice President—Design
Larry E. Justice, Vice President—Corporate Business Systems
Roy E. Keech, Vice President—Distribution Resources
Philip J. Mercorella, Vice President—Sales
Gary S. Miller, Vice President—Development Engineering
Thomas C. Pratt, Vice President—Corp. Design and Development
Richard H. Ruch, Vice President—Corp. Resources and Subsidiaries
James G. Schreiber, Vice President and Controller
Joseph N. Schwartz, Vice President—Sales and Marketing
William H. Simmons, Vice President—Operations
Edward R. Simon, Jr., Vice President—Finance and CFO
Gary J. Ten Harmsel, Vice President—Logistics
Adrian R. Van Donkelaar, Vice President—Health/Science Division
James A. Von Ins, Treasurer
Sherman A. Walters, Vice President—Central Purchasing and Services
Thomas D. Wolterink, Vice President—Facility Management

Statement of Income (Year ends 6/1/85 and 6/2/84—$ figures in 000's)

	1985	1984
Net Sales	$491,919	$402,524
Cost of Sales	$278,485	$226,094
Gross Profit on Sales	$213,434	$176,430
Selling, General and Administrative Expenses	$121,428	$108,298
Design and Research Expenses	16,604	13,943
Operating Income	$ 75,402	$ 54,189
Interest Expense	$ 6,734	$ 7,836
Interest (Income)	(3,954)	(5,011)
Income before Income Taxes	$ 76,622	$ 51,364
Income Taxes	31,700	22,800
Net Income	$ 40,922	$28,564

Stockholder's Equity, Jobs, and Labor Productivity ($ figures in 000's)

Year	Stockholder's Equity	Net Sales	Number of Employees	Index of Labor Productivity
1975	$ 17,010	$ 50,788	1,099	46.213
1976	20,773	81,212	1,600	50.758
1977	30,757	119,617	2,701	44.286
1978	48,904	174,699	3,097	56.409
1979	59,644	230,295	3,211	71.721
1980	83,830	252,740	3,288	76.867
1981	100,937	314,019	3,595	87.349
1982	118,677	314,946	3,202	98.359
1983	143,197	402,524	3,703	108.702
Change, 1983/1975	+742 %	+693 %	+237 %	+135 %

Capital Productivity ($ figures in 000's)

Year	Total Invested Capital	Net Income	Index of Capital Productivity
1975	$ 25,711	$ 2,671	.104
1976	41,823	4,138	.099
1977	61,106	5,468	.089
1978	80,809	9,005	.111
1979	105,780	12,108	.114
1980	141,549	13,881	.098
1981	164,666	18,117	.110
1982	177,917	18,851	.106
1983	195,534	28,564	.146
Change, 1983/1975	+661 %	+969 %	+41 %

Stock Prices and Earnings per Share*

	Stock Prices			Earnings**
Year	High	Low	Close	Per Share
1975	$ 1.184	$ .576	$ .768	$ .290
1976	1.960	.780	1.880	.307
1977	3.450	1.850	3.100	.466
1978	5.550	2.800	3.350	.528
1979	5.406	3.313	4.688	.690
1980	9.938	3.875	9.188	.883
1981	11.500	7.063	11.500	.940
1982	13.875	9.125	12.875	1.140
1983	27.000	12.375	26.875	1.160
1984	36.250	20.500	34.625	1.710

Change, 1975–84 +4,409%; change, S&P 500 Index, 1975–84 +82%

*Adjusted for stock splits and stock dividends   **Includes extraordinary items

Note: The fiscal year financial results in the tables above are shown in the year in which most of the results were achieved.

The company's principal business consists of the research, design, development, manufacture, and sale of furniture systems, products, and related services. Most of these systems and products are coordinated in design so that they may be used together and interchangeably. The company's systems and products and related services are purchased primarily for office/institution and health/science use, with sales for such uses representing more than 98 percent of the company's total revenues. The company is a leader in design and development of furniture and furniture systems. In particular, the Action Office^R system, the company's freestanding office partition and furnishing system, was the first such system introduced and nationally marketed as an "open plan" approach to space utilization. This system has accounted for most of its growth over the last five years. The company's products are marketed worldwide by its own sales staffs of approximately 200 serving office/institutional customers and 25 serving health/science customers. Approximately 75 percent of the company's sales were made to or through approximately 375 nonexclusive, independent dealers. The remaining sales (25 percent) were made directly to end-users, including federal, state, and local governments and several major corporations.

MULTIMEDIA, INC.

Corporate Headquarters: 305 South Main Street, PO Box 1688
                          Greenville, South Carolina 29602

Telephone: (803) 298-4373
Incorporated in South Carolina
Over the Counter—MMED

Business: Operates newspapers, TV stations, radio stations, cable TV franchises, and produces and syndicates TV programming.

Officers:
   Walter E. Bartlett, President and Chief Executive Officer
   Wilson C. Wearn, Chairman of the Board
   Donald J. Barhyte, Chief Financial Officer, Treasurer
   Vice Presidents: Donald L. Dahlman, James T. Lynaugh, Donald D. Sbarra, Myron B. Weinblatt
   Robert E. Hamby, Jr., Vice President, Controller

Statement of Income (Year ends 12/31—$ figures in 000's)

	1984	1983
Operating Revenues		
Broadcasting	$135,319	$125,881
Newspapers	102,995	90,659
Cablevision	66,047	53,180
Total Operating Revenues	304,361	269,720
Operating Costs and Expenses		
Production	104,883	94,353
Selling, General and Administrative	97,131	86,913
Depreciation and Amortization	21,523	18,411
Total Operation Costs and Expenses	223,537	199,677
Operating Profit	80,824	70,043
Interest Expense	(8,289)	(8,198)
Loss on Investment in Joint Venture	(11,000)	—
Other Income (Net)	2,632	3,413
Earnings before Income Taxes	64,167	65,258
Income Taxes	30,479	30,084
Net Income	$ 33,688	$ 35,174

Stockholder's Equity, Jobs, and Labor Productivity ($ figures in 000's)

Year	Stockholder's Equity	Net Sales	Number of Employees	Index of Labor Productivity
1975	$ 20,689	$ 57,467	1,600	35.917
1976	23,562	79,008	1,800	43.893
1977	30,663	92,489	1,900	48.678
1978	40,993	110,630	1,950	56.733
1979	36,479	133,487	2,200	60.676
1980	37,374	163,563	2,800	58.415
1981	55,473	195,276	3,000	65.092
1982	80,422	225,463	3,100	72.730
1983	113,857	269,720	3,000	89.907
Change, 1983/1975	+ 450 %	+ 369 %	+ 88 %	+ 150 %

Capital Productivity ($ figures in 000's)

Year	Total Invested Capital	Net Income	Index of Capital Productivity
1975	$ 63,244	$ 6,926	.110
1976	85,358	9,958	.117
1977	95,061	12,013	.126
1978	96,594	15,601	.162
1979	128,932	18,676	.145
1980	167,459	21,618	.129
1981	202,048	25,824	.128
1982	227,024	28,974	.128
1983	304,152	35,174	.116
Change, 1983/1975	+ 381 %	+ 408 %	+ 6 %

Stock Prices and Earnings per Share[*]

Year	Stock Prices			Earnings[**] Per Share
	High	Low	Close	
1975	$ 4.222	$ 2.593	$ 4.148	$ .468
1976	6.593	4.222	6.519	.673
1977	8.296	6.222	8.296	.809
1978	12.778	7.167	10.889	1.044
1979	14.889	10.333	14.778	1.249
1980	22.167	8.750	20.000	1.433
1981	24.833	18.000	23.333	1.700
1982	33.667	18.167	32.667	1.900
1983	43.750	31.000	37.250	2.150
1984	42.500	29.750	36.750	2.020

Change, 1975–84 + 786%; change, S&P 500 Index, 1975–84 + 82%

[*]Adjusted for stock splits and stock dividends   [**]Includes extraordinary items

243

The company is a media communications company with corporate headquarters located in Greenville, South Carolina. Multimedia's divisions now publish 13 daily and 31 nondaily newspapers; own and operate 5 television and 12 radio broadcasting stations; operate more than 100 cable television franchises in 4 states; and produce and syndicate television programming. The company's long tradition of success in the communications industry began with its predecessor company, founded in 1888. 1984 marked the 96th consecutive profitable year for the company, even though results that year were depressed because of an $11 million charge on its investment in a joint venture in Sports Time, a regional pay-cable sports network. The company expects to show earnings growth in fiscal 1985; a return to historical growth patterns is anticipated.

NATIONAL CONVENIENCE STORES, INCORPORATED

Corporate Headquarters: 100 Waugh Drive
 Houston, TX 77007

Telephone: (713) 863-2200

Incorporated in Delaware

New York Stock Exchange—NCS

Business: Operates 1,081 specialty convenience retail stores under the names "Stop N Go," "Shop N Go," "Hot Stop" and "Colonial."

Officers:

V. H. Van Horn, President and Chief Executive Officer

Thomas W. Ewens, Senior Vice President—Corporate Development

Jerry R. Welch, Senior Vice President—Stores

A. J. Gallerano, Vice President—General Counsel and Secretary

J. C. Brewster, Vice President—Finance and Chief Financial Officer

Patricia A. Raybon, Vice President—Internal Audit

Terry D. Parks, Vice President—Real Estate

Ned E. Dickey, Vice President—Midwestern Division

Raymond P. Springer, Vice President—West Texas Division

Statement of Income (Year ends 6/30—$ figures in 000's)

	1985	1984
Sales	$927,507	$818,988
Costs and Expenses		
Cost of Sales	$683,555	$597,896
Operating, General and Administrative Expenses	201,229	177,242
Interest Expense	19,185	14,835
	$903,969	$789,973
Earnings before Income Taxes	$ 23,538	$ 29,015
Income Taxes	8,029	10,565
Net Earnings	$ 15,509	$ 18,450

Stockholder's Equity, Jobs, and Labor Productivity ($ figures in 000's)

Year	Stockholder's Equity	Net Sales	Number of Employees	Index of Labor Productivity
1975	$13,918	$196,226	3,900	50.314
1976	16,272	212,606	4,079	52.122
1977	17,891	233,208	3,971	58.728
1978	21,296	263,705	4,089	64.491
1979	18,359	320,363	4,559	70.270
1980	24,078	434,430	5,200	83.544
1981	47,086	527,447	6,541	80.637
1982	60,361	617,438	6,439	95.890
1983	74,289	632,310	6,250	101.008
Change, 1983/1975	+434 %	+222 %	+61 %	+101 %

Capital Productivity ($ figures in 000's)

Year	Total Invested Capital	Net Income	Index of Capital Productivity
1975	$ 24,912	$ 1,259	.051
1976	23,295	2,652	.114
1977	25,183	3,536	.140
1978	30,594	5,011	.164
1979	72,772	6,005	.083
1980	79,694	8,050	.101
1981	99,592	10,180	.102
1982	146,354	12,185	.083
1983	201,894	14,226	.070
Change, 1983/1975	+710 %	+1,030 %	+39 %

Stock Prices and Earnings per Share[*]

Year	Stock Prices			Earnings[**] Per Share
	High	Low	Close	
1975	$ .847	$ .397	$ .661	$.090
1976	1.323	.661	.979	.183
1977	2.361	.944	2.195	.243
1978	3.233	1.800	2.933	.341
1979	4.500	2.667	4.167	.400
1980	4.733	2.933	3.733	.536
1981	7.244	3.200	7.022	.604
1982	10.560	5.333	8.000	.691
1983	17.600	7.867	16.800	.747
1984	18.100	11.200	14.800	.936

Change, 1975–84 +2,138%; change, S&P 500 Index, 1975–84 +82%

[*]Adjusted for stock splits and stock dividends   [**]Includes extraordinary items

246

National Convenience Stores Incorporated, headquartered in Houston, Texas, operated 1,081 specialty convenience stores at fiscal yearend 1984 in 11 Sunbelt states: Arizona, California, Colorado, Florida, Georgia, Louisiana, Mississippi, Nevada, Oklahoma, Tennessee, and Texas. The stores operate primarily under the names Stop N Go, Shop N Go, Hot Stop, and Colonial. They are open every day of the year; most operate around the clock. The stores carry more than 2,500 items, representing a diverse range of frequently purchased products. The company expects its outstanding growth record of the past to continue at least through 1987. In fact, the company is unusual in that it has provided forecasts in its 1984 annual report of sales and earnings for the year 1987. The forecast, if it materializes, will result in an additional 450 new stores, total sales of nearly $1.5 billion, and earnings before taxes of nearly $60 million. This company has set ambitious and aggressive goals for itself. It will be an interesting growth organization to monitor during the next few years.

NATIONAL MEDICAL ENTERPRISES, INC.

Corporate Headquarters: 11620 Wilshire Boulevard
Los Angeles, CA 90025

Telephone: (213) 479-5526

Incorporated in Nevada

New York Stock Exchange—NME

Business: Owns, manages or operates acute, psychiatric, rehabilitative and long term care hospitals, retail outlets for medical supplies, etc.

Officers:

Richard K. Eamer, Chairman and Chief Executive Officer

Leonard Cohen, President and Chief Operating Officer

John C. Bedrosian, Senior Vice President

Executive Vice Presidents: James P. Livingston, Peter de Wetter, Daniel R. Baty, Gerard A. Smith, Michael H. Focht

Taylor R. Jenson, Executive Vice President and Chief Financial Officer

Maris Andersons, Senior Vice President and Treasurer

Marcus E. Powers, Senior Vice President and General Counsel

Gerald L. Stevens, Senior Vice President

Sidney F. Tyler, Jr., Senior Vice President

Scott M. Brown, Vice President and Secretary

Steven Dominguez, Senior Vice President—Government Programs

Edward A. Elliot, Senior Vice President—Corporate Finance

Leon Leonian, Senior Vice President—Real Estate

Statement of Income (Year ends 5/31—$ figures in 000,000's)

	1985	1984
Net Operating Revenues	$3,304	$2,559
Operating and Administrative Expenses	$2,568	$2,187
Depreciation and Amortization	111	84
Interest	114	92
Total Costs and Expenses	$2,793	$2,363
Income from Operations	$ 241	$ 196
Investment Earnings	26	25
Income before Taxes on Income	$ 267	$ 221
Taxes on Income	118	97
Net Income	$ 149	$ 124

Stockholder's Equity, Jobs, and Labor Productivity ($ figures in 000's)

Year	Stockholder's Equity	Net Sales	Number of Employees	Index of Labor Productivity
1975	$ 46,656	$ 109,198	5,665	19.276
1976	52,865	159,319	7,332	21.759
1977	66,578	210,775	8,557	24.632
1978	109,194	277,611	10,995	25.249
1979	200,186	608,639	25,283	24.073
1980	376,183	881,009	28,200	31.241
1981	451,882	1,138,552	40,100	28.393
1982	648,000	1,747,000	50,200	34.801
1983	766,000	2,065,000	55,100	37.477
Change, 1983/1975	+ 1,542 %	+ 1,791 %	+ 873 %	+ 94 %

Capital Productivity ($ figures in 000's)

Year	Total Invested Capital	Net Income	Index of Capital Productivity
1975	$ 145,187	$ 5,420	.037
1976	163,453	6,890	.042
1977	176,232	9,807	.056
1978	245,866	13,849	.056
1979	463,836	29,493	.064
1980	663,862	51,799	.078
1981	932,142	75,237	.081
1982	1,497,000	93,000	.062
1983	1,712,000	121,000	.071
Change, 1983/1975	+ 1,079 %	+ 2,133 %	+ 89 %

Stock Prices and Earnings per Share[*]

Year	Stock Prices			Earnings[**] Per Share
	High	Low	Close	
1975	$ 1.117	$ .397	$ .793	$ .246
1976	1.568	.760	1.535	.297
1977	2.756	1.444	2.711	.398
1978	5.633	2.500	4.200	.467
1979	7.533	3.333	7.433	.731
1980	15.200	6.500	14.800	.992
1981	23.000	12.500	13.900	1.280
1982	23.750	9.750	23.250	1.470
1983	32.375	20.125	23.000	1.740
1984	25.625	17.625	23.375	2.049

Change, 1975–84 + 2,846%; change, S&P 500 Index, 1975–84 + 82%

[*]Adjusted for stock splits and stock dividends   [**]Includes extraordinary items

National Medical Enterprises, Inc., is an international health care provider that at fiscal yearend 1985 owned, operated, or managed more than 400 acute psychiatric, rehabilitative, and long-term care hospitals having in excess of 50,000 beds. The company also operates retail outlets for durable medical equipment and supplies; offers prepaid and preferred-provider health insurance programs to employers and group insurers; and operates urgent care centers, retail and institutional pharmacies, and home health agencies. It has achieved exceptional growth in virtually all performance measures and continues its aggressive stance toward acquisition opportunities. In addition, it exploits geographic expansion and internal growth.

National Medical Enterprises is one of the big four medical care providers. (See American Medical Enterprises for details.) However, NME has developed a somewhat different mix of hospital care services than the other three. For instance, NME is the only one with a major presence in psychiatric hospitals. NME, Charter Medical, and Community Psychiatric Centers now operate a full 50 percent of the 215 hospitals that belong to the National Association of Private Psychiatric Hospitals. (Both Charter Medical and Community Psychiatric Centers also are among America's 101 Best Performing Companies.)

NME's Recovery Centers of America, with its "New Beginnings" program, is a growing factor in the developing substance abuse, drug and alcohol dependence area of health care.

250

NUCOR CORPORATION

Corporate Headquarters: 4425 Randolph Rd.
Charlotte, NC 28211
Telephone: (704) 366-7000
Incorporated in Delaware
New York Stock Exchange—NUE

Business: Operates steel mills and sells steel products.
Officers:
F. Kenneth Iverson, Chairman and Chief Executive Officer
Hugh D. Aycock, President and Chief Operating Officer
Samuel Siegle, Vice President, Chief Financial Officer, Treasurer, Secretary
Vice Presidents: Hasting M. Crapse, John A. Doherty, Donald N. Holloway, William J. Kontor, Richard L. Havekost, Keith E. Busse, John D. Correnti, Larry A. Roos, William E. Dauksch, James W. Cunningham

Statement of Income (Year ends 12/31—$ figures in 000's)

	1984	1983
Net Sales	$660,260	$542,531
Costs and Expenses		
Cost of Products Sold	$539,731	$461,728
Marketing and Administration Expenses	45,939	33,988
Interest Expense (Income)	(3,959)	(749)
	$581,711	$494,967
Earnings before Federal Income Taxes	$ 78,548	$ 47,564
Federal Income Taxes	34,000	19,700
Net Income	$ 44,548	$ 27,864

251

Stockholder's Equity, Jobs, and Labor Productivity ($ figures in 000's)

Year	Stockholder's Equity	Net Sales	Number of Employees	Index of Labor Productivity
1975	$ 44,550	$121,467	2,300	52.812
1976	54,085	175,768	2,300	76.421
1977	66,295	212,953	2,500	85.181
1978	92,129	306,940	2,800	109.621
1979	133,258	428,682	3,100	138.285
1980	177,604	482,420	3,300	146.188
1981	212,376	544,821	3,700	147.249
1982	232,281	486,018	3,600	135.005
1983	258,130	542,531	3,700	146.630
Change, 1983/1975	+479 %	+347 %	+61 %	+178 %

Capital Productivity ($ figures in 000's)

Year	Total Invested Capital	Funds from Operations	Index of Capital Productivity
1975	$ 72,802	$11,973	.164
1976	85,752	14,396	.168
1977	94,428	19,179	.203
1978	133,602	34,704	.260
1979	174,656	52,877	.303
1980	217,209	60,956	.281
1981	296,130	64,429	.218
1982	280,510	57,879	.206
1983	303,861	63,174	.208
Change, 1983/1975	+317 %	+428 %	+26 %

Stock Prices and Earnings per Share*

| Year | Stock Prices | | | Earnings** Per Share |
	High	Low	Close	
1975	$ 3.189	$ 1.849	$ 2.466	$ .616
1976	5.272	2.466	4.464	.682
1977	6.131	3.839	6.131	.960
1978	11.000	5.792	10.417	1.953
1979	20.313	10.063	19.938	3.146
1980	37.125	15.000	34.938	3.310
1981	41.125	24.500	29.875	2.510
1982	31.750	17.063	31.250	1.590
1983	42.750	30.125	42.750	1.980
1984	44.250	26.000	32.250	3.160

Change, 1975–84 +1,208%; change, S&P 500 Index, 1975–84 +82%

*Adjusted for stock splits and stock dividends   **Includes extraordinary items

The company operates scrap-based steel mills in four locations. These mills use modern steelmaking techniques and produce steel at a cost competitive with steel manufactured anywhere in the world. Steel sales in 1984 were 990,000 tons, slightly lower than the 1,030,000 tons in 1983. This represented about 65 percent of the mills' production; the balance was used by the company's Vulcraft, Cold Finish, and Grinding Balls Divisions. Steel sales in 1985 are projected to be at least 10 percent higher than in 1984. Ninety-nine percent of Nucor's sales are from its primary business—the manufacture of steel products. During the last five years, Nucor's sales have increased 54 percent. All of this growth has been internally generated. The company's ability to compete effectively in the steel industry is an outstanding example of sound strategic focus and management attention. The outlook for 1985 is for growth over 1984. Funds from operations are expected to reach an all time high.

PACIFIC SCIENTIFIC

Corporate Headquarters: 1350 South State College Blvd.
Anaheim, CA 92805

Telephone: (714) 535-8141
Incorporated in California
New York Stock Exchange—PSX

Business: Manufactures high technology electronic instruments, specialty motors, aerospace products and restraint systems.

Officers:

Harry R. Goff, Chairman

Edgar S. Brower, President and Chief Executive Officer

Richard V. Plat, Vice President, Finance and Administration and Secretary

Thomas J. Pope, Senior Vice President

Vice Presidents: Douglas D. Flockler, Albert F. Hartung, Jerome Harrington, Joseph T. Sacco, Jr.

William L. Nothwang, Controller

Peet A. Swan, Treasurer

Statement of Income (Year ends 12/28/84 and 12/30/83—$ figures in 000's)

	1984	1983
Revenues		
Net Sales	$88,912	$78,886
Investment and Other Income	3,380	2,535
Total Revenues	92,192	81,421
Costs and Expenses		
Cost of Sales	54,649	42,506
Selling, General and Administrative	18,262	14,387
Research and Development	4,453	2,512
Interest	2,469	1,860
Total Costs and Expenses	79,833	61,265
Income before Taxes	12,359	20,156
Income Taxes	5,359	9,310
Net Income	$ 7,000	$10,846

Stockholder's Equity, Jobs, and Labor Productivity ($ figures in 000's)

Year	Stockholder's Equity	Net Sales	Number of Employees	Index of Labor Productivity
1975	$ 6,960	$18,236	450	40.524
1976	7,697	20,364	517	39.389
1977	11,331	26,054	449	58.027
1978	18,761	33,266	479	69.449
1979	21,291	44,220	713	62.020
1980	27,525	62,784	722	86.958
1981	34,461	74,313	886	83.875
1982	36,038	84,902	879	96.589
1983	46,467	81,421	728	111.842
Change, 1983/1975	+ 568 %	+ 347 %	+ 62 %	+ 176 %

Capital Productivity ($ figures in 000's)

Year	Total Invested Capital	Net Income	Index of Capital Productivity
1975	$ 7,899	$ 562	.071
1976	9,710	893	.092
1977	12,283	2,850	.232
1978	19,692	4,479	.227
1979	28,986	5,161	.178
1980	30,273	7,153	.236
1981	37,401	8,444	.226
1982	38,671	9,240	.239
1983	79,272	10,846	.137
Change, 1983/1975	+ 904 %	+ 1,830 %	+ 92 %

Stock Prices and Earnings per Share*

Year	Stock Prices			Earnings** Per Share
	High	Low	Close	
1975	$ .776	$ .406	$ .741	$ .126
1976	1.111	.593	1.111	.199
1977	3.722	1.111	3.722	.580
1978	10.444	2.667	5.444	.827
1979	7.056	4.333	6.444	.898
1980	20.667	4.917	17.000	1.220
1981	22.875	12.000	14.750	1.420
1982	21.500	8.000	19.125	1.600
1983	39.875	16.250	17.250	1.980
1984	19.000	11.875	14.250	1.290

Change, 1975–84 + 1,824%; change, S&P 500 Index, 1975–84 + 82%

*Adjusted for stock splits and stock dividends   **Includes extraordinary items

The company's operations are grouped in three industry segments. Restraint equipment is the responsibility of the Kin-Tech Division. These products include both mechanical shock arrestors and aerospace products. Instruments and components are the responsibility of the HIAC/Royco, Gardner/Neotec, and Belfab divisions. Motors and controls are the responsibility of the Motor and Control Division, which was acquired in February 1984. This product line consists of low-inertia motors sold mainly to the data processing industry. In recent years, a great deal of progress has been made in reducing the company's dependence on the construction of nuclear power plants. In 1983, mechanical shock arrestors for the nuclear industry accounted for 39 percent of the company's revenues and an even greater share of earnings; arrestor sales in 1984 accounted for only 11 percent of revenues. This lost sales volume has been replaced. However, the products that provide the replacement revenue do not have the same high profit margin as arrestors, which accounts for the lower profit result in 1984. As a result of restructuring its product/market emphasis, the company is expected to resume its growth pattern.

PACIFIC TELECOM, INC.

Corporate Headquarters: 805 Broadway, PO Box 9901
                         Vancouver, WA 98668
Telephone: (206) 696-0983
Incorporated in Washington
Over the Counter—PTCM

Business: Provides telecommunications service to 171 communities in eight Pacific Northwest states.

Officers:

A. M. Gleason, Chairman and Chief Executive Officer
Charles E. Robinson, President and Chief Operating Officer
Dennis W. Elliott, Executive Vice President
Vern K. Dunham, Vice President, Revenue Requirements
Charles E. Peterson, Vice President
James P. Best, Vice President, Controller
Robert W. Bunke, Vice President
Edward R. Beiger, Vice President, Administration
Charles Kegley, Jr., Vice President, Industrial Relations
John E. McGill, Vice President, Regulatory Affairs
B. Charles Russell, Vice President, Engineering
James C. Warwick, Vice President, Plans and Programs
Brian M. Wirkkala, Vice President, Treasurer

Statement of Income (Year ends 12/31—$ figures in 000's)

	1984	1983
Operating Revenues	$399,064	$386,205
Operating Expenses Other than Income Taxes	273,507	249,141
Income Taxes	58,596	60,045
Total Operating Expenses	332,103	309,186
Net Operating Income	66,961	77,019
Income (Losses) from Nonregulated Activities (Net)	(31,391)	4,702
Other Income (Expenses), (Net)	(11,176)	(10,276)
Net Income	$ 24,394	$ 71,445

Stockholder's Equity, Jobs, and Labor Productivity ($ figures in 000's)

Year	Stockholder's Equity	Net Sales	Number of Employees	Index of Labor Productivity
1975	$ 34,993	$ 28,836	585	49.292
1976	37,531	32,248	618	52.181
1977	41,531	37,155	659	56.381
1978	46,994	44,698	735	60.814
1979	52,104	54,170	877	61.767
1980	56,104	64,982	996	65.243
1981	62,490	77,771	1,161	66.986
1982	298,632	341,078	2,651	128.660
1983	374,115	386,205	2,895	133.404
Change, 1983/1975	+ 969 %	+ 1,239 %	+ 395 %	+ 171 %

Capital Productivity ($ figures in 000's)

Year	Total Invested Capital	Net Income	Index of Capital Productivity
1975	$ 90,570	$ 4,211	.046
1976	94,324	4,791	.051
1977	96,943	5,806	.060
1978	100,206	7,818	.078
1979	92,999	9,135	.098
1980	136,817	9,909	.072
1981	147,652	10,656	.072
1982	556,063	56,931	.102
1983	651,599	71,445	.110
Change, 1983/1975	+ 619 %	+ 1,597 %	+ 136 %

Stock Prices and Earnings per Share*

Year	Stock Prices			Earnings** Per Share
	High	Low	Close	
1975	$ 3.125	$ 1.563	$ 2.375	$ .440
1976	3.250	2.250	3.126	.505
1977	5.500	3.000	4.375	.610
1978	6.000	4.375	5.500	.825
1979	7.250	5.000	5.875	.975
1980	7.250	4.750	6.250	1.060
1981	8.250	5.500	8.000	1.125
1982	20.000	7.250	18.000	1.620
1983	29.000	15.500	20.250	1.920
1984	20.250	10.000	14.500	.650

Change, 1975–84 + 511%; change, S&P 500 Index, 1975–84 + 82%

*Adjusted for stock splits and stock dividends   **Includes extraordinary items

Pacific Telecom is a diversified telecommunications firm with assets approaching $1 billion. The company's long lines operations provide a full range of services to all areas of Alaska and between Alaska and the rest of the world through a system of over 190 earth stations and the company's satellite, Aurora I. Ten local telephone operating companies provide service to 171 communities in an eight-state geographic area, concentrated primarily in the Pacific Northwest. Diversified activities include communications-related enterprises, and investments in developmental-stage companies offering information processing and display products or services. The telecommunications industry continues to be in a state of flux, challenging the management of this company to adapt to the rapidly shifting external environment. Over time, the company's earnings performance has been somewhat erratic. It will be interesting to monitor this firm's progress through the balance of the decade.

PHH GROUP INC.

Corporate Headquarters: 11333 McCormick Rd.
Hunt Valley, MD 21031

Telephone: (301) 667-4000
Incorporated in Maryland
New York Stock Exchange—PHH

Business: Provides a variety of relocation services, fleet management vices and aviation management services.

Officers:

Jerome W. Geckle, Chairman of the Board and Chief Executive Officer
Robert D. Kunisch, President and Chief Operating Officer
Executive Vice Presidents: A. Samuel Penn, Frank J. Schmieder
Philip W. Taff, Senior Vice President and Chief Financial Officer
Duncan H. Cocroft, Vice President and Treasurer
John T. Connor, Jr., Vice President and General Counsel
Donald V. Freiert, Jr. Vice President and Controller
Edwin F. Miller, Vice President and Secretary
Samuel H. Wright, Vice President, Government Relations
Edwin K. Bell, Assistant Treasurer
Philip J. Lange, Assistant Controller
William R. MacIntosh, Assistant Treasurer
Lawrence D. Sugar, Assistant Controller
Charles G. Wise, III, Assistant Controller

Statement of Income (Year ends 4/30—$ figures in 000's)

	1985	1984
Revenues		
Automotive and Aviation Services	$226,940	$200,542
Relocation Services	473,137	330,791
	$700,077	$531,333
Operating Expenses		
Costs of Carrying and Reselling Homes	$418,832	$296,990
Interest	118,314	96,693
Selling, General and Administrative	92,252	72,802
Operating Income	$ 70,679	$ 64,927
Other Income (Net)	177	1,079
Income before Income Taxes	$ 70,856	$ 64,848
Provision for Income Taxes	30,081	29,515
Net Income	$ 40,775	$ 36,412

Stockholder's Equity, Jobs, and Labor Productivity ($ figures in 000's)

Year	Stockholder's Equity	Net Sales	Number of Employees	Index of Labor Productivity
1975	$ 39,074	$ 29,006	1,020	28.437
1976	45,269	37,500	1,136	33.011
1977	53,034	142,254	1,370	103.835
1978	62,660	197,067	1,466	134.425
1979	75,139	280,013	1,770	158.199
1980	138,615	395,831	2,245	176.317
1981	159,638	471,714	2,260	208.723
1982	187,717	576,543	2,390	241.231
1983	211,660	538,440	2,491	216.154
Change, 1983/1975	+412 %	+1,756 %	+144 %	+660 %

Capital Productivity ($ figures in 000's)

Year	Total Invested Capital	Funds from Operations	Index of Capital Productivity
1975	$ 135,580	$ 5,546	.041
1976	144,462	7,025	.049
1977	431,935	20,392	.047
1978	486,606	25,110	.052
1979	834,406	30,705	.037
1980	965,285	44,127	.046
1981	1,107,986	46,098	.042
1982	1,024,678	62,594	.061
1983	1,294,725	61,418	.047
Change, 1983/1975	+855 %	+1,007 %	+16 %

Stock Prices and Earnings per Share[*]

Year	Stock Prices High	Low	Close	Earnings[**] Per Share
1975	$ 6.500	$ 3.125	$ 5.250	$ .580
1976	7.750	5.250	6.625	.695
1977	8.500	6.500	7.375	.835
1978	10.125	6.500	7.938	1.020
1979	11.750	7.563	10.813	1.295
1980	22.000	9.500	20.750	1.690
1981	25.750	17.625	24.000	1.930
1982	38.000	17.250	37.500	2.200
1983	47.000	29.570	36.000	2.300
1984	36.250	18.000	24.875	2.560

Change, 1975–84 +374%; change, S&P 500 Index, 1975–84 +82%

[*]Adjusted for stock splits and stock dividends   [**]Includes extraordinary items

PHH Group companies provide the following services: Home Equity relocation services, including the purchase, management and resale of homes for the transferred employees of corporate clients; Fantus site selection and location planning; Peterson, Howell and Heather car, truck and equipment fleet management, leasing and national account purchasing, vehicle maintenance and expense control programs; Executive Air Fleet management, charter, and brokerage programs for corporate aircraft; PHH Aviation Systems information for flight planning, weather, fuel, and support services; NTS Inc. fuel purchase programs for truck fleets. The company's outstanding growth record continued during fiscal 1985, marking the 39th year of consecutive growth. PHH Group has the stated objective of continuing to increase earnings at a rate in excess of 15 percent per year.

PHH is the ultimate service company: it sells nothing but information. PHH manages over 300,000 automobiles for over 800 U.S., Canadian, and British customers saving them 10 to 15 percent on their automobile operating costs by knowing more about auto fleet management than they do. This is an interesting example of how the definition of a business can shape its direction. PHH sees itself as a provider of services and has broadened those services to provide customers with such things as credit cards for fuel, tire, and battery purchases. In contrast, Gelco Corp., PHH's major competitor, defines itself as a company in the transportation business and, therefore, has diversified into container and truck leasing.

PIC 'N' SAVE CORP.

Corporate Headquarters: 2430 East Del Amo Blvd.
Carson, CA 90749

Telephone (213) 537-9220
Incorporated in Delaware
Over the Counter—PICN

Business: Owns and operates 90 + retail outlets that specialize in low price close-out merchandise.

Officers:
Lewis B. Merrifield, III, Chairman of the Board
Arthur Frankel, President and Chief Executive Officer
Arthur Borie, Executive Vice President and Chief Operating Officer
Bill M. Thomas, Executive Vice President and Chief Financial Officer
Richard A. Frankel, Vice President, Merchandise Manager
Kenneth Johnson, Vice President, Store Operations
Sheldon S. McClusky, Vice President, Warehousing and Distribution
Martin S. Tepper, Vice President, Merchandise Manager
Raymond L. Kugel, Assistant Treasurer

Statement of Income (Year ends 12/31—$ figures in 000's)

	1984	1983
Net Sales	$235,147	$227,130
Costs and Expenses		
Cost of Sales	$108,954	$102,486
Store Expenses	40,425	38,458
Warehouse and Administrative Expenses	13,487	12,487
	$162,866	$153,431
Earnings before Income Taxes	$ 72,281	$ 73,699
Income Taxes	35,771	37,248
Net Income	$ 36,510	$ 36,451

Stockholder's Equity, Jobs, and Labor Productivity ($ figures in 000's)

Year	Stockholder's Equity	Net Sales	Number of Employees	Index of Labor Productivity
1975	$ 12,306	$ 34,671	850	40.798
1976	16,933	43,591	900	48.434
1977	22,576	53,982	1,000	53.982
1978	29,511	63,363	1,100	57.603
1979	37,329	85,325	1,500	56.883
1980	52,480	113,550	1,600	70.969
1981	71,536	129,413	1,700	76.125
1982	98,548	172,654	2,100	82.216
1983	136,346	220,750	2,300	95.978
Change, 1983/1975	+ 1,008 %	+ 537 %	+ 171 %	+ 135 %

Capital Productivity ($ figures in 000's)

Year	Total Invested Capital	Net Income	Index of Capital Productivity
1975	$ 15,486	$ 3,085	.199
1976	18,726	4,592	.245
1977	24,333	5,522	.227
1978	31,444	6,917	.220
1979	39,420	10,259	.260
1980	54,494	14,761	.271
1981	73,467	18,512	.252
1982	100,390	27,009	.269
1983	138,091	36,451	.264
Change, 1983/1975	+ 792 %	+ 1,082 %	+ 33 %

Stock Prices and Earnings per Share[*]

Year	Stock Prices			Earnings[**] Per Share
	High	Low	Close	
1975	$ .604	$ .146	$ .542	$ .103
1976	1.042	.542	.917	.153
1977	1.333	.813	1.188	.182
1978	1.958	.979	1.958	.227
1979	3.292	1.750	3.292	.343
1980	7.000	2.958	5.367	.492
1981	9.750	5.500	8.000	.605
1982	19.375	6.750	19.375	.875
1983	25.375	16.750	19.875	1.170
1984	24.125	14.375	19.875	1.250

Change, 1975–84 + 3,569%; change, S&P 500 Index, 1975–84 + 82%

[*]Adjusted for stock splits and stock dividends   [**]Includes extraordinary items

264

Pic 'N' Save operates a chain of 90 retail stores in California, Arizona, Texas, Nevada, New Mexico, Utah, and Colorado. The company follows a niche strategy by stocking merchandise that it can purchase at price levels that give customers substantial reductions from original retail yet still maintains its gross profit margins. Major store departments include wearing apparel, hardware, housewares, luggage, wine, gifts, toys, stationery, books, candles and beauty aids. Availability of merchandise continues to increase each year with more than 2,000 suppliers now looking to the company to distribute their close-out merchandise without conflicting with their normal distribution channels. Fiscal 1985 should once again show the company achieving new highs in sales and net earnings.

PIEDMONT AVIATION, INC.

Corporate Headquarters: Smith Reynolds Airport
                         Winston-Salem, NC 27156

Telephone: (919) 767-5100
Incorporated in North Carolina
New York Stock Exchange—PIE

Business: Provides domestic air transportation for passengers, property and mail.

Officers:

William R. Howard, President and Chief Executive Officer
Gordon M. Bethune, Senior Vice President, Operations
Joseph F. Healy, Jr., Senior Vice President, Legal Affairs and Secretary
W. Howard Mackinnon, Senior Vice President, Finance and Treasurer
William G. McGee, Senior Vice President, Marketing
Wilbur A. Blackmon, Vice President, Station Properties and Leases
Howard M. Cartwright, Vice President, Maintenance and Engineering
Joe H. Culler, Vice President, General Aviation
Audree F. Long, Vice President, Controller and Assistant Secretary
Joseph B. Wilson, Vice President, Employee Relations
James B. Bradley, Asst. Vice President, Industrial Relations
Samuel K. Carter, Asst. Vice President, Computer and Communication Services
Alan J. Schneider, Asst. Secretary

Statement of Income (Year ends 12/31—$ figures in 000's)

	1984	1983
Operating Revenues		
Airline	$1,159,018	$858,010
Other	123,861	84,424
Total Operating Revenues	1,282,879	942,434
Operating Expenses		
Salaries and Related Costs	360,212	287,117
Aircraft Fuel	253,273	207,079
Depreciation and Amortization	85,371	66,622
Other Operating Expenses	444,743	319,272
Total Operating Expenses	1,143,599	880,090
Operating Income	139,280	62,344
Non-Operating Expenses (Income)		
Interest Expense	54,976	45,206
Interest Capitalized	(3,080)	(1,988)
Sales of Tax Benefits	—	(12,757)
Miscellaneous Income (Net)	(4,654)	(4,387)
Total Non-Operating Expenses	47,242	26,074
Income before Income Taxes	92,038	26,270
Provision for Income Taxes	33,863	10,731
Net Income	$ 58,175	$ 25,539

Stockholder's Equity, Jobs, and Labor Productivity ($ figures in 000's)

Year	Stockholder's Equity	Net Sales	Number of Employees	Index of Labor Productivity
1975	$ 19,809	$163,494	3,335	49.024
1976	23,962	186,784	3,437	54.345
1977	30,966	222,650	3,711	59.997
1978	39,147	254,924	4,324	58.956
1979	59,034	352,055	5,217	67.482
1980	98,110	473,378	5,702	83.020
1981	153,063	629,904	6,796	92.687
1982	254,373	701,767	8,091	86.734
1983	279,189	942,434	9,908	95.125
Change, 1983/1975	+ 1,309 %	+ 477 %	+ 197 %	+ 94 %

Capital Productivity ($ figures in 000's)

Year	Total Invested Capital	Net Income	Index of Capital Productivity
1975	$ 87,976	$ 204	.002
1976	86,141	4,398	.051
1977	117,510	7,495	.064
1978	135,186	5,591	.041
1979	194,904	11,164	.057
1980	265,043	16,062	.061
1981	346,747	32,585	.094
1982	623,271	30,463	.049
1983	792,652	25,539	.032
Change, 1983/1975	+ 801 %	+ 12,419 %	+ 1,290 %

Stock Prices and Earnings per Share[*]

Year	Stock Prices			Earnings[**] Per Share
	High	Low	Close	
1975	$ 3.993	$ 1.997	$ 2.083	$ .056
1976	3.733	2.170	3.385	1.222
1977	4.427	3.038	4.167	2.049
1978	10.069	4.340	6.163	1.417
1979	13.889	6.076	10.503	2.382
1980	13.368	7.378	10.503	2.764
1981	26.771	9.583	22.500	3.675
1982	32.500	18.438	24.271	2.667
1983	35.104	22.604	20.104	1.900
1984	32.500	22.917	30.000	4.158

Change, 1975–84 + 1,340%; change, S&P 500 Index, 1975–84 + 82%

[*]Adjusted for stock splits and stock dividends   [**]Includes extraordinary items

Piedmont Airlines is the principal division of this corporation, which at the end of 1984, operated a fleet of more than 100 jet aircraft linking 65 airports. The company's route network now stretches from the Atlantic to the Pacific coasts, with a major presence in Florida. Piedmont now ranks among the nation's top major airlines, with annual revenues in excess of $1 billion. It serves more than one million travelers each month. The company also, through an affiliated subsidiary, services and sells private business aircraft and operates a general aviation overhaul facility. Through a second wholly owned subsidiary, the company also is in the aircraft parts and equipment business in several southeastern states. This company seems to have prospered in the airline industry's climate of deregulation; company management is particularly proud to have received the "Airline of the Year" award for 1984 from *Air Transport World* magazine.

Piedmont's basic strategy has been to service the small- and medium-size markets abandoned by the major carriers when deregulation swept the airline industry. Piedmont started with a hub at Charlotte, North Carolina and served cities near there, such as Asheville and Jacksonville. The strategy was so successful that Piedmont has added hubs in Dayton, Ohio and the Baltimore-Washington Airport.

In 1985, Piedmont added nonstop flights from Dayton and Charlotte to Los Angeles and San Francisco on the simple theory that those two markets were on the top of the list of unserviced cities that Piedmont passengers wanted to travel to.

PLENUM PUBLISHING CORP.

Corporate Headquarters: 233 Spring Street
New York, NY 10013

Telephone: (212) 620-8000
Incorporated in New York
Over the Counter—PLEN

Business: Publishes books and journals on scientific, technical and medical subjects and provides specialized database products.

Officers:

Martin E. Tash, Chairman, President and Treasurer

Mark Shaw, Executive Vice President and Director

John Matzka, Vice President and Managing Editor

Frank Columbus, Vice President, Electronic Information Services Division

Alan Harris, Controller and Assistant Secretary

Harry Allcock, Vice President, IFI/Plenum Data, and Career Placement Registry, Inc.

Marshall Lebowitz, Vice President, J. S. Canner & Co.

Statement of Income (Year ends 12/31—$ figures in 000's)

	1984	1983
Income		
Subscriptions, Books, Outside Journals and Other Sales (Net)	$34,139	$31,304
Dividends and Interest	1,723	1,567
Gain on Sales of Marketable Securities	187	1,013
	$36,049	$33,884
Costs and Expenses (Net)		
Cost of Sales	14,914	13,782
Royalties	2,295	2,069
Selling, General and Administrative Expenses	7,477	7,772
Interest	143	171
	24,829	23,794
Income before Taxes	11,220	10,090
Income Taxes	4,575	3,870
Net Income	$ 6,645	$ 6,220

Stockholder's Equity, Jobs, and Labor Productivity ($ figures in 000's)

Year	Stockholder's Equity	Net Sales	Number of Employees	Index of Labor Productivity
1975	$ 1,194	$13,028	280	46.529
1976	2,558	14,450	280	51.607
1977	3,334	17,854	280	63.764
1978	7,458	20,123	280	71.868
1979	8,397	22,363	280	79.868
1980	6,675	23,500	280	83.929
1981	7,991	25,764	310	83.110
1982	12,236	28,988	310	93.510
1983	15,882	31,304	310	100.981
Change, 1983/1975	+ 1,230 %	+ 140 %	+ 11 %	+ 117 %

Capital Productivity ($ figures in 000's)

Year	Total Invested Capital	Net Income	Index of Capital Productivity
1975	$ 6,692	$ 756	.113
1976	7,724	1,282	.166
1977	8,106	2,262	.279
1978	9,875	2,663	.270
1979	10,618	3,247	.306
1980	8,746	3,510	.401
1981	9,957	3,728	.374
1982	12,437	5,184	.417
1983	16,047	6,220	.388
Change, 1983/1975	+ 240 %	+ 723 %	+ 243 %

Stock Prices and Earnings per Share[*]

	Stock Prices			Earnings[**]
Year	High	Low	Close	Per Share
1975	$ .926	$ .444	$ .852	$ .299
1976	2.111	.852	2.111	.453
1977	4.000	1.944	3.833	.827
1978	7.389	3.500	6.389	.871
1979	10.000	6.333	9.667	1.058
1980	10.833	7.000	9.333	1.240
1981	12.667	8.833	12.333	1.447
1982	24.000	12.167	21.333	2.053
1983	32.000	21.333	26.667	2.480
1984	26.625	20.750	22.000	2.680

Change, 1975–84 + 2,483%; change, S&P 500 Index, 1975–84 + 82%

[*]Adjusted for stock splits and stock dividends   [**]Includes extraordinary items

270

CORPORATE PROFILE—PLENUM PUBLISHING CORPORATION

This company, while small, is an important supplier of information to the international, scientific, medical, and industrial research communities. Its growth has been through internal development. The company has achieved well-balanced growth in its subscription business, its book business, and its data base products. Its subscription business revenues are derived primarily from the Plenum Press Division, which publishes more than 60 journals under the direction of internationally renowned boards of specialized research scientists. Its other major division publishes scientific, technical, and medical books, publishing a total of 342 new titles in 1984. The company, through other divisions and subsidiaries, publishes books under the name Da-Capo Press, supplies back-issue periodicals through its J. S. Canner & Company, and also has a London-based subsidiary to serve the UK, European and Middle East markets. The company is conservatively financed and earns high margins on sales. Its backlist of titles, which number in excess of 5,000, represent an important intangible resource. The company seems extremely well positioned to remain a high-growth organization.

PORTA SYSTEMS CORPORATION

Corporate Headquarters: 575 Underhill Boulevard
Syosset, NY 11791

Telephone: (516) 364-9300
Incorporated in Delaware
American Stock Exchange—PSI

Business: Develops, designs, and manufactures telecommunications equipment for sale, primarily to telephone operating companies, worldwide.

Officers:
Paul V. DeLuca, Chairman and Chief Executive Officer
Vincent F. Santulli, President and Chief Operating Officer
Garet M. Romeo, Executive Vice President
William V. Carney, Senior Vice President—Connector Products
Michael A. Tancredi, Vice President—Finance and Treasurer
John J. Gazzo, Vice President—Research and Development
Eladio Rodriguez, Vice President—Caribbean Operations
Geoffrey W. Crowley, Vice President—Connector Products
Warren Marcus, Vice President—Electronic Products
Jane M. Jozefek, Vice President and General Counsel
Daniel J. Fleming, Controller

Statement of Income (Year ends 12/31—$ figures in 000's)

	1984	1983
Sales	$29,434	$22,953
Cost of Sales	16,919	13,035
Gross Profit	$12,515	$ 9,918
Selling, General and Administrative Expenses	$ 7,201	$ 6,293
Research and Development Expenses	3,109	2,543
Total Expenses	$10,310	$ 8,836
Operating Income	$ 2,205	$ 1,082
Interest Income (Expense)	$(1,145)	$ (509)
Accounting Change for Inventories	737	—
Net Income	$ 1,798	$ 572

272

Stockholder's Equity, Jobs, and Labor Productivity ($ figures in 000's)

Year	Stockholder's Equity	Net Sales	Number of Employees	Index of Labor Productivity
1975	$ 1,141	$ 3,837	151	25.411
1976	1,432	6,001	251	23.948
1977	2,289	10,610	422	25.142
1978	10,380	15,082	384	39.276
1979	11,155	12,747	284	44.884
1980	11,761	15,123	231	65.468
1981	13,835	19,097	343	55.676
1982	16,334	23,121	317	72.937
1983	16,910	22,953	366	62.713
Change, 1983/1975	+ 1,382 %	+ 498 %	+ 142 %	+ 147 %

Capital Productivity ($ figures in 000's)

Year	Total Invested Capital	Net Income	Index of Capital Productivity
1975	$ 1,197	$ 32	.027
1976	1,488	279	.188
1977	3,668	840	.229
1978	10,499	1,747	.166
1979	11,215	765	.068
1980	11,812	606	.051
1981	13,876	1,973	.142
1982	16,389	2,469	.151
1983	16,985	572	.034
Change, 1983/1975	+ 1,319 %	+ 1,688 %	+ 26 %

Stock Prices and Earnings per Share*

	Stock Prices			Earnings**
Year	High	Low	Close	Per Share
1975	$ .250	$ .187	$ .187	$.008
1976	.292	.208	.208	.075
1977	2.667	1.417	2.500	.223
1978	5.583	2.250	3.000	.380
1979	3.708	1.333	1.542	.143
1980	2.625	1.167	2.000	.113
1981	10.125	1.792	9.917	.367
1982	10.625	4.125	9.188	.455
1983	17.000	8.250	12.500	.110
1984	14.125	7.375	8.750	.330

Change, 1975–84 + 4,579%; change, S&P 500 Index, 1975–84 + 82%

*Adjusted for stock splits and stock dividends   **Includes extraordinary items

Since Porta Systems' inception, its focus has been on establishing the company as a major supplier to the Bell System. Each year for over a decade, Bell has accounted for more than 50 percent of the firm's domestic sales. With a sales force already organized on the same regional basis as the newly configured Regional Bell Operating Companies, Porta Systems emerged in 1984 as a timely alternative to Western Electric. While the company's net income pattern has been erratic in recent years, it is expected to benefit from the AT&T divestiture.

Porta Systems has an interesting definition of its market:

> Despite the obvious diversity of today's emerging technologies, they all share one common denominator . . . at some point the vital information they transmit is carried on a simple wire pair, or telephone line. And every telephone line needs to be:
> Connected
> Protected
> Tested

The company concentrates its entire business on these three functions.

PRIME COMPUTER INC.

Corporate Headquarters: Prime Park
Natick, Massachusetts, 01760
Telephone: (617) 655-8000
Incorporated in Delaware
New York Stock Exchange—PRM

Business: Manufactures and markets superminicomputers primarily for the engineering and scientific, commercial office and CAD/CAM markets.
Officers:
  Joe M. Henson, President and Chief Executive Officer
  Andrew C. Knowles, III, Vice President, CAD/CAM & Workstations/ Terminals Group
  Gale R. Aguilar, Vice President, Corporate Business Development and Strategy
  Roland D. Pampel, Vice President, Research and Development
  D. Cheesman, Vice President, International Development
  E. J. Christiansen, Vice President, Operations and Custom Systems
  Leonard F. Halio, Vice President, Video Products
  Richard B. Snyder, Vice President, Software Development
  David J. Collar, Vice President, Finance, Administration and Planning, and Chief Financial Officer
  Richard L. Ballantyne, Vice President, General Counsel and Secretary
  Bernard F. Bradstreet, Treasurer
  Richard B. Goldman, Corporate Controller
  John T. Maske, Vice President, Manufacturing and Service
  Ian R. G. Edmonds, Vice President, Systems and Product Marketing
  W. L. Brubaker, Vice President, Sales
  Marvin G. Kirby, Vice President, Domestic Sales

Statement of Income (Year ends 12/31—$ figures in 000's)

	1984	1983
Product Revenue	$479,059	$391,680
Service and Other Revenue	163,720	124,823
Total Revenue	624,779	516,503
Costs and Expenses		
Cost of Sales	301,663	242,934
Selling and Administrative	203,702	170,530
Research Development and Engineering	64,062	52,074
	569,427	465,538
Operating Income	73,352	50,965
Interest Expense, Net of Interest	1,014	1,686
Other Expense (Net)	2,035	1,483
	3,049	3,168
Income before Taxes	70,303	47,797
Provision for Income Taxes	19,591	15,294
Reversal of Deferred Taxes on DISC Income	(9,000)	—
	10,591	32,503
Net Income	$ 59,712	$ 32,503

Stockholder's Equity, Jobs, and Labor Productivity ($ figures in 000's)

Year	Stockholder's Equity	Net Sales	Number of Employees	Index of Labor Productivity
1975	$ 2,764	$ 11,387	239	47.644
1976	5,251	22,797	520	43.840
1977	15,280	50,032	1,070	46.759
1978	25,073	93,554	1,665	56.189
1979	44,399	152,943	2,570	59.511
1980	98,898	267,637	4,011	66.726
1981	142,458	364,787	4,636	78.686
1982	228,907	435,826	5,311	82.061
1983	268,179	516,503	5,927	87.144
Change, 1983/1975	+9,603 %	+4,436 %	+2,380 %	+83 %

Capital Productivity ($ figures in 000's)

Year	Total Invested Capital	Net Income	Index of Capital Productivity
1975	$ 6,534	$ 692	.106
1976	13,153	2,429	.185
1977	26,908	3,926	.146
1978	56,716	8,406	.148
1979	91,161	16,940	.186
1980	159,670	31,222	.196
1981	200,548	37,678	.188
1982	246,080	44,926	.183
1983	284,458	32,503	.114
Change, 1983/1975	+4,254 %	+4,597 %	+8 %

Stock Prices and Earnings per Share[*]

Year	Stock Prices			Earnings[**] Per Share
	High	Low	Close	
1975	$ .444	$ .130	$ .296	$ .025
1976	1.315	.296	1.259	.079
1977	1.852	.917	1.852	.108
1978	6.611	1.519	4.463	.216
1979	7.630	4.111	7.370	.427
1980	27.583	6.000	27.500	.713
1981	32.833	11.500	15.750	.833
1982	25.833	10.417	23.083	.987
1983	30.250	13.250	17.625	.680
1984	21.500	11.750	18.000	1.250

Change, 1975–84 +5,975%; change, S&P 500 Index, 1975–84 +82%

[*]Adjusted for stock splits and stock dividends   [**]Includes extraordinary items

Since its founding in 1972, this outstanding growth company has been a leader in the super-minicomputer industry. Prime exemplifies a company that has grown to be a major corporation in a relatively short period of time, partially through an aggressive level of expenditures for research and development. In addition to selling hardware systems the company offers more than 1,100 third-party applications software packages to meet the needs of its three major markets: engineering and scientific; commercially distributed data processing; and computer-aided design/computer-aided manufacturing (CAD/CAM). The engineering and scientific market accounts for nearly 45 percent of Prime's business and the company expects this segment to continue to grow at a 20 to 25 percent rate during the next several years. The distributed data processing market which accounts for nearly 40 percent of Prime's business is currently reported to be growing at a rate between 20 and 30 percent. The remaining portion of Prime's business is in the CAD/CAM marketplace, which the company entered approximately three years ago. It is expected to be a strong growth market since the company is able to offer a broader range of integrated solutions to customers than its competitors currently can.

PUBLIC SERVICE CO. OF NEW MEXICO

Corporate Headquarters: Alvarado Square
Albuquerque, NM 87158
Telephone: (505) 848-2700
Incorporated in New Mexico
New York Stock Exchange—PNM

Business: Generates and distributes electric power primarily in New Mexico and Arizona.

Officers:
- J. D. Geist, Chairman and President
- J. B. Mulcock, Jr., Senior Vice President, Corporate Affairs and Assistant Secretary
- A. J. Robison, Senior Vice President and Chief Financial Officer
- R. B. Rountree, Senior Vice President & Chairman, Meadows Resources, Inc. & Sunbelt Mining
- M. A. Clifton, Vice President, Financial Planning
- B. D. Lackey, Vice President and Corporate Controller

Statement of Income (Year ends 12/31—$ figures in 000's)

	1984	1983
Operating Revenues		
Electric	$438,974	$391,947
Water	6,354	5,527
	445,328	397,474
Operating Expenses		
Fuel and Purchased Power	95,904	59,365
Other Operation Expenses	68,278	72,760
Maintenance and Repairs	34,075	32,028
Depreciation and Amortization	48,975	47,172
Taxes, Other than Income Taxes	19,246	18,694
Income Taxes	32,356	31,208
Total Operating Expenses	298,834	261,227
Operating Income	146,494	136,247
Other Income and Deductions		
Allowance for Equity Funds Used during Construction	52,754	45,789
Equity in Earnings of Unconsolidated Affiliates, Net of Taxes	7,975	6,373
Gain on Sale of Equity Interest in Trust, Net of Taxes	—	24,129
Other, Net of Taxes	8,865	779
Net Other Income and Deductions	69,594	77,070
Income before Interest Charge	216,088	213,317
Interest Charges		
Interest on Long-Term Debt	98,463	80,922
Other Interest Charges	8,421	11,182
Allowance for Borrowed Funds Used during Construction	(23,636)	(19,306)
Net Interest Charges	83,248	72,798
Net Earnings	132,840	140,519

Stockholder's Equity, Jobs, and Labor Productivity ($ figures in 000's)

Year	Stockholder's Equity	Net Sales	Number of Employees	Index of Labor Productivity
1975	$106,701	$ 84,978	1,326	64.086
1976	154,371	97,586	1,476	66.115
1977	191,447	136,023	1,751	77.683
1978	276,289	184,604	2,054	89.875
1979	347,328	241,826	2,294	105.417
1980	381,525	277,911	2,498	111.253
1981	589,517	336,165	2,787	120.619
1982	780,601	426,543	2,973	143.472
1983	855,571	397,474	2,783	142.822
Change, 1983/1975	+ 702 %	+ 368 %	+ 110 %	+ 123 %

Capital Productivity ($ figures in 000's)

Year	Total Invested Capital	Net Income	Index of Capital Productivity
1975	$ 293,265	$ 14,216	.048
1976	392,804	17,357	.044
1977	516,168	24,921	.048
1978	738,636	37,464	.051
1979	924,983	54,803	.059
1980	1,144,715	71,436	.062
1981	1,492,988	107,958	.072
1982	1,823,254	115,822	.064
1983	2,059,560	140,519	.068
Change, 1983/1975	+ 602 %	+ 888 %	+ 41 %

Stock Prices and Earnings per Share[*]

Year	Stock Prices			Earnings[**] Per Share
	High	Low	Close	
1975	$21.250	$11.375	$18.625	$ 2.440
1976	24.375	17.625	24.000	2.160
1977	24.000	20.000	21.500	2.460
1978	22.375	18.375	19.875	2.830
1979	21.500	17.375	18.250	2.970
1980	21.750	15.250	19.750	3.360
1981	24.875	19.250	23.750	4.230
1982	28.125	21.625	26.000	3.220
1983	29.625	22.750	25.375	3.530
1984	26.625	19.500	24.375	3.110

Change, 1975–84 + 31%; change, S&P 500 Index, 1975–84 + 82%

[*]Adjusted for stock splits and stock dividends   [**]Includes extraordinary items

This company is organized to accomplish two complementary tasks. Its electric and gas utility divisions serve as New Mexico's primary energy resources while its investment group, headed by Meadows Resources, Inc., attempts to enhance corporate profitability, spread investment risk, and create economic opportunities in New Mexico and the Southwest. Meadows has developed a broad base of interests, with investments in forest products, minerals, land, and new technologies. It accounted for 14 percent of net earnings in calendar year 1984. The company is expected to show a modest increase in earnings in 1985, even though revenues will show a substantial increase from its 1985 acquisition of the utility assets of the Southern Union Company. This acquisition will add approximately $400 million in new revenues.

PULTE HOME CORPORATION

Corporate Headquarters: 6400 Farmington Rd.
West Bloomfield, MI 48033

Telephone: (313) 661-1500
Incorporated in Michigan
New York Stock Exchange—PHM

Business: Builds and sells moderately priced single-family homes.
Officers:

James Grosfeld, Chairman of the Board, Member, Office of Chief
Executive

C. Howard Johnson, President, Member, Office of Chief Executive
William J. Pulte, Chairman of the Exec. Committee of the Board
Senior Vice Presidents: Glen W. Barnard, Robert K. Burgess
Richard C. Staky, Vice President, Finance
David Ebling, Vice President and Controller
Mark P. Layton, Vice President, Manufacturing
Bryan C. Noreen, Treasurer

Statement of Income (Year ends 12/31—$ figures in 000's)

	1984	1983
Revenues		
Sales (Settlements)	$839,081	$863,314
Other Income—Net	2,907	3,432
	841,988	866,746
Costs and Expenses		
Cost of Sales	731,918	688,613
Selling, General and Administrative	95,758	96,754
	827,676	785,367
Operating Income	14,312	81,379
Income Taxes	6,933	39,325
	7,379	42,054
Equity in Net Income of Unconsolidated Subsidiaries	9,905	6,876
Net Income	$ 17,284	$ 48,930

Stockholder's Equity, Jobs, and Labor Productivity ($ figures in 000's)

Year	Stockholder's Equity	Net Sales	Number of Employees	Index of Labor Productivity
1975	$ 14,346	$ 53,738	322	167.043
1976	17,037	84,627	434	194.993
1977	22,979	138,305	671	206.118
1978	32,552	203,412	1,089	186.788
1979	46,368	294,143	1,548	190.015
1980	56,064	325,825	1,326	245.720
1981	64,622	383,516	975	393.350
1982	87,158	478,473	1,273	375.863
1983	133,936	863,314	2,100	411.102
Change, 1983/1975	+ 834 %	+ 1,505 %	+ 552 %	+ 146 %

Capital Productivity ($ figures in 000's)

Year	Total Invested Capital	Net Income	Index of Capital Productivity
1975	$ 24,824	$ 278	.011
1976	27,502	2,661	.097
1977	37,743	5,926	.157
1978	61,552	10,542	.171
1979	85,468	14,543	.170
1980	104,789	11,936	.114
1981	93,497	9,603	.103
1982	115,912	23,434	.202
1983	160,366	48,930	.305
Change, 1983/1975	+ 546 %	+ 7,501 %	+ 2,625 %

Stock Prices and Earnings per Share[*]

Year	Stock Prices			Earnings[**] Per Share
	High	Low	Close	
1975	$ .302	$ .094	$ .177	$ .012
1976	.583	.188	.521	.107
1977	.781	.510	.667	.229
1978	1.208	.573	.917	.422
1979	2.016	.922	1.688	.570
1980	3.719	1.125	3.219	.473
1981	4.344	2.563	3.813	.375
1982	19.438	3.250	19.375	.905
1983	37.500	17.625	24.750	1.840
1984	27.000	10.125	18.500	.650

Change, 1975–84 + 3,130%; change, S&P 500 Index, 1975–84 + 82%

[*]Adjusted for stock splits and stock dividends   [**]Includes extraordinary items

Note: The fiscal year financial results in the tables above are shown in the year in which most of the results were achieved.

This company is one of the largest independent publicly owned home building companies in the United States. Its operations are concentrated in the following states: Arizona, California, Colorado, Florida, Georgia, Illinois, Maryland, Michigan, Texas, Virginia, Wyoming, and Puerto Rico. The company's principal business is the construction and sale of moderately priced single-family homes. For example, during 1984 its average sales price approximated $76,000. In line with the housing cycle, there can be considerable fluctuations in the company's year-to-year sales volume. It delivered 11,000, 12,000, and 7,000 homes in 1984, 1983, and 1982, respectively. The company's basic policy is to purchase land only with the intent of using it in its building operations. The company achieved spectacular growth during the last decade but, given the cyclicality of the housing market, is dependent upon an industry turnaround to surpass its peak net income year in 1983.

RAI RESEARCH CORPORATION

Corporate Headquarters: 225 Marcus Boulevard
                          Hauppauge, Long Island, NY 11788
Telephone: (516) 273-0911
Incorporated in New York
American Stock Exchange—RAC

Business: Expertise in membrane technology produces a line of sophisticated battery separators for use in digital watches, hearing aids, smoke alarms, and other applications where critical performance is required.

Officers:

Sol J. Arditti, Chairman, President and Treasurer
Vincent F. D'Agostino, Vice President and Secretary
Charles P. Lipari, Vice President
Dr. Joseph Y. Lee, Director, RAIPORE Division
George R. Wallis, Director, RAICOUP Division
Robert J. Pascuzzi, Vice President

Statement of Income (Year ends 5/31—$ figures in 000's)

	1985	1984
Net Sales	$7,022	$5,452
Cost of Goods Sold	4,231	3,344
Gross Profit	$2,791	$2,108
Selling and Administrative Costs	$1,325	$1,198
Research and Development Expenses	165	229
Interest Expense	52	64
	$1,541	$1,491
Operating Income	$1,249	$ 617
Other Income (Principally Interest)	404	314
Income before Income Taxes	$1,653	$ 931
Income Taxes	472	430
Net Income	$1,180	$ 501

Stockholder's Equity, Jobs, and Labor Productivity ($ figures in 000's)

Year	Stockholder's Equity	Net Sales	Number of Employees	Index of Labor Productivity
1975	$ 831	$1,276	46	27.739
1976	1,034	2,069	80	25.863
1977	1,526	3,290	77	42.727
1978	2,044	3,535	89	39.719
1979	2,953	4,787	93	51.473
1980	3,903	5,630	105	53.619
1981	4,804	6,038	136	44.397
1982	5,568	5,529	135	40.956
1983	6,119	5,452	107	50.953
Change, 1983/1975	+ 636 %	+ 327 %	+ 133 %	+ 84 %

Capital Productivity ($ figures in 000's)

Year	Total Invested Capital	Funds from Operations	Index of Capital Productivity
1975	$ 988	$ 112	.113
1976	1,380	266	.193
1977	2,089	573	.274
1978	2,621	652	.249
1979	3,460	1,067	.308
1980	5,140	1,278	.249
1981	6,020	1,264	.210
1982	6,603	1,238	.187
1983	6,926	927	.134
Change, 1983/1975	+ 601 %	+ 728 %	+ 18 %

Stock Prices and Earnings per Share[*]

Year	Stock Prices			Earnings[**] Per Share
	High	Low	Close	
1975	$ .365	$ .209	$ .209	$.042
1976	.686	.439	.658	.103
1977	2.742	.548	1.783	.219
1978	2.664	1.296	1.296	.248
1979	4.589	1.296	4.589	.432
1980	10.798	2.915	8.854	.397
1981	9.070	3.671	3.887	.501
1982	10.431	3.628	10.204	.345
1983	16.667	7.738	8.929	.238
1984	10.500	4.750	6.750	.430

Change, 1975–84 + 3,130%; change, S&P 500 Index, 1975–84 + 82%

[*]Adjusted for stock splits and stock dividends [**]Includes extraordinary items

Note: The fiscal year financial results in the tables above are shown in the year in which most of the results were achieved.

This company is engaged in the manufacture of specialty products related to radiation and polymer chemistry, electrochemistry, and electronic instrumentation and engineering. The company's expertise in membrane technology has led to the development of a line of sophisticated Permion battery separators sold to battery manufacturers throughout the world. This membrane technology represents the company's core business, and efforts continue to expand and broaden the product base, not only in increased applications for batteries, but in membranes for industrial applications and for use in metal recovery systems. Sales of the Membrane division accounted for 77 percent of the company's revenues during the most recent fiscal year. The company, which is among the smallest of those profiled, achieved a major recovery in net income during fiscal year 1985.

RESEARCH INDUSTRIES CORPORATION

Corporate Headquarters: 1847 West 2300 South
                          Salt Lake City, UT 84119
Telephone: (801) 972-5500
Incorporated in Utah
Over the Counter—REIC

Business: This is a real estate developer in the process of becoming an ethical pharmaceuticals producer.

Officers:
Gary L. Crocker, President and Chief Executive Officer
Louis M. Haynie, Vice President
Paul R. Green, Secretary
F. Lynn Michelsen, Treasurer and Controller

Statement of Income (Year ends 6/30—$ figures in 000's)

	1985	1984
Revenues		
Net Sales	$6,189	$5,307
Research and Development Contract	30	267
Interest and Other	152	205
	$6,371	$5,778
Costs and Expenses		
Cost of Sales	$3,173	$2,729
Research and Development	599	396
Interest	619	428
Selling, General and Administrative	1,573	1,342
	$5,964	$4,894
Income before Income Tax Expense	$ 406	$ 885
Income Tax Expense	100	330
Net Income	$ 306	$ 555

287

Stockholder's Equity, Jobs, and Labor Productivity ($ figures in 000's)

Year	Stockholder's Equity	Net Sales	Number of Employees	Index of Labor Productivity
1975	$1,000	$ 976	30	32.533
1976	1,180	1,606	55	29.200
1977	1,358	1,006	30	33.533
1978	1,416	1,665	40	41.625
1979	1,839	2,399	40	59.975
1980	2,020	3,820	40	95.500
1981	3,709	4,961	40	124.025
1982	3,840	4,310	40	107.750
1983	4,700	3,735	40	93.375
Change, 1983/1975	+370 %	+283 %	+33 %	+187 %

Capital Productivity ($ figures in 000's)

Year	Total Invested Capital	Net Income	Index of Capital Productivity
1975	$1,701	$ 27	.016
1976	2,125	19	.009
1977	1,960	25	.013
1978	2,212	37	.017
1979	3,849	73	.019
1980	4,223	117	.028
1981	6,002	1,203	.200
1982	4,075	102	.025
1983	5,519	412	.075
Change, 1983/1975	+225 %	+1,426 %	+370 %

Stock Prices and Earnings per Share*

Year	Stock Prices			Earnings** Per Share
	High	Low	Close	
1975	$ 2.500	$1.313	$2.188	$.005
1976	4.875	2.250	3.500	.005
1977	8.875	3.500	6.500	.005
1978	10.500	5.750	5.750	.010
1979	7.500	5.375	5.750	.020
1980	7.750	4.000	4.250	.030
1981	6.375	3.750	5.250	.280
1982	7.125	4.875	6.500	.025
1983	12.000	6.000	9.000	.090
1984	12.250	5.000	7.000	.120

Change, 1975–84 +220%; change, S&P 500 Index, 1975–84 +82%

*Adjusted for stock splits and stock dividends   **Includes extraordinary items

The company is a major developer, manufacturer, and marketer of proprietary "through-the-skin" drug delivery products and innovative disposable hospital supplies. During the past two years, Research Industries Corporation has aggressively pursued the development of several patented medical products, including open-heart surgical catheters, biochemical tissue gas measuring catheters, nerve regeneration implants, and transdermal drug delivery pharmaceuticals for viral diseases and scleroderma. Research Industries' successful development of its innovative drug delivery systems and disposables businesses builds upon its historical technology base of proprietary drugs and sterile medical solutions.

In many ways, Research Industries is the most unusual of all of the 101 companies. Although it clearly intends to become a high-technology health care company, in 1985, two-thirds of the company's revenues and *all* of its profits came from its real estate operations. It is the only company among the 101 to attempt such a radical change in operations. It will be interesting to see if Research Industries can execute it.

SCI SYSTEMS, INC.

Corporate Headquarters: 5000 Technology Drive
                          Huntsville, AL 35807
Telephone: (205) 882-4800
Incorporated in Delaware
Over the Counter—SCIS

Business: Produces electronic components for military aircraft, supplies data management systems to DOD, microcomputers and does volume contract manufacturing for commercial customers, esp. IBM.

Officers:

Olin B. King, Chairman and Chief Executive Officer

A. Eugene Sapp, Jr., President and Chief Operating Officer

Senior Vice Presidents: Ronald F. Borelli, Thomas O. Cook, Juan Sandoval, G. Thomas Scott

Vice Presidents: Walter J. Conroy, P. Michael Dunn, Irwin O. Goldstein, Charles H. Gunselman, James H. Lawson, Leonard L. Mitchum, Jr., Thomas H. Southerland, Jerry F. Thomas, Edmund F. Turek

Harvey D. Harkness, Secretary and Treasurer

Statement of Income (Year ends 6/30—$ figures in 000's)

	1985	1984
Net Sales	$538,110	$437,351
Other Income, Principally Interest	787	2,393
	$538,897	$439,744
Costs and Expenses		
Cost of Sales, Including General and Administrative Expense	$504,611	$407,507
Interest Expense	1,137	9,099
Other Expense	10,174	2,807
	$515,922	$419,414
Income before Income Taxes	$ 22,975	$ 20,330
Income Taxes	9,240	8,815
Net Income	$ 13,735	$ 11,516

Stockholder's Equity, Jobs, and Labor Productivity ($ figures in 000's)

Year	Stockholder's Equity	Net Sales	Number of Employees	Index of Labor Productivity
1975	$ 2,866	$ 25,054	1,012	24.757
1976	3,274	27,273	1,113	24.504
1977	5,348	28,633	880	32.538
1978	6,901	26,247	1,192	22.019
1979	16,324	36,772	1,352	27.198
1980	18,107	46,737	1,619	28.868
1981	21,187	59,383	2,085	28.481
1982	33,904	90,014	2,920	30.827
1983	44,136	182,499	3,220	56.677
Change, 1983/1975	+ 1,440 %	+ 628 %	+ 218 %	+ 130 %

Capital Productivity ($ figures in 000's)

Year	Total Invested Capital	Net Income	Index of Capital Productivity
1975	$ 9,141	$ 710	.078
1976	8,997	417	.046
1977	8,271	714	.086
1978	12,068	933	.077
1979	19,874	1,412	.071
1980	25,589	2,120	.083
1981	28,647	3,101	.108
1982	47,652	4,110	.086
1983	84,305	6,570	.079
Change, 1983/1975	+ 822 %	+ 825 %	+ 1 %

Stock Prices and Earnings per Share[*]

Year	Stock Prices			Earnings[**] Per Share
	High	Low	Close	
1975	$ .368	$ .140	$ .254	$.112
1976	1.410	.254	1.371	.064
1977	2.794	1.302	2.571	.104
1978	4.889	1.603	1.825	.114
1979	2.400	1.467	2.333	.146
1980	5.333	2.089	5.200	.213
1981	8.833	4.167	7.083	.313
1982	15.250	5.250	14.875	.377
1983	30.500	14.250	22.500	.570
1984	25.500	10.750	14.000	.910

Change, 1975–84 + 5,413%; change, S&P 500 Index, 1975–84 + 82%

[*]Adjusted for stock splits and stock dividends   [**]Includes extraordinary items

Prior to July 1, 1984, SCI conducted its business as a single operating company. On that date, however, the company was restructured and now operates as a parent company (SCI Systems, Inc.) with two operating subsidiaries (SCI Technology, Inc. and SCI Manufacturing, Inc.). The Government, Computer, and Systems Divisions are operated by SCI Technology, Inc. Each of these divisions is characterized by major engineering activities in high-technology areas. The frequent interchange of significant technology and personnel favors the organizational grouping of these divisions, as do common accounting practices, control systems, and equipment sharing. The company supplies a variety of instrumentation, computer, and communications systems to the U.S. government and its prime contractors. Sales of the Government Division are generally under fixed-price, fixed-price-incentive, and cost-plus-incentive-fee contracts. Contracts of the Government Division include substantial follow-on work as well as new awards. The company experienced explosive growth in 1985, which will challenge management's ability to cope with its new status as a half billion dollar corporation.

SMITHFIELD FOODS, INC.

Corporate Headquarters: Suite 811
1777 North Kent Street
Arlington, VA 22209

Telephone: (703) 276-7200
Incorporated in Delaware
Over the counter—SFDS

Business: Manufactures and markets fresh pork and a wide variety of processed meats.

Officers:

Joseph W. Luter, III, Chairman, President and Chief Executive Officer
Henry L. Morris, Vice President—Engineering
J. Sam Sawyer, Vice President—Credit
P. Edward Schenk, Vice President—Technical Services
John P. Schroeder, Vice President—Livestock Procurement
Aaron D. Trub, Vice President, Secretary and Treasurer
C. Larry Pope, Controller
Alan T. Anderson, President—Patrick Cudahy Inc.
Kenneth W. Brown, President—Gwaltney of Smithfield, Ltd.
George E. Hamilton, Jr., President—Smithfield Packing Company, Inc.

Statement of Income (Year ends 4/28/85 and 4/29/84—$ figures in 000's)

	1985	1984
Net Sales	$669,130	$541,641
Costs and Expenses:		
Cost of Sales	$604,023	$486,732
Selling, General and Administrative	45,289	38,945
Depreciation	6,990	5,885
Interest	6,004	4,534
Loss on Disposition of Plant	—	1,800
	$662,306	$537,896
Income before Income Taxes	$ 6,824	$ 3,745
Income Taxes	3,366	1,310
Net Income	$ 3,485	$ 2,435

Stockholder's Equity, Jobs, and Labor Productivity ($ figures in 000's)

Year	Stockholder's Equity	Net Sales	Number of Employees	Index of Labor Productivity
1975	$ 1,811	$138,255	2,350	58.832
1976	3,343	143,736	2,275	63.181
1977	5,520	139,125	1,420	97.975
1978	11,071	170,756	1,750	97.575
1979	13,800	192,914	2,134	90.400
1980	12,292	218,255	2,070	105.437
1981	14,447	344,364	3,450	99.816
1982	17,372	570,615	3,000	190.205
1983	18,399	541,641	3,150	171.950
Change, 1983/1975	+916 %	+292 %	+34 %	+192 %

Capital Productivity ($ figures in 000's)

Year	Total Invested Capital	Net Income	Index of Capital Productivity
1975	$16,602	$ 393	.024
1976	17,357	1,532	.088
1977	17,450	2,177	.125
1978	20,287	6,579	.316
1979	27,169	3,511	.129
1980	25,763	873	.034
1981	53,605	1,612	.030
1982	54,466	2,946	.054
1983	54,278	2,435	.045
Change, 1983/1975	+270 %	+520 %	+90 %

Stock Prices and Earnings per Share[*]

Year	Stock Prices			Earnings[**] Per Share
	High	Low	Close	
1975	$ 1.625	$1.125	$1.500	$ .160
1976	2.750	1.500	2.250	.580
1977	3.000	1.875	2.750	.840
1978	5.750	2.625	4.750	2.660
1979	8.625	4.750	8.000	1.480
1980	8.375	4.875	4.875	.450
1981	6.125	4.750	5.750	.720
1982	7.750	4.625	7.250	1.000
1983	11.750	7.125	8.625	.860
1984	9.500	6.125	7.625	1.220

Change, 1975–84 +408%; change, S&P 500 Index, 1975–84 +82%

[*]Adjusted for stock splits and stock dividends   [**]Includes extraordinary items

Note: The fiscal year financial results in the tables above are shown in the year in which most of the results were achieved.

294

CORPORATE PROFILE—SMITHFIELD FOODS, INC.

This company manufactures and markets fresh pork and a wide variety of processed meats. The company's product lines include bacon, ham, franks, sausage, and luncheon meats marketed under the Smithfield, Luter, Gwaltney, and Williamsburg brand names, canned hams and dry sausage marketed under the Patrick Cudahy name, and the "Great" line of processed poultry products. The company distributes its products throughout the United States, with major concentrations in the Northeast, the Mid-Atlantic, the Southeast, and the Midwest. Compared to other meat processors, Smithfield has performed exceptionally well. However, its 1985 results remain well below the net income achieved in fiscal 1978.

SMITHKLINE BECKMAN CORPORATION

Corporate Headquarters: One Franklin Plaza
                          Philadelphia, PA 19101
Telephone: (215) 751-4000
Incorporated in Pennsylvania
New York Stock Exchange—SKB

Business: Manufactures and markets worldwide a broadline of prescription and proprietary products for human and animal health care as well as diagnostic and analytical products and services that facilitate the detion and treatment of disease and the advancement of biomedical research.

Officers:

Robert F. Dee, Chairman
Henry Wendt, President and Chief Executive Officer
Arnold O. Beckman, Ph.D., Vice Chairman
Donald van Roden, Vice Chairman
Executive Vice Presidents: Alan J. Dalby, George W. Ebright
Vice Presidents: Norman H. Blanchard, Robert J. Byrnes, James H. Cavanaugh, Ph.D., John F. Chappell, Thomas M. Collins, Stanley T. Crooke, M.D., Ph.D., Bryce Douglas, Ph.D., Harry C. Groome, Gavin S. Herbert, Richard V. Holmes, William E. Learnard, Kurt W. Reiss, Richard W. Rodney, Louis T. Rosso, William C. Shepard

Statement of Income (Year ends 12/31—$ figures in 000,000's)

	1984	1983
Sales	$2,949	$2,835
Operating Costs and Expenses		
Cost of Sales	$1,031	$ 962
Marketing, Administrative and General	938	903
Research, Development and Engineering	279	264
	$2,249	$2,130
Operating Income	$ 700	$ 705
Non-Operating Income (Expense)		
Interest Income	84	66
Interest Expense	(46)	(54)
Other, (Net)	(24)	(7)
	$ 12	$ 4
Earnings from Continuing Operations before		
Income Taxes	$ 712	$ 709
Income Taxes	212	223
Earnings from Continuing Operations	$ 500	$ 486
Discontinued Operations	3	3
Net Earnings	$ 503	$ 489

Stockholder's Equity, Jobs, and Labor Productivity ($ figures in 000's)

Year	Stockholder's Equity	Net Sales	Number of Employees	Index of Labor Productivity
1975	$ 269,060	$ 588,728	13,722	42.904
1976	315,222	673,501	14,222	47.356
1977	376,260	780,337	15,134	51.562
1978	503,770	1,112,039	16,589	67.035
1979	667,468	1,351,145	18,056	74.831
1980	923,723	1,771,937	21,196	83.598
1981	1,138,456	1,985,341	22,914	86.643
1982	1,749,406	2,968,666	35,831	82.852
1983	1,970,792	2,835,390	31,317	90.538
Change, 1983/1975	+633 %	+382 %	+128 %	+111 %

Capital Productivity ($ figures in 000's)

Year	Total Invested Capital	Net Income	Index of Capital Productivity
1975	$ 416,602	$ 63,592	.153
1976	465,919	72,027	.155
1977	528,688	89,271	.169
1978	663,697	164,075	.247
1979	831,098	233,837	.281
1980	1,127,093	307,994	.273
1981	1,381,866	370,000	.268
1982	2,036,352	455,157	.224
1983	2,144,800	489,500	.228
Change, 1983/1975	+414 %	+670 %	+50 %

Stock Prices and Earnings per Share*

	Stock Prices			Earnings**
Year	High	Low	Close	Per Share
1975	$14.750	$10.813	$14.750	$1.070
1976	20.625	14.625	19.844	1.210
1977	25.188	15.375	24.875	1.490
1978	51.250	23.063	45.750	2.725
1979	63.250	38.500	62.875	3.850
1980	80.625	43.500	80.000	4.650
1981	88.375	63.875	67.625	5.550
1982	77.625	57.375	69.000	5.510
1983	76.500	55.250	56.500	5.890
1984	60.250	50.000	52.250	6.230

Change, 1975–84 +254%; change, S&P 500 Index, 1975–84 +82%

*Adjusted for stock splits and stock dividends   **Includes extraordinary items

CORPORATE PROFILE—SMITHKLINE BECKMAN CORPORATION

This company is a high-technology, worldwide health care company operating in two primary business segments. The Therapeutics segment includes products regulated under the food and drug laws of the United States and other countries, and distributed principally through the food and drug trade, hospitals, and veterinarians. The Diagnostic/Analytical segment includes diagnostic and analytical products and clinical laboratory services. Diagnostic and analytical products include instruments and systems, and related chemical consumables and supplies, for health care, biomedical research, and scientific applications. Clinical laboratory services are provided by a network of laboratories located primarily in the United States. SmithKline Beckman has compiled a record of steady increases in sales and net earnings during the past decade. It also has shown a major improvement in capital productivity and, as one of the larger of the 101 companies profiled, has a record few large firms can come close to matching.

Without a doubt, this is a company with exceptional management. During the 1950s and 1960s it made a smooth transition from family to professional management. During that period, the company was a pioneer in the development of tranquilizers and generated healthy profits from products like Thorazine. It invested those profits in carefully selected R & D projects, one of which produced Tagamet, the first cure for ulcers and one of the most successful prescription drugs ever introduced. Management has now reinvested Tagamet's enormous profits with the goal of becoming a truly first-class international company. SmithKline Beckman aims to be a provider of an array of health care products for an aging population. The firm is set for the rest of the century.

STANDARD-PACIFIC CORP.

Corporate Headquarters: 1565 West Macarthur Blvd.
Costa Mesa, CA 92626
Telephone: (714) 546-1161
Incorporated in Delaware
New York Stock Exchange—SPF

Business: Builds medium priced single family houses, primarily in the major cities of the South and West.

Officers:

Arthur E. Svendsen, Chairman of the Board and Chief Executive Offi-
Ronald R. Foell, President
Robert J. St. Lawrence, Vice President, Finance, Secretary and Treasurer

Statement of Income (Year ends 12/31—$ figures in 000's)

	1984	1983
Sales and Revenues		
Residential Housing	$164,921	$116,187
Manufacturing	26,229	17,724
Interest and Other Income	1,792	639
	192,941	134,551
Cost and Expenses		
Residential Housing	140,564	103,182
Manufactured	15,251	10,425
General and Administrative	11,575	8,420
Interest Expense	291	303
	167,681	122,330
Income from Operations before Provision for Taxes on Income and Equity in Net Income of Unconsolidated Subsidiary	25,260	12,221
Provision for Taxes on Income	12,553	5,986
Income before Equity in Net Income of Unconsolidated Subsidiary	12,708	6,235
Equity in Net Income of Unconsolidated Subsidiary	347	92
Net Income	$ 13,055	$ 6,327

Stockholder's Equity, Jobs, and Labor Productivity ($ figures in 000's)

Year	Stockholder's Equity	Net Sales	Number of Employees	Index of Labor Productivity
1975	$11,743	$ 44,615	240	185.896
1976	19,345	79,087	298	265.225
1977	26,046	87,779	373	235.332
1978	34,001	106,946	385	277.782
1979	42,519	129,091	419	308.093
1980	48,109	120,746	361	334.476
1981	48,932	79,325	330	240.379
1982	48,543	95,641	310	308.519
1983	73,416	133,911	397	337.307
Change, 1983/1975	+525 %	+200 %	+65 %	+81 %

Capital Productivity ($ figures in 000's)

Year	Total Invested Capital	Funds from Operations	Index of Capital Productivity
1975	$ 32,837	$ 1,896	.058
1976	32,324	4,495	.139
1977	30,585	7,910	.259
1978	37,798	10,346	.274
1979	69,351	12,275	.177
1980	78,754	12,773	.162
1981	77,382	10,970	.142
1982	97,335	4,165	.043
1983	109,543	8,850	.081
Change, 1983/1975	+234 %	+367 %	+40 %

Stock Prices and Earnings per Share[*]

Year	Stock Prices			Earnings[**] Per Share
	High	Low	Close	
1975	$ 2.121	$ .606	$ 1.263	$ .396
1976	4.394	1.313	3.939	.925
1977	4.773	2.803	3.939	1.206
1978	7.417	3.417	4.917	1.547
1979	8.417	4.917	6.667	1.747
1980	10.583	5.667	9.333	1.400
1981	12.083	5.750	6.917	.567
1982	9.667	2.833	7.917	.113
1983	15.333	7.333	11.667	.913
1984	12.167	6.500	12.000	1.720

Change, 1975–84 +850%; change, S&P 500 Index, 1975–84 +82%

[*]Adjusted for stock splits and stock dividends   [**]Includes extraordinary items

300

The company's business is homebuilding—medium-priced, single-family homes, primarily in major market areas of the South and West. It has 72 active residential development projects in Texas, California, Illinois, and the Pacific Northwest. A subsidiary, SP Financial Services, Inc., provides permanent mortgage financing for many of its home buyers at attractive rates. In addition, the company has two manufacturing subsidiaries, which accounted for 14 percent of revenues in 1984. Panel Concepts manufactures office furniture systems—high-quality, movable office partitions, workstation modules, and accessory units for business office use. Its products are manufactured in Southern California and North Carolina and are marketed nationwide. Panel-Air manufactures components of fiberglass, metal, and advanced composite materials for commercial and military aircraft.

STATE-O-MAINE, INC.

Corporate Headquarters: One Astor Plaza
New York, NY 10036

Telephone: (212) 869-3333
Incorporated in Delaware
Over the Counter—DSIF

Business: Manufactures men's robes, swim wear, lounge wear, outer wear, and active sportswear sold as "State-O-Maine:" and "Christian Dior."

Officers:

Milton Weinick, Chairman and Secretary
Harvey L. Sanders, President and Treasurer
Van Baalen Pacific Corp. (Subsidiary)
Steve Taglia, President
Harris Cohen, Treasurer
Nautica Apparel, Inc. (Subsidiary)
David Chu, President

Statement of Income (Year ends 2/28/85 and 2/29/84—$ figures in 000's)

	1985	1984
Net Sales	$26,251	$20,120
Costs and Expenses		
Cost of Goods Sold	$16,510	$13,069
Designing, Selling, Shipping, General and Administrative Expenses	6,249	4,962
Interest Expense	404	371
Operating Income	$ 3,088	$ 1,717
Other Income	9	—
Earnings before Provision for Income Taxes	$ 3,097	$ 1,717
Income Taxes	1,569	806
Net Earnings	$ 1,528	$ 912

Stockholder's Equity, Jobs, and Labor Productivity ($ figures in 000's)

Year	Stockholder's Equity	Net Sales	Number of Employees	Index of Labor Productivity
1975	$ 635	$ 7,912	250	28.048
1976	1,150	9,884	337	29.329
1977	1,685	11,300	395	28.608
1978	2,080	11,775	395	29.810
1979	2,325	12,686	395	32.116
1980	2,797	14,210	302	47.053
1981	3,293	17,751	302	58.778
1982	3,801	19,177	302	63.500
1983	4,713	20,120	302	66.623
Change, 1983/1975	+642 %	+187 %	+21 %	+138 %

Capital Productivity ($ figures in 000's)

Year	Total Invested Capital	Net Income	Index of Capital Productivity
1975	$1,635	$123	.075
1976	1,976	509	.258
1977	2,344	536	.229
1978	3,025	394	.130
1979	3,052	245	.080
1980	3,188	472	.148
1981	3,509	574	.164
1982	3,975	509	.128
1983	4,869	912	.187
Change, 1983/1975	+198 %	+642 %	+149 %

Stock Prices and Earnings per Share[*]

Year	Stock Prices			Earnings[**] Per Share
	High	Low	Close	
1975	$ .315	$ .010	$ .010	$ .080
1976	.337	.125	.125	.340
1977	.562	.187	.187	.360
1978	.837	.250	.250	.260
1979	.500	.337	.337	.160
1980	.375	.187	.187	.310
1981	1.250	.500	1.000	.390
1982	1.250	.750	.875	.350
1983	1.750	.750	1.750	.640
1984	3.750	2.000	3.500	1.070

Change, 1975–84 +34,900%; change, S&P 500 Index, 1975–84 +82%

[*]Adjusted for stock splits and stock dividends   [**]Includes extraordinary items

Note: The fiscal year financial results in the tables above are shown in the year in which most of the results were achieved.

303

CORPORATE PROFILE—STATE-O-MAINE, INC.

The company is a manufacturer of men's robes, swimwear, lounge-wear, outerwear, and active sportswear sold across the United States under various trade names including "State-O-Maine," "Nautica," and "Christian Dior." The firm has showrooms in New York and Los Angeles and one manufacturing plant in Rockland, Maine. While the company has operated in the volatile fashion industry, it nevertheless has been able to compile a consistent record of growth in sales and net income. The last three years have seen net earnings triple.

STEWART INFORMATION SERVICES CORPORATION

Corporate Headquarters: 2200 West Loop South
                         Houston, TX 77027
Telephone: (713) 871-1100
Incorporated in Delaware
Over the Counter—SISC

Business: Title insurance and related services for the real estate market.
Officers:
  Carloss Morris, Chairman of the Board, Co-Chief Executive Officer
  Stewart Morris, President, Co-Chief Executive Officer
  Max Crisp, Vice President, Finance and Secretary-Treasurer
  Malcolm S. Morris, Vice President, Operations
  Stewart Morris, Jr., Vice President, Operations

Statement of Income (Year ends 12/31—$ figures in 000's)

	1984	1983
Revenues		
Title Premiums, Fees and Related Revenues	$121,244	$113,685
Mapping	2,910	1,131
Total Revenues	$124,154	$114,816
Investment Income	6,982	4,842
Other Income, Including Equity Earnings	357	473
Sales of Title Plant Copies	458	48
	$131,951	$120,179
Expenses		
Employee Costs	58,272	48,976
Other Operating Expenses	41,712	37,959
Depreciation and Amortization	3,084	2,751
Mapping	2,682	1,300
Interest	1,255	1,190
Minority Interests	648	707
	$121,291	$102,567
Operating Income before Taxes	10,660	17,612
Income Taxes	3,846	7,818
Operating Income	6,814	9,794
Realized Investment Gains, Net of		
Taxes and Minority Interests	225	187
Net Income	$ 7,039	$ 9,981

Stockholder's Equity, Jobs, and Labor Productivity ($ figures in 000's)

Year	Stockholder's Equity	Net Sales	Number of Employees	Index of Labor Productivity
1975	$13,561	$ 30,308	1,200	25.257
1976	16,169	38,835	1,370	28.420
1977	23,330	45,866	1,650	27.798
1978	29,632	57,143	1,760	32.468
1979	35,284	66,192	1,960	33.771
1980	38,969	64,228	1,810	35.485
1981	42,091	73,006	1,775	41.130
1982	44,680	79,284	1,855	42.741
1983	64,014	114,816	2,225	50.916
Change, 1983/1975	+ 372 %	+ 279 %	+ 88 %	+ 102 %

Capital Productivity ($ figures in 000's)

Year	Total Invested Capital	Net Income	Index of Capital Productivity
1975	$19,140	$1,062	.055
1976	21,728	2,874	.132
1977	28,624	5,505	.192
1978	37,375	7,950	.213
1979	45,583	7,652	.168
1980	48,937	4,215	.086
1981	54,202	3,955	.073
1982	54,977	4,189	.076
1983	74,878	9,981	.133
Change, 1983/1975	+ 291 %	+ 840 %	+ 140 %

Stock Prices and Earnings per Share[*]

Year	Stock Prices			Earnings[**] Per Share
	High	Low	Close	
1975	$ 3.375	$ 1.750	$ 2.250	$ .600
1976	7.250	2.250	6.625	1.605
1977	10.125	6.000	8.000	2.635
1978	17.125	6.875	11.500	3.515
1979	16.625	9.250	11.125	3.385
1980	15.125	8.750	11.750	1.815
1981	13.375	10.500	12.000	1.660
1982	19.375	9.125	19.250	1.750
1983	33.500	17.750	29.500	3.920
1984	28.750	16.750	22.750	2.440

Change, 1975–84 + 911%; change, S&P 500 Index, 1975–84 + 82%

[*]Adjusted for stock splits and stock dividends   [**]Includes extraordinary items

306

Stewart's primary business is title insurance. The company operates in 43 states and the District of Columbia. Through more than 1,400 issuing offices and agents, and as part of a single process, Stewart searches, examines, closes, and insures the titles to homes and other real property. Customers include home buyers and sellers, attorneys, builders, lenders, and real estate brokers. Stewart is the leading title company in Texas. Its other major markets are in Arizona, California, and Florida. Stewart also provides computer-related services to the real estate industry from the computer data base systems used in its operations. This highly focused company has shown virtually uninterrupted growth in sales during the last decade. Its net income, however, has fluctuated to a much greater extent, with 1984 results being the second highest achieved during the company's history. It would appear that 1985 will show a continued roller coaster ride.

TANDY CORPORATION

Corporate Headquarters: 1800 One Tandy Center
Fort Worth, TX 76102

Telephone: (817) 390-3700
Incorporated in Delaware
New York Stock Exchange—TAN

Business: Manufactures and markets electronic products for the home and for business through approximately 6,000 owned retail stores and 3,000 franchisees.

Officers:

> John Roach, Chairman of the Board, Chief Executive Officer and President
> John McDaniel, Senior Vice President and Controller
> Charles Tindall, Senior Vice President and Treasurer
> Herschel Winn, Senior Vice President and Secretary
> Billy Roland, Vice President
> Loyd Turner, Vice President
> Donald Bock, Assistant Treasurer
> Louis Neumann, Assistant Secretary

Statement of Income (Year ends 6/30—$ figures in 000's)

	1985	1984
Net Sales and Operating Revenues	$2,841,434	$2,775,496
Other Income	11,530	8,983
	$2,852,964	$2,784,479
Costs and Expenses:		
Cost of Products Sold	$1,291,789	$1,184,531
Selling, General and Administrative	1,102,135	1,014,827
Depreciation and Amortization	51,947	46,079
Interest (Net)	55,682	4,363
Income from Continuing Operations before Income Taxes	$ 351,411	$ 534,679
Income Taxes	162,351	252,808
Net Income	$ 186,060	$ 281,871

Stockholder's Equity, Jobs, and Labor Productivity ($ figures in 000's)

Year	Stockholder's Equity	Net Sales	Number of Employees	Index of Labor Productivity
1975	$ 190,356	$ 724,488	16,000	45.281
1976	205,882	741,722	15,000	49.488
1977	164,337	949,267	18,000	52.737
1978	138,996	1,059,324	20,000	52.966
1979	208,353	1,215,483	20,700	58.719
1980	283,125	1,384,637	22,000	58.719
1981	571,863	1,691,373	26,000	65.053
1982	812,677	2,032,553	31,000	65.566
1983	1,120,872	2,475,187	32,000	77.350
Change, 1983/1975	+ 489 %	+ 424 %	+ 100 %	+ 71 %

Capital Productivity ($ figures in 000's)

Year	Total Invested Capital	Net Income	Index of Capital Productivity
1975	$ 300,360	$ 34,596	.115
1976	242,140	67,524	.279
1977	294,623	69,042	.234
1978	376,211	66,146	.176
1979	439,086	83,229	.190
1980	511,822	112,235	.219
1981	698,193	169,602	.243
1982	955,985	224,085	.234
1983	1,259,291	278,521	.221
Change, 1983/1975	+ 319 %	+ 705 %	+ 92 %

Stock Prices and Earnings per Share[*]

Year	Stock Prices			Earnings[**] Per Share
	High	Low	Close	
1975	$ 3.297	$ .727	$ 3.250	$ .238
1976	5.922	3.250	5.266	.466
1977	5.359	2.625	4.375	.521
1978	8,656	3.734	6.813	.688
1979	8.000	4.406	7.813	.808
1980	25.563	7.063	24.688	1.118
1981	39.125	20.125	33.750	1.650
1982	60.750	22.750	50.750	2.170
1983	64.500	33.250	43.375	2.670
1984	43.375	23.250	24.250	2.750

Change, 1975–84 + 646%; change, S&P 500 Index, 1975–84 + 82%

[*]Adjusted for stock splits and stock dividends   [**]Includes extraordinary items

Tandy/Radio Shack manufactures and markets electronics for the home and office. Distribution is through approximately 6,100 company-owned stores and 3,000 dealer/franchise locations in more than 80 countries. The company has the largest number of retail electronics outlets in the world. The 1985 Radio Shack-U.S. catalog features about 2,700 items, including audio and video products, telephone equipment, radios, scanners, citizens band radios, security devices, electronic kits and games, clocks, and parts, plus 20 pages of selected computer products. The current Radio Shack-U.S. computer catalog contains more than 1,000 items. Tandy owns or operates in 30 factories in the United States, Asia, Canada, and France. About 39 percent of the products in the 1985 Radio Shack-U.S. catalog are manufactured, assembled, or packaged in the company's plants. While Tandy incurred a decrease in net income for fiscal 1985 (its first in 23 years), management projects a 30 percent increase for fiscal 1986. The company appears to be positioned to benefit from the long-term growth in computer and electronic components and systems in light of its strong distribution/retail network.

TELEFLEX, INCORPORATED

Corporate Headquarters: 155 South Limerick Road
                          Limerick, PA 19468
Telephone: (215) 948-5100
Incorporated in Delaware
American Stock Exchange—TFX

Business: Applications engineering that designs, develops and markets specialized technologies to aerospace, medical, automotive, marine, defense and other markets.

Officers:

- Lennox K. Black, Chairman and Chief Executive Officer
- John H. Remer, Senior Vice President, Administration
- John J. Sickler, Senior Vice President & Chief Financial Officer
- Ira Albom, President and Chief Operating Officer, Defense/Aerospace Group
- David S. Boyer, Vice President & General Manager, Automotive Products
- Dr. Roy C. Carriker, President and Chief Operating Officer, Sermatech
- Steven K. Chance, Director of Legal Services
- Thomas A. Coneys, President and Chief Operating Officer, Medical Group
- Claude Jacquemin, Director of International Marketing Services
- David R. Loveless, President & Chief Operating Officer, Commercial Products
- John F. Schoenfelder, Secretary and Treasurer
- August E. Tschanz, Vice President and General Manager, Development and Training

Statement of Income (Year ends 12/30/84 and 12/25/83—$ figures in 000's)

	1984	1983
Revenues		
Net Sales	$153,311	$129,341
Other Income	2,426	1,388
	155,736	130,729
Costs and Expenses		
Materials, Labor and Other Product Costs	106,687	88,593
Selling, Engineering and Administrative Expenses	28,543	24,587
Interest Expense	1,396	1,448
	136,626	114,628
Income from Operations	19,110	16,101
Income before Taxes	19,110	16,101
Estimated Taxes on Income	7,800	6,600
Net Income	$ 11,310	$ 9,501

Stockholder's Equity, Jobs, and Labor Productivity ($ figures in 000's)

Year	Stockholder's Equity	Net Sales	Number of Employees	Index of Labor Productivity
1975	$10,226	$ 32,500	1,167	27.849
1976	11,424	41,778	1,250	33.422
1977	13,057	47,670	1,300	36.669
1978	14,726	54,845	1,400	39.175
1979	19,054	66,791	1,427	46.805
1980	23,782	78,501	1,780	44.102
1982	30,265	103,220	1,870	55.198
1982	40,107	111,689	1,750	63.822
1983	63,563	129,341	1,940	66.671
Change, 1983/1975	+522 %	+298 %	+66 %	+139 %

Capital Productivity ($ figures in 000's)

Year	Total Invested Capital	Net Income	Index of Capital Productivity
1975	$18,588	$ 393	.021
1976	21,351	1,212	.057
1977	24,094	1,790	.074
1978	27,834	2,668	.096
1979	31,941	3,872	.121
1980	38,771	4,759	.123
1981	57,897	7,106	.123
1982	57,692	10,954	.190
1983	77,690	9,501	.122
Change, 1983/1975	+318 %	+2,318 %	+478 %

Stock Prices and Earnings per Share[*]

Year	Stock Prices			Earnings[**] Per Share
	High	Low	Close	
1975	$ 1.493	$ .945	$ 1.285	$ .095
1976	2.778	1.310	2.778	.287
1977	4.125	2.375	4.042	.420
1978	9.167	3.625	5.333	.600
1979	10.667	5.250	10.042	.860
1980	17.000	6.167	14.750	1.047
1981	25.875	12.625	19.750	1.520
1982	31.375	15.500	29.875	2.330
1983	39.000	28.250	30.750	1.830
1984	32.000	21.250	27.750	2.150

Change, 1975–84 +2,060%; change, S&P 500 Index, 1975–84 +82%

[*]Adjusted for stock splits and stock dividends [**]Includes extraordinary items

312

Teleflex is an applications engineering company dedicated to solving problems through the design, development, and marketing of specialized technologies. Its business is divided into two segments. The technical segment serves the aerospace, defense, medical, and transportation industries. These products and services require a high degree of sophisticated engineering and are generally produced in limited quantities. The Commercial segment serves the automotive, pleasure marine, outdoor power equipment, and general industrial markets. These products tend to be less complex and are produced in much higher volume. This company, which is solid record of growth with only one down year during the decade, is committed to achieving $500 million in revenues by 1990. This objective, if realized, would represent more than a tripling of 1984 revenues.

TELEX CORPORATION

Corporate Headquarters: 6422 East 41st Street, PO Box 1526
Tulsa, OK 74101

Telephone: (918) 627-2333
Incorporated in Delaware
New York Stock Exchange—TC

Business: Manufactures and markets computer terminals, peripheral equipment, as well as audio, audiovisual and communications products.

Officers:

Stephen J. Jatras, Chairman of the Board and President

George L. Bragg, Group Vice President, Chairman of the Board, Telex Computer

Ansel Kleiman, Group Vice President, Chairman of the Board Telex Communications

J. B. Bailey, Vice President, General Counsel and Secretary

E. G. Frank, Vice President, Finance and Treasurer

David E. Gannon, Assistant Treasurer

Jess Mitchell, Director in Internal Auditing

Serge Novovich, Assistant Secretary

Bhrent E. Waddell, Controller

Statement of Income (Year ends 3/31—$ figures in 000's)

	1985	1984
Revenues		
Sales, Rental and Service	$591,038	$318,295
Other	10,561	7,137
Total Revenues	$601,599	$325,432
Costs and Expenses		
Cost of Sales, Rental and Service	$351,006	$185,435
Engineering and Development	24,639	14,927
Reduction in Spare Parts Carrying Value	15,778	7,292
Selling, General and Administrative	86,515	45,128
Interest	16,500	4,738
Other	6,398	3,430
Total Costs and Expenses	$500,836	$260,950
Income before Income Taxes & Extraordinary Credit	$100,763	$ 64,482
Income Tax Expense		
Current	41,029	24,136
Deferred	6,391	4,232
Total Income Tax Expense	$ 47,420	$ 28,368
Net Income	$ 55,343	$ 36,114

314

Stockholder's Equity, Jobs, and Labor Productivity ($ figures in 000's)

Year	Stockholder's Equity	Net Sales	Number of Employees	Index of Labor Productivity
1975	$ 8,733	$101,676	2,350	43.266
1976	14,200	112,149	3,149	35.614
1977	22,742	133,534	3,120	42.799
1978	40,665	142,722	3,847	37.100
1979	41,682	157,037	4,026	39.006
1980	49,822	178,466	3,902	45.737
1981	61,165	203,412	3,618	56.222
1982	110,900	271,181	3,973	68.256
1983	147,208	318,295	4,193	75.911
Change, 1983/1975	+ 1,586 %	+ 213 %	+ 78 %	+ 76 %

Capital Productivity ($ figures in 000's)

Year	Total Invested Capital	Net Income	Index of Capital Productivity
1975	$ 49,785	$ 6,600	.133
1976	51,009	6,285	.123
1977	57,939	8,454	.146
1978	108,632	5,358	.049
1979	105,514	991	.009
1980	115,300	8,083	.070
1981	123,239	11,835	.096
1982	145,774	28,778	.197
1983	173,325	26,114	.208
Change, 1983/1975	+ 248 %	+ 447 %	+ 57 %

Stock Prices and Earnings per Share[*]

Year	Stock Prices			Earnings[**] Per Share
	High	Low	Close	
1975	$ 3.500	$ .875	$ 2.000	$ .620
1976	4.625	1.875	3.125	.580
1977	3.375	1.875	3.125	.780
1978	9.250	2.750	5.375	.450
1979	7.125	3.250	4.000	.080
1980	6.500	2.500	4.875	.640
1981	9.375	4.250	6.500	.940
1982	27.750	6.000	22.000	2.050
1983	32.500	19.500	25.875	2.480
1984	36.125	18.625	35.875	3.650

Change, 1975–84 + 1,694%; change, S&P 500 Index, 1975–84 + 82%

[*]Adjusted for stock splits and stock dividends   [**]Includes extraordinary items

Note: The fiscal year financial results in the tables above are shown in the year in which most of the results were achieved.

The company is engaged in the manufacture and sale of such products as computer terminals; magnetic tape drives; aircraft high-fidelity stereo devices, cartridge players, and recorders; tape duplicating systems; reel-to-reel tape recorders and players; hearing aids; microphones; headsets; high-fidelity components; and military and instrumentation tape recorders. During fiscal 1985 the company acquired Raytheon Data Systems. This acquisition, a record number of new product introductions, and new highs in sales and earnings combined to make 1985 a significant one for Telex. The Raytheon acquisition substantially increased the size of the company in both revenues and resources and brought a very important 53 percent market share position in a market not previously served by Telex—worldwide airline reservation systems. It also solidified the company's presence in the rapidly expanding advanced workstation market. Its latest fiscal year results added further evidence of the company's ability to achieve dramatic growth both via acquisition and internal new product development.

TERADYNE, INC.

Corporate Headquarters: 321 Harrison Ave.
                         Boston, MA 02118
Telephone (617) 482-2700
Incorporated in Massachusetts
New York Stock Exchange—TER

Business: Manufactures and markets automatic test equipment and back-plane connection systems for the electronics and other markets.

Officers:

Alexander V. d'Arbeloff, President and Chairman of the Board

Vice Presidents: G. Russell Ashdown, George W. Chamillard, George V. Arbeloff, Loren G. Eaton, Windsor H. Hunter, Lennart B. Johnson, Joseph B. Lassiter, III, Thomas B. Newman, Jr., Dennis P. O'Connell, James A. Prestridge, Owen W. Robbins, Edward Rogas, Jr., Frederick T. Van Veen

John P. McCabe, Controller

Stuart M. Osattin, Treasurer

Richard J. Testa, Secretary, Clerk and Director

Statement of Income (Year ends 12/31—$ figures in 000's)

	1984	1983
Net Sales	$389,278	$251,422
Expenses		
Cost of Sales	193,724	128,176
Engineering and Development	44,218	30,597
Selling and Administrative	79,336	55,937
Interest Expense	5,163	6,167
	322,441	220,876
Income before Taxes	66,837	30,546
Provision (Credit) for Income Taxes		
Federal	14,017	6,287
Foreign	6,366	1,402
State	3,300	1,475
	23,683	9,164
Net Income	$ 43,154	$ 21,382

317

Stockholder's Equity, Jobs, and Labor Productivity ($ figures in 000's)

Year	Stockholder's Equity	Net Sales	Number of Employees	Index of Labor Productivity
1975	$ 23,666	$ 37,872	1,120	33.814
1976	26,829	53,731	1,387	38.739
1977	32,079	67,815	1,573	43.112
1978	39,801	91,663	1,980	46.294
1979	68,205	122,447	2,550	48.018
1980	83,392	164,970	3,050	54.089
1981	90,541	159,942	3,050	52.440
1982	98,229	176,305	3,200	55.095
1983	176,460	251,422	3,900	64.467
Change, 1983/1975	+646 %	+564 %	+248 %	+91 %

Capital Productivity ($ figures in 000's)

Year	Total Invested Capital	Net Income	Index of Capital Productivity
1975	$ 23,939	$ 380	.016
1976	27,060	2,299	.085
1977	32,268	4,864	.151
1978	49,948	6,704	.134
1979	85,865	7,966	.093
1980	113,194	11,370	.100
1981	137,458	4,267	.031
1982	177,971	4,298	.024
1983	204,772	21,382	.104
Change, 1983/1975	+755 %	+5,527 %	+558 %

Stock Prices and Earnings per Share[*]

Year	Stock Prices			Earnings[**] Per Share
	High	Low	Close	
1975	$ 4.000	$ 1.438	$ 2.625	$ .030
1976	5.375	2.625	3.563	.178
1977	4.969	2.813	4.625	.375
1978	7.625	3.750	4.125	.508
1979	9.313	3.625	8.875	.590
1980	14.938	7.750	12.094	.688
1981	12.781	7.290	8.750	.250
1982	17.750	6.063	14.250	.245
1983	39.375	13.625	36.000	1.080
1984	39.375	21.250	26.000	1.870

Change, 1975–84 +891%; change, S&P 500 Index, 1975–84 +82%

[*]Adjusted for stock splits and stock dividends   [**]Includes extraordinary items

The company is one of the leading manufacturers of automatic test equipment and backplane connection systems for the electronics industry and other industries using electronic devices. As such, the company designs, manufactures, markets, and services test systems and associated software used by component manufacturers both for the incoming inspection of components and for the testing of subassemblies, such as completed circuit boards. The company sells its products across most sectors of the electronics industry and to companies in other industries that use electronic devices in high volume. No single customer accounted for as much as 10 percent of net sales in 1984. Direct sales to U.S. government agencies accounted for less than 1 percent of net sales in 1984, while export sales, consisting almost entirely of automatic test equipment, accounted for 31 percent of net sales in 1984. During 1985 the company experienced a slowdown in overall order volumes, particularly relating to the general slump in the semiconductor industry. As such, it appears probable that 1985 results will be below those achieved in 1984.

TEXAS OIL & GAS CORP.

Corporate Headquarters: First City Center, 1700 Pacific Avenue
Dallas, TX 75201
Telephone: (214) 954-2000
Incorporated in Delaware
New York Stock Exchange—TXO

Business: Wholesale domestic natural gas supply business including gathering and processing, exploring and producing natural gas and crude oil.
Officers:
William L. Hutchison, Chairman of the Board
Forrest E. Hoglund, President and Chief Executive Officer
A. D. Carter, Jr., Executive Vice President
T. E. Lohman, Executive Vice President
Senior Vice Presidents: Charles L. Canfield, Donald Chase, John R. Morgan
Richard F. Doyle, Senior Vice President, Finance and Administration
Bob F. Young, Vice President and General Counsel
Martin B. McNamara, Vice President, Assoc. General Counsel and Secretary
Hamilton P. Schrauff, Vice President, Finance and Treasurer
R. G. Schweers, Vice President and Controller
Charles D. Williams, Vice President, Investor Affairs
Vice Presidents: J. E. Cannon, Larry Carpenter, Jack E. Coffman, Barnard P. Deitz, John D. Huppler, David M. Kihneman, Louis E. Little, H. M. Rutledge

Statement of Income (Year ends 8/31—$ figures in 000's)

	1985	1984
Revenues		
Gas Gathering	$ 902,121	$1,290,588
Oil and Gas	739,485	727,177
Drilling	34,441	34,876
Miscellaneous	33,694	41,799
Total Revenues	**$1,709,741**	**$2,094,440**
Costs and Expenses		
Gas Purchases	$ 679,869	$1,021,578
Operating and General	121,859	101,732
Taxes, Other than Federal Income Taxes	65,423	68,897
Depreciation and Depletion	282,849	229,694
Drilling (including Depreciation)	30,498	29,352
Interest and Financing	51,482	60,982
Total Costs and Expenses	**$1,231,980**	**$1,512,235**
Income before Federal Income Taxes	$ 477,761	$ 582,205
Income Taxes	201,000	236,000
Net Income	**$ 276,761**	**$ 346,205**

Stockholder's Equity, Jobs, and Labor Productivity ($ figures in 000's)

Year	Stockholder's Equity	Net Sales	Number of Employees	Index of Labor Productivity
1975	$ 179,166	$ 232,935	1,125	206.686
1976	223,456	348,217	1,317	264.402
1977	286,019	597,183	1,607	371.614
1978	359,389	621,576	1,927	322.561
1979	393,661	791,561	2,219	356.720
1980	523,224	1,062,371	2,673	297.445
1981	699,554	1,433,925	3,262	439.585
1982	923,257	1,658,824	3,459	479.568
1983	1,192,827	1,838,496	3,405	539.940
Change, 1983/1975	+ 566 %	+ 689 %	+ 202 %	+ 161 %

Capital Productivity ($ figures in 000's)

Year	Total Invested Capital	Net Income	Index of Capital Productivity
1975	$ 364,962	$ 40,112	.110
1976	409,235	48,208	.118
1977	532,942	66,662	.125
1978	703,808	78,865	.112
1979	782,321	97,277	.124
1980	987,233	141,116	.143
1981	1,282,308	191,924	.150
1982	1,616,145	247,093	.153
1983	1,867,526	295,703	.158
Change, 1983/1975	+ 412 %	+ 736 %	+ 44 %

Stock Prices and Earnings per Share[*]

	Stock Prices			Earnings[**]
Year	High	Low	Close	Per Share
1975	$ 1.996	$ 1.092	$ 1.244	$ .193
1976	2.641	1.244	2.536	.231
1977	3.287	2.348	3.146	.319
1978	3.428	2.313	3.322	.378
1979	6.741	3.306	6.327	.465
1980	18.982	6.069	16.348	.465
1981	18.977	12.727	15.909	.914
1982	16.875	8.920	15.455	1.177
1983	26.875	15.125	23.875	1.405
1984	27.875	17.000	17.876	1.650

Change, 1975–84 + 1,337%; change, S&P 500 Index, 1975–84 + 82%

[*]Adjusted for stock splits and stock dividends   [**]Includes extraordinary items

321

This company is committed to one basic business: the wholesale supply of domestic natural gas. Its primary activities include exploring for and producing low-cost natural gas and crude oil, gathering and processing natural gas, extracting natural gas liquids, and contract drilling. Fiscal 1985 saw the company's revenues and net income both decline, thus ending a 28-year record of continuous growth. Industry conditions in the gas industry finally caught up with this outstanding growth company. The impact of deregulation is expected to be a critical factor affecting the company's ability to resume its growth pattern.

TRANSTECHNOLOGY CORP.

Corporate Headquarters: Ste. 500 Union Bank Plaza
                         15233 Ventura Blvd.
                         Sherman Oaks, CA 91403

Telephone: (213) 990-5920
Incorporated in California
American Stock Exchange—TT

Business: Develops, manufactures and markets technically sophisticated products to aerospace, defense and industrial markets such as cargo control products.

Officers:

Dr. Arch C. Scurlock, Chairman
Dan McBride, President and Chief Executive Officer
Paul Grosher, Senior Vice President and Treasurer
Vice Presidents: Burl Alison, Wellem F. Bakker, Joseph R. Cabaret, Thomas E. Hanrahan, Ralph E. Hutchins, John B. Reilly
Jeffrey A. Norton, Vice President and Secretary

Statement of Income (Year ends 3/31—$ figures in 000's)

	1985	1984
Revenues		
Sales	$110,688	$103,416
Interest Income	1,652	1,016
Other Income	601	4,154
	$112,941	$108,586
Cost and Expenses		
Cost of Sales	$ 72,964	$ 71,674
General, Administrative and Selling Expense	21,973	20,135
Interest Expense	1,698	1,217
	$ 96,635	$ 93,026
Income before Income Taxes	$ 16,306	$ 15,560
Income Taxes	7,888	7,158
Net Income	$ 8,418	$ 8,402

Stockholder's Equity, Jobs, and Labor Productivity ($ figures in 000's)

Year	Stockholder's Equity	Net Sales	Number of Employees	Index of Labor Productivity
1975	$ 3,878	$ 18,715	507	36.913
1976	4,644	21,965	754	29.131
1977	5,234	29,573	633	46.719
1978	5,840	28,693	707	40.584
1979	7,052	36,399	835	43.592
1980	14,916	47,144	774	60.910
1981	18,107	47,412	783	60.552
1982	33,407	69,429	1,408	49.319
1983	52,813	103,416	1,487	69.547
Change, 1983/1975	+1,262 %	+453 %	+193 %	+88 %

Capital Productivity ($ figures in 000's)

Year	Total Invested Capital	Net Income	Index of Capital Productivity
1975	$ 5,447	$ 610	.112
1976	8,512	947	.111
1977	10,608	605	.057
1978	11,953	895	.075
1979	12,818	1,586	.124
1980	34,356	2,767	.081
1981	36,746	3,723	.101
1982	52,768	5,766	.109
1983	69,996	8,402	.120
Change, 1983/1975	+1,185 %	+1,277 %	+7 %

Stock Prices and Earnings per Share*

	Stock Prices			Earnings**
Year	High	Low	Close	Per Share
1975	$ 1.875	$ .875	$ 1.500	$ .360
1976	3.000	1.500	2.500	.550
1977	4.000	2.375	2.750	.340
1978	5.000	2.750	3.125	.500
1979	9.250	2.750	9.125	.870
1980	14.250	6.625	12.750	1.170
1981	14.750	7.250	8.375	1.420
1982	16.500	7.750	15.500	1.900
1983	25.285	13.500	16.625	1.780
1984	19.250	11.250	13.625	1.750

Change, 1975–84 +808%; change, S&P 500 Index, 1975–84 +82%

*Adjusted for stock splits and stock dividends **Includes extraordinary items

Note: The fiscal year financial results in the tables above are shown in the year in which most of the results were achieved.

324

Transtechnology develops, manufactures, and sells a wide range of technically sophisticated products. The company is either the leader or an important factor in most of its product lines. Its aerospace-defense products, which represent about two-thirds of the company's revenues, include: (1) cargo restraint and control products—principally helicopter rescue hoists and external hook systems, winches and hoists for aircraft and other weapons systems, and aircraft and cargo tie-down devices; (2) a spectrum of high-reliability devices containing solid propellants, high explosives, or pyrotechnic materials, and law enforcement products; (3) custom electrical-interconnection systems and their components, and industrial security products; and (4) weather instruments. The company's line of industrial products include: (1) gear-driven fasteners, tachometers, and related equipment, and crane accessories and other construction-related equipment, and (2) textile-finishing machinery and related supplies, and elastomer products. Over time this company has turned in a strong record of growth in both revenues and earnings; however, the cyclical nature of its markets tends to make earnings performance somewhat erratic. Also, historically, the company has been somewhat dependent on acquisitions to maintain its growth.

TYCO LABORATORIES, INC.

Corporate Headquarters: Tyco Park
                         Exeter, NH 03833
Telephone: (603) 778-7331
Incorporated in Massachusetts
New York Stock Exchange—TYC

Business: Manufactures electronic components, packaging materials and fire protection systems.
Officers:
  John F. Fort, President and Chief Executive Officer
  Joshua M. Berman, Secretary
  James T. Gard, Vice President, Operations
  John J. Guarnieri, Treasurer
  Irving Gutin, Vice President
  Elliot F. Honan, Vice President, Corporate Development
  William A. Hartley, Vice President, Tax Counsel
  Richard D. Power, Vice President, Finance
  John D. Ryder, Corporate Controller

Statement of Income (Year ends 5/31—$ figures in 000's)

	1985	1984
Net Revenues	$673,932	$650,064
Costs and Expenses		
Cost of Sales	$525,935	$513,056
Selling, General and Administrative	89,142	85,288
Interest	2,797	6,883
	$617,874	$605,227
Non-Operating Income	$ 4,568	$ 3,980
Income before Income Taxes	$ 60,626	$ 48,817
Income Taxes	25,521	18,722
Net Income	$ 35,105	$ 30,095

Stockholder's Equity, Jobs, and Labor Productivity ($ figures in 000's)

Year	Stockholder's Equity	Net Sales	Number of Employees	Index of Labor Productivity
1975	$ 25,905	$ 92,157	3,558	25.901
1976	31,567	163,843	3,675	44.583
1977	44,847	165,940	3,745	44.310
1978	59,019	216,285	4,285	50.475
1979	87,382	320,268	5,170	61.947
1980	126,313	360,873	5,430	66.459
1981	123,323	552,160	7,470	73.917
1982	148,269	573,930	7,135	80.439
1983	176,428	650,064	7,443	87.339
Change, 1983/1975	+581 %	+605 %	+109 %	+237 %

Capital Productivity ($ figures in 000's)

Year	Total Invested Capital	Net Income	Index of Capital Productivity
1975	$ 79,229	$ 4,352	.055
1976	80,520	6,291	.078
1977	137,246	12,179	.089
1978	125,093	17,799	.142
1979	143,331	22,583	.158
1980	195,359	22,519	.115
1981	312,602	23,200	.074
1982	240,510	21,475	.089
1983	243,334	30,095	.124
Change, 1983/1975	+207 %	+592 %	+125 %

Stock Prices and Earnings per Share[*]

Year	Stock Prices			Earnings[**] Per Share
	High	Low	Close	
1975	$ 9.688	$ 4.250	$ 5.625	$ .720
1976	9.625	5.750	9.500	1.020
1977	12.250	6.563	6.875	1.960
1978	11.875	6.250	8.375	2.840
1979	14.500	8.125	14.250	3.410
1980	25.313	11.625	24.313	2.685
1981	24.375	10.625	12.375	2.560
1982	18.875	10.000	17.500	2.470
1983	29.375	16.750	28.000	3.220
1984	37.875	25.500	34.000	3.730

Change, 1975–84 +504%; change, S&P 500 Index, 1975–84 +82%

[*]Adjusted for stock splits and stock dividends   [**]Includes extraordinary items

Note: The fiscal year financial results in the tables above are shown in the year in which most of the results were achieved.

The company is engaged in the manufacture and sale of fire protection equipment, electrical and electronic components, and packaging and consumer materials. Its major subsidiary in the fire protection equipment area is Grinnell Fire Products Systems Company, Inc., which is the largest North American manufacturer of automatic sprinkler devices and the largest company engaged in the design, engineering, fabrication, and installation of fire protection sprinkler systems. This segment of the business, which represented approximately one-third of corporate sales, has experienced profit problems since fiscal year 1981 and has recently accounted for less than 10 percent of income from operations. The electrical and electronic component segment, while only approximately 20 percent of sales, has been contributing slightly more than 50 percent of income from operations. It is primarily conducted by the Simplex Wire and Cable Company, which is one of the world's major manufacturers of underwater communications cable and cable assemblies. The third major segment of the company includes Ludlow Corporation, a manufacturer of materials used in flexible packaging applications and a producer of specialty paper products. This company's performance during the last five years has been somewhat erratic. It will be interesting to see if its fire protection operations can return to the historic profit levels that contributed so significantly to Tyco's profitability during the early 1980s.

UNITRODE CORPORATION

Corporate Headquarters: 5 Forbes Road
Lexington, MA 02173
Telephone: (617) 861-6540
Incorporated in Maryland
New York Stock Exchange—UTR

Business: Manufactures and markets electronic products such as discrete semiconductors, analog integrated circuits, ceramic capacitors and EMI filters.

Officers:

George M. Berman, Chairman
William B. Mitchell, President
Gerald C. Bellis, Senior Vice President
Arthur H. Bruno, Vice President, Microelectronics
William T. Campbell, Jr., Controller
John F. Catrambone, Vice President, Components Marketing
Robert R. Feier, Vice President, Capacitors
Walter B. Gates, Vice President, Finance, Treasurer
Richard S. Morse, Jr., Secretary
Arthur A. Pappas, President, Power General Corp.
Alan R. Shoolman, Vice President, Planning and Development
Edward Simon, Vice President, Research and Engineering
Howard F. Wasserman, Senior Vice President, Strategic Operations

Statement of Income (Year ends 1/31—$ figures in 000's)

	1985	1984
Net Sales	$200,113	$159,571
Cost of Sales	111,377	87,002
Research and Development Expenses	12,124	8,813
Selling, General and Administrative Expenses	42,487	36,541
Interest Expense	1,342	1,593
Interest Income	(442)	(907)
	166,888	133,042
Income before Income Taxes	33,225	26,528
Provision for Income Taxes		
Federal and Foreign	9,314	8,428
State	1,696	1,361
	11,010	9,789
Net Income	$ 22,215	$ 16,739

Stockholder's Equity, Jobs, and Labor Productivity ($ figures in 000's)

Year	Stockholder's Equity	Net Sales	Number of Employees	Index of Labor Productivity
1975	$19,806	$ 27,753	1,009	27.505
1976	21,849	30,594	1,255	24.378
1977	25,089	38,789	1,208	32.110
1978	30,891	48,421	1,232	39.303
1979	46,383	81,609	2,009	40.622
1980	42,538	103,601	1,985	52.192
1981	54,556	112,408	2,068	54.356
1982	69,871	120,081	2,113	56.830
1983	92,600	159,571	3,094	51.574
Change, 1983/1975	+ 368 %	+ 475 %	+ 207 %	+ 88 %

Capital Productivity ($ figures in 000's)

Year	Total Invested Capital	Net Income	Index of Capital Productivity
1975	$ 20,277	$ 1,727	.085
1976	22,284	2,182	.098
1977	26,824	3,390	.126
1978	32,969	6,817	.207
1979	51,992	8,270	.159
1980	50,782	10,402	.205
1981	72,110	11,233	.156
1982	87,351	12,912	.148
1983	109,151	16,739	.153
Change, 1983/1975	+ 438 %	+ 869 %	+ 80 %

Stock Prices and Earnings per Share[*]

Year	Stock Prices			Earnings[**] Per Share
	High	Low	Close	
1975	$ 2.281	$ .875	$ 1.125	$ .175
1976	2.406	1.125	1.906	.218
1977	2.813	1.656	2.781	.335
1978	5.156	2.438	4.094	.678
1979	9.375	4.063	8.563	.680
1980	11.500	5.938	9.750	.843
1981	15.250	8.125	15.250	.965
1982	21.563	10.688	20.625	1.090
1983	36.750	20.125	32.250	1.250
1984	36.875	22.000	27.125	1.650

Change, 1975–84 + 2,311%; change, S&P 500 Index, 1975–84 + 82%

[*]Adjusted for stock splits and stock dividends   [**]Includes extraordinary items

Note: The fiscal year financial results in the tables above are shown in the year in which most of the results were achieved.

The company is a manufacturer of electronic products that include discrete semiconductors, analog integrated circuits, ceramic capacitors, EMI filters, data conversion products, and switching power supplies. These products are sold throughout the world for a variety of military, data processing, telecommunications, industrial, and consumer applications. The company marked its 25th year in business during 1985; since its first profitable quarter in 1962, Unitrode has not had a single quarterly loss. The company has continued to broaden its marketing programs to minimize dependence on any one segment, product family, or customer. Its success in pursuing this strategy is reflected in its steady growth in sales and net income.

VARI-CARE, INC.

Corporate Headquarters: 800 Medical Arts Building
                          277 Alexander Street
                          Rochester, NY 14607

Telephone: (716) 325-6940
Incorporated in Delaware
Over the Counter—VCRE

Business: Operates nursing homes, provides meals-on-wheels, and home health care services.

Officers:

Robert H. Hurlburt, President
William F. Doud, Vice President and Treasurer
Sheldon L. Smith, Vice President, Operations

Statement of Income (Year ends 9/30—$ figures in 000's)

	1984	1983
Patient Revenue	$26,699	$22,707
Other Income (including Interest)	807	732
Total Revenues	$27,507	$23,439
Operating Costs	$18,130	$15,527
Depreciation and Amortization	887	768
Rent	595	602
General and Administrative Costs	5,320	4,565
Interest	1,055	943
Total Costs and Expenses	$25,987	$22,404
Income before Income Taxes	$ 1,520	$ 1,035
Income Taxes	636	387
Net Income	$ 884	$ 649

Stockholder's Equity, Jobs, and Labor Productivity ($ figures in 000's)

Year	Stockholder's Equity	Net Sales	Number of Employees	Index of Labor Productivity
1975	$ 491	$ 7,524	924	8.143
1976	598	9,532	954	9.532
1977	868	10,322	961	10.322
1978	1,234	10,937	1,029	10.937
1979	989	13,304	1,198	13.304
1980	1,242	15,717	1,272	15.717
1981	1,397	18,195	1,335	18.195
1982	1,643	20,763	1,361	20.763
1983	2,285	22,707	1,352	22.707
Change, 1983/1975	+ 365 %	+ 202 %	+ 46 %	+ 202 %

Capital Productivity ($ figures in 000's)

Year	Total Invested Capital	Funds from Operations	Index of Capital Productivity
1975	$ 3,774	$ 420	.111
1976	3,845	283	.074
1977	4,075	466	.114
1978	4,356	638	.146
1979	7,453	744	.100
1980	9,012	851	.094
1981	9,352	963	.103
1982	9,466	1,188	.126
1983	10,376	1,425	.137
Change, 1983/1975	+ 175 %	+ 239 %	+ 23 %

Stock Prices and Earnings per Share[*]

	Stock Prices			Earnings[**]
Year	High	Low	Close	Per Share
1975	n.a.	n.a.	n.a.	$.083
1976	$ .187	$ .062	$ .062	.030
1977	.062	.031	.031	.079
1978	.406	.093	.093	.113
1979	.437	.250	.250	.067
1980	.312	.250	.250	.079
1981	1.250	.187	.187	.086
1982	3.000	.469	2.250	.128
1983	7.406	2.158	4.313	.173
1984	5.813	3.938	4.781	.225

Change, 1976–84 + 7,611%; change, S&P 500 Index, 1976–84 + 82%

[*]Adjusted for stock splits and stock dividends   [**]Includes extraordinary items

333

Founded 16 years ago, Vari-Care provides a full range of recuperative and health care services including skilled nursing and intermediate care, meals-on-wheels, and home health care. The company operates 18 long-term health care facilities with a capacity of 1,772 patients. In the past five years, revenues and earnings have increased at a compound annual rate of 15 percent and 32 percent, respectively. Vari-Care has a successful record of acquiring and operating well-located health care facilities, particularly those that had previously been unprofitable or produced less than average returns. These situations have provided the company with opportunities to purchase or lease ongoing operations at reasonable prices, thus minimizing the risks and hazards associated with most startup operations. During September 1985, the company announced that it acquired a 150-bed nursing center in Kerrville, Texas. The company's ability to maintain its record of growth will be aided by this and other acquisitions expected in the future.

VERSA TECHNOLOGIES, INC.

Corporate Headquarters: 1300 South Green Bay Road, P.O. Drawer S
Racine, WI 53405

Telephone: (414) 554-7575
Incorporated in Wisconsin
Over-the-Counter—VRSA

Business: Manufactures and markets close tolerance silicone rubber components, hydraulic and pneumatic cylinders and fabricates custom parts for medical markets.

Officers:

James E. Mohrhauser, President and Chief Executive Officer

Donald W. Peterson, Vice President, Finance, Treasurer & Assistant Secretary

Lawrence Block, Secretary

Frederick H. Meyer, Director, Human Resources

Moxness Products Inc.

Charles E. Kind, President and Chief Operating Officer

Jack I. Leeds, Senior Vice President

Chester C. Layman, Vice President, Manufacturing

Milwaukee Cylinder

David J. McKendrey, President and Chief Operating Officer

George A. Verhaeghe, Senior Vice President

Versa Medical Technologies, Inc.

Thomas A. Mohrhauser, President and Chief Operating Officer

Mox-Med, Inc.

Russell W. Garrett, Director, Marketing and Sales

Statement of Income (Year ends 3/31—$ figures in 000's)

	1985	1984
Net Sales	$35,145	$30,070
Cost of Sales	23,693	19,764
Gross Profit	11,452	10,307
Selling, Engineering and Administrative Expenses	6,583	5,608
Operating Income	4,868	4,699
Operating Income (Deductions)		
Interest Expense	(89)	(71)
Interest Income	302	310
Miscellaneous (Net)	57	33
	297	271
Earnings before Income Taxes	5,138	4,970
Income Taxes	2,052	2,240
Net Income	$ 3,086	$ 2,730

Stockholder's Equity, Jobs, and Labor Productivity ($ figures in 000's)

Year	Stockholder's Equity	Net Sales	Number of Employees	Index of Labor Productivity
1975	$ 2,489	$ 9,638	275	35.047
1976	3,533	11,745	319	36.818
1977	4,866	13,956	361	38.659
1978	6,482	16,742	409	40.934
1979	7,649	17,930	329	54.498
1980	8,299	18,759	384	48.852
1981	10,134	24,406	403	60.561
1982	11,084	24,676	411	60.039
1983	12,742	30,070	492	61.118
Change, 1983/1975	+412 %	+212 %	+79 %	+74 %

Capital Productivity ($ figures in 000's)

Year	Total Invested Capital	Net Income	Index of Capital Productivity
1975	$ 4,906	$ 592	.121
1976	5,189	1,079	.208
1977	6,483	1,496	.231
1978	8,039	1,891	.235
1979	9,145	1,366	.149
1980	9,736	1,351	.139
1981	12,023	2,187	.182
1982	12,792	1,988	.155
1983	14,116	2,730	.193
Change, 1983/1975	+188 %	+361 %	+60 %

Stock Prices and Earnings per Share*

| Year | Stock Prices | | | Earnings** Per Share |
	High	Low	Close	
1975	$ 2.816	$ .512	$ .768	$ .232
1976	1.451	.683	1.451	.416
1977	2.987	1.536	2.475	.573
1978	5.440	2.400	3.947	.721
1979	6.080	3.840	4.480	.521
1980	5.973	2.347	5.333	.533
1981	11.867	4.667	10.667	.869
1982	10.667	7.333	9.000	.807
1983	15.000	7.625	15.000	1.150
1984	16.000	13.500	15.750	1.300

Change, 1975–84 +1,951%; change, S&P 500 Index, 1975–84 +82%

*Adjusted for stock splits and stock dividends   **Includes extraordinary items

Note: The fiscal year financial results in the tables above are shown in the year in which most of the results were achieved.

Versa/Tek is engaged in three manufacturing technologies: (1) extrusion and molding of close tolerance silicone rubber components for the industrial marketplace; (2) production of engineered fluid power products, principally hydraulic and pneumatic cylinders, special lifting devices and related products; and (3) custom fabrication of parts and devices for the medical marketplace.

Versa/Tek's strategy is to concentrate on market niches where customers' needs for technological and engineering expertise, product quality, and superior service will command above-average returns. Three operating divisions serve diverse market niches: Moxness Products, Inc. concentrates on silicone rubber fabrication for special sectors of the industrial market. Milwaukee Cylinder manufactures custom-engineered cylinders for the automotive, robotics, petrochemical, machine tool, and other capital goods industries. Mox-Med, Inc. extrudes, molds, and fabricates silicone components for medical and health care markets.

VISHAY INTERTECHNOLOGY, INC.

Corporate Headquarters: 63 Lincoln Highway
                          Malvern, PA 19355
Telephone: (215) 644-1300
Incorporated in Delaware
New York Stock Exchange—VSH

Business: Manufactures a variety of instruments for stress measurement
in advanced, high precision applications for industrial and military use.
Officers:

   Alfred P. Slaner, Chairman
   Dr. Felix Zandman, President and Chief Executive Officer
   Robert A. Freece, Vice President, Treasurer and Chief Financial Officer
   Moshe Shamir, Vice President
   William J. Spires, Vice President and Secretary

Statement of Income (Year ends 6/30—$ figures in 000's)

	1985	1984
Net Sales	$56,536	$48,532
Cost of Products Sold	29,818	26,614
Gross Profit	$26,718	$21,917
Selling, Administrative and General Expenses	$16,734	$14,304
Operating Income	$ 9,984	$ 7,613
Other Income (Expense)		
Interest Expense	$(1,735)	$(1,450)
Other Income	2,411	1,799
Earnings before Income Taxes	$10,661	$ 7,962
Income Taxes	2,758	1,859
Net Earnings	$ 7,903	$ 6,103

338

Stockholder's Equity, Jobs, and Labor Productivity ($ figures in 000's)

Year	Stockholder's Equity	Net Sales	Number of Employees	Index of Labor Productivity
1975	$ 7,654	$15,784	850	18.569
1976	8,990	16,725	800	20.906
1977	9,704	20,074	1,100	18.249
1978	11,656	24,667	1,100	22.425
1979	16,341	30,408	1,250	24.326
1980	16,942	37,101	1,400	26.501
1981	18,200	37,418	1,000	37.418
1982	21,413	41,069	1,100	37.335
1983	35,287	42,161	1,000	42.161
Change, 1983/1975	+361 %	+167 %	+18 %	+127 %

Capital Productivity ($ figures in 000's)

Year	Total Invested Capital	Net Income	Index of Capital Productivity
1975	$13,511	$1,192	.088
1976	12,875	1,281	.099
1977	13,254	1,027	.077
1978	16,729	1,945	.116
1979	20,858	3,007	.144
1980	26,126	609	.023
1981	32,957	1,550	.047
1982	35,944	3,236	.090
1983	39,047	4,422	.113
Change, 1983/1975	+189 %	+271 %	+28 %

Stock Prices and Earnings per Share[*]

Year	Stock Prices			Earnings[**] Per Share
	High	Low	Close	
1975	$ 2.537	$ 1.119	$ 1.418	$ .334
1976	2.761	1.269	1.567	.358
1977	3.731	1.492	3.134	.287
1978	7.611	2.836	6.492	.543
1979	9.246	4.231	8.776	.827
1980	13.657	5.594	8.885	.158
1981	9.502	4.492	6.824	.401
1982	11.973	4.717	10.249	.834
1983	17.524	9.429	15.238	1.036
1984	16.700	11.500	14.400	1.256

Change, 1975–84 +916%; change, S&P 500 Index, 1975–84 +82%

[*]Adjusted for stock splits and stock dividends   [**]Includes extraordinary items

The business of Vishay is based on two interrelated technologies: stress measurement (electronic and optical sensors and instruments) and high-precision resistors (electronic components). Vishay stress measurement products and techniques can determine the areas of high stress that need strengthening. Also, they show areas of low stress so engineers can reduce structural weight, with resultant savings in manufacturing cost and energy. Electronic sensors used for stress measurement are also used in the production of digital scales. Vishay resistor products, an outgrowth of the company's stress measurement technology, are used in space projects, navigation and communications systems, specialized computers, and military projects—in fact, in all areas where stability is crucial. With the exception of the 1980-1981 recession period, this high-technology firm has reported impressive results. During late 1985, the company acquired Dale Electronics from the Lionel Corporation through a joint venture with Mezzanine Capital Corporation. This major acquisition will add significantly to the company's sales and net income results for 1986.

WANG LABORATORIES, INC.

Corporate Headquarters: One Industrial Avenue
                           Lowell, MA 01851
Telephone: (617) 459-5000
Incorporated in Massachusetts
American Stock Exchange—WAN

Business: Manufactures computer systems and related products for office automation, including word, data and audio processing systems.

Officers:

An Wang, Chairman and Chief Executive Officer

Harry H. S. Chou, Vice Chairman, Treasurer and Chief Financial Officer

J. Carl Masi, Executive Vice President

Fredrick A. Wang, Executive Vice President

Eugene M. Bullis, Senior Vice President and Controller

Senior Vice Presidents: Dodge Chu, Raymond C. Cullen, Jr., Edward J. Devin, Robert L. Doretti, Robert S. Kolk, Johannes Spanjaard, Horace Tsiang

Edward D. Grayson, Senior Vice President, General Counsel and Secretary

Statement of Income (Year ends 6/30—$ figures in 000's)

	1985	1984
Net Product Sales, Service and Rental Income	$2,351,700	$2,184,700
Cost of Goods and Services Sold	1,398,400	1,117,100
Gross Profit	$ 953,300	$1,117,100
Selling, General and Administrative Expenses	$ 767,800	$ 619,300
Research and Development Expenses	181,100	160,500
Operating Income	$ 4,400	$ 287,800
Interest Expense	$ 58,900	$ 26,600
Income (Losses) before Provision for Income Taxes	$ (54,500)	$ 261,200
Income Taxes	(70,000)	51,000
Net Income	$ 15,500	$ 210,200

341

Stockholder's Equity, Jobs, and Labor Productivity ($ figures in 000's)

Year	Stockholder's Equity	Net Sales	Number of Employees	Index of Labor Productivity
1975	$ 36,981	$ 75,525	2,350	32.138
1976	42,311	96,693	2,600	37.190
1977	51,390	134,129	3,200	41.915
1978	74,997	197,951	4,600	43.033
1979	118,239	321,301	7,725	41.592
1980	191,496	543,272	11,670	46.553
1981	465,596	856,376	15,770	54.304
1982	577,110	1,159,309	19,759	58.672
1983	937,800	1,538,000	24,769	62.094
Change, 1983/1975	+2,436 %	+1,936 %	+954 %	+93 %

Capital Productivity ($ figures in 000's)

Year	Total Invested Capital	Net Income	Index of Capital Productivity
1975	$ 58,870	$ 3,255	.055
1976	68,241	6,172	.090
1977	93,264	9,124	.098
1978	130,971	15,592	.119
1979	229,417	28,585	.125
1980	405,613	52,113	.128
1981	709,836	78,073	.110
1982	905,629	107,139	.118
1983	1,301,100	152,000	.117
Change, 1983/1975	+2,110 %	+4,570 %	+111 %

Stock Prices and Earnings per Share*

Year	Stock Prices			Earnings** Per Share
	High	Low	Close	
1975	$ .844	$ .331	$ .488	$ .040
1976	1.070	.609	.766	.076
1977	1.531	.719	1.469	.110
1978	4.156	1.203	3.641	.173
1979	8.688	3.500	8.406	.293
1980	22.625	7.125	20.500	.500
1981	22.813	12.000	16.625	.680
1982	31.688	12.313	29.500	.880
1983	42.500	28.000	35.625	1.160
1984	37.625	23.000	25.875	1.520

Change, 1975–84 +5,208%; change, S&P 500 Index, 1975–84 +82%

*Adjusted for stock splits and stock dividends   **Includes extraordinary items

This company has, through its technological innovations, been able to achieve phenomenal growth. The company's business is the design, manufacture, and marketing of computer systems and related products and services directed towards the worldwide office automation marketplace. The systems sold by the company are used for data, text, image, and voice processing. These systems can be incorporated into an office network, thus providing extensive communications abilities among interconnected systems. Its growth from less than $100 million in sales a decade ago to its present $1.5 billion size is an accomplishment that has been equaled by few firms in American business history. Its early entry into office automation during the 1970s, coupled with the introduction of innovative systems and products, propelled the company to its major status in that market. Today, however, many of the company's competitors have been aggressively developing new products that address the same customer needs. Wang continues to rely on its core technologies of voice processing, image processing, data processing, word processing, and networking, and through the integration of these, plans to remain a market leader and high-growth organization.

Wang is another company that is very much the lengthened shadow of its founder, An Wang. It will be necessary for the company to make the transition from family management to professional management without losing its vitality or its direction.

THE WASHINGTON POST CO.

Corporate Headquarters: 1150 15th Street, N.W.
Washington, D.C. 20071

Telephone: (202) 334-6670
Incorporated in Delaware
American Stock Exchange—WPOB

Business: Owns and operates newspapers, television stations, *Newsweek* magazine, a news service and cellular telephone systems.

Officers:

Katherine Graham, Chairman of the Board, Chief Executive Officer
Richard D. Simmons, President, Chief Operating Officer
Vice Presidents: Joel Chaseman, Mark M. Edmiston, Gordon C. King, Jr.
Martin Cohen, Vice President, Finance and Treasurer
Alan R. Finberg, Vice President, General Counsel and Secretary
Guyon Knight, Vice President, Corporate Communications
Edward N. Van Gombos, Vice President, Information Systems
Howard E. Wall, Vice President and Chief Accounting Officer

Statement of Income (Year ends 12/30/84 and 1/1/83—$ figures in 000's)

	1984	1983
Operating Revenues		
Advertising	$749,673	$659,896
Circulation	215,294	201,706
Other	19,336	16,112
	984,303	877,714
Operating Costs and Expenses		
Operating	594,552	542,555
Selling, General and Administrative	199,465	180,451
Depreciation and Amortization of Property, Plant and Equipment	21,740	20,080
Amortization of Goodwill and other Intangibles	2,251	2,213
	818,008	745,299
Income from Operations	166,295	132,415
Equity in (Losses) Earnings of Affiliates	(5,731)	399
Interest Income	8,667	6,101
Interest Expense, Net of Capitalized Interest of $833 in 1982	(1,792)	(2,725)
Other Income (Expense) (Net)	(1,296)	(1,571)
Income before Income Taxes	166,143	134,619
Provision for Income Taxes	80,257	68,225
Net Income	$ 85,886	$ 68,394

344

Stockholder's Equity, Jobs, and Labor Productivity ($ figures in 000's)

Year	Stockholder's Equity	Net Sales	Number of Employees	Index of Labor Productivity
1975	$ 34,902	$309,335	4,700	65.816
1976	49,315	375,729	4,700	79.942
1977	67,253	436,102	4,700	92.788
1978	83,029	520,398	4,800	108.416
1979	72,270	593,262	5,200	114.089
1980	95,861	659,535	5,400	122.136
1981	134,589	753,447	5,400	139.527
1982	181,236	800,824	5,300	151.099
1983	239,801	877,714	5,300	165.606
Change, 1983/1975	+587 %	+188 %	+13 %	+152 %

Capital Productivity ($ figures in 000's)

Year	Total Invested Capital	Net Income	Index of Capital Productivity
1975	$150,581	$12,042	.080
1976	153,488	24,490	.160
1977	163,286	35,469	.217
1978	198,071	49,720	.251
1979	183,162	29,468	.161
1980	231,546	34,335	.148
1981	236,993	32,710	.138
1982	270,033	52,413	.194
1983	327,390	68,394	.209
Change, 1983/1975	+117 %	+468 %	+161 %

Stock Prices and Earnings per Share[*]

Year	Stock Prices			Earnings[**] Per Share
	High	Low	Close	
1975	$ 7.500	$ 4.219	$ 5.375	$ .638
1976	12.625	5.438	12.500	1.360
1977	18.000	10.750	17.875	2.090
1978	24.375	15.500	23.250	3.060
1979	26.750	18.750	21.000	1.890
1980	24.750	15.875	22.625	2.440
1981	33.000	19.375	31.375	2.320
1982	60.875	27.375	55.250	3.700
1983	73.250	54.500	73.250	4.820
1984	85.000	60.750	80.250	6.110

Change, 1975–84 +1,393%; change, S&P 500 Index, 1975–84 +82%

[*]Adjusted for stock splits and stock dividends   [**]Includes extraordinary items

CORPORATE PROFILE—THE WASHINGTON POST COMPANY

This company consists of newspaper publishing (the *Washington Post* and the *Everett* (Washington) *Herald*, magazine publishing (*Newsweek* magazine) and television broadcasting (through ownership and operation of four network-affiliated stations). Its four television stations are located in Detroit, Michigan, (an NBC affiliate), in Miami, Florida, (an ABC network affiliate), and in Hartford, Connecticut and Jacksonville, Florida, (as CBS network affiliates). Newspaper publishing accounts for approximately 52 percent of revenues and 57 percent of income from operations. Magazine publishing—which accounts for approximately one-third of the company's revenues—has accounted for only 13 percent of the company's income from operations in its most recent fiscal year. The most profitable portion of the company is its broadcasting business, which represented only 14 percent of operating revenues but contributed approximately 30 percent of income from operations.

WASTE MANAGEMENT, INC.

Corporate Headquarters: 3003 Butterfield Road
Oakbrook, IL 60521

Telephone: (312) 654-8800
Incorporated in Delaware
New York Stock Exchange—WMX

Business: Provides waste management services for integrated solid waste recovery systems. Also mines lime, aggregates and coal.

Officers:
Dean L. Buntrock, Chairman
Jerry E. Dempsey, Vice Chairman
Phillip B. Rooney, President
Donald F. Flynn, Senior Vice President, Chief Financial Officer and Treasurer
Harold Gershowitz, Senior Vice President
J. Steven Bergerson, Vice President and General Counsel
David C. Coleman, Vice President, Labor Relations
John J. Cull, Controller
James G. DeBoer, Vice President, Midwest Region
Jerome D. Girsch, Vice President
Peter H. Huizenga, Vice President and Secretary
Francis B. Moore, Vice President, Government Affairs
Robert A. Paul, Vice President, Administration
Peter Vardy, Environmental Management

Statement of Income (Year ends 12/31—$ figures in 000's)

	1984	1983
Revenue	$1,314,761	$1,039,989
Costs and Expenses		
Operating	$ 846,364	$ 657,536
Selling and Administrative	195,217	167,973
Income from Operations	$ 273,180	$ 214,480
Other Expense		
Interest, Net	$ 24,508	$ 3,337
Sundry (Net) including Minority Interest	695	1,828
Income before Income Taxes	$ 247,977	$ 209,315
Provision for Income Taxes	$ 105,468	$ 88,868
Net Income	$ 142,509	$ 120,447

347

Stockholder's Equity, Jobs, and Labor Productivity ($ figures in 000's)

Year	Stockholder's Equity	Net Sales	Number of Employees	Index of Labor Productivity
1975	$ 62,242	$ 158,691	3,800	41.761
1976	69,507	179,179	3,660	48.956
1977	78,032	233,095	3,850	57.947
1978	135,369	307,112	4,450	69.014
1979	165,042	381,522	5,150	74.082
1980	263,621	560,149	6,070	92.282
1981	376,419	772,690	7,290	105.993
1982	547,697	966,548	7,900	122.348
1983	627,864	1,039,989	9,100	114.285
Change, 1983/1975	+909 %	+555 %	+140 %	+174 %

Capital Productivity ($ figures in 000's)

Year	Total Invested Capital	Net Income	Index of Capital Productivity
1975	$163,271	$ 8,915	.054
1976	161,521	11,647	.072
1977	166,895	18,236	.109
1978	232,993	27,429	.118
1979	274,578	36,725	.134
1980	403,779	54,855	.136
1981	545,735	84,033	.154
1982	830,173	106,524	.128
1983	935,804	120,447	.129
Change, 1983/1975	+473 %	+1,251 %	+139 %

Stock Prices and Earnings per Share[*]

Year	Stock Prices			Earnings[**] Per Share
	High	Low	Close	
1975	$ 3.917	$ 1.333	$ 2.292	$ .300
1976	4.583	2.250	4.500	.393
1977	6.375	4.000	6.333	.613
1978	10.625	5.708	9.042	.840
1979	14.917	8.750	14.625	1.033
1980	33.333	12.042	30.500	1.437
1981	41.125	25.875	33.875	1.950
1982	55.750	25.500	53.500	2.400
1983	61.875	37.500	46.375	2.500
1984	47.875	27.250	43.875	2.930

Change, 1975–84 +1,814%; change, S&P 500 Index, 1975–84 +82%

[*]Adjusted for stock splits and stock dividends   [**]Includes extraordinary items

348

CORPORATE PROFILE—WASTE MANAGEMENT, INC.

This diversified and fast-growing firm provides waste management services through its various operating units. The largest of these businesses is Waste Management of North America, which represented approximately 69 percent of the company's revenues in 1984. This business unit operates solid waste disposal facilities in the United States and Canada. The company's customers number more than 325,000 commercial/industrial businesses and more than 4,500,000 households in 430 communities. The Chemical Waste Management group deals with hazardous waste disposal and during 1984 represented approximately 15 percent of the company's revenues. Waste Management International, which accounts for about 10 percent of revenues, serves international customers in Australia, Saudi Arabia, and South America. The remainder of Waste Management's business is conducted by Chem-Nuclear Systems, which is the leading company providing low-level radioactive waste management services. Waste Management has been creative both in the means it has used to finance growth and in its approach to planning and managing what is essentially a collection of local businesses. This represents a true testament to corporate management's skills.

WHITEHALL CORPORATION

Corporate Headquarters: P.O. Box 29709, 2659 Nova Drive
Dallas, TX 75229

Telephone: (214) 247-8747
Incorporated in Delaware
New York Stock Exchange—WHT

Business: Provides products and services in four major areas: earth sciences (geophysical exploration), aircraft maintenance, systems engineering in defense electronics and quartz crystals.

Officers:

Lee D. Webster, President and Chairman of the Board
Carl R. Anderson, Vice President and Controller
Daniel J. Hampton, Vice President, Corporate Planning & Marketing
George M. Pavey, Vice President

Statement of Income (Year ends 12/31—$ figures in 000's)

	1984	1983
Net Sales	$63,277	$64,537
Other Income	1,086	775
	64,363	65,312
Costs and Expenses		
Cost of Sales	39,278	37,790
Selling, Engineering and Administration	7,793	6,993
Interest	272	301
	47,344	45,084
Income before Income Taxes	17,019	20,228
Provision for Income Taxes	7,638	8,750
Net Income	$ 9,381	$11,478

Stockholder's Equity, Jobs, and Labor Productivity ($ figures in 000's)

Year	Stockholder's Equity	Net Sales	Number of Employees	Index of Labor Productivity
1975	$ 6,907	$26,794	1,261	21.248
1976	7,532	25,210	1,353	18.633
1977	8,728	29,275	1,416	20.674
1978	10,158	32,971	1,379	23.909
1979	11,852	35,017	1,464	23.919
1980	13,789	45,554	1,428	31.901
1981	18,795	53,911	1,457	27.001
1982	27,622	63,084	1,427	44.207
1983	38,729	64,537	1,392	46.363
Change, 1983/1975	+461 %	+141 %	+10 %	+118 %

Capital Productivity ($ figures in 000's)

Year	Total Invested Capital	Net Income	Index of Capital Productivity
1975	$11,196	$ 1,033	.092
1976	11,394	736	.065
1977	12,094	1,250	.103
1978	13,049	1,422	.109
1979	14,263	1,349	.095
1980	15,721	1,877	.119
1981	20,022	4,906	.245
1982	28,441	8,827	.310
1983	39,140	11,478	.293
Change, 1983/1975	+250 %	+1,011 %	+218 %

Stock Prices and Earnings per Share[*]

Year	Stock Prices			Earnings[**] Per Share
	High	Low	Close	
1975	$ 1.875	$ .750	$ .938	$ .275
1976	1.625	.938	1.125	.200
1977	2.500	1.063	2.188	.350
1978	3.938	1.875	2.750	.390
1979	3.563	2.188	3.376	.365
1980	11.188	2.563	9.688	.500
1981	25.500	8.375	22.750	1.300
1982	34.500	12.250	31.000	2.350
1983	65.375	29.375	38.500	3.050
1984	41.750	17.625	21.625	2.520

Change, 1975–84 +2,207%; change, S&P 500 Index, 1975–84 +82%

[*]Adjusted for stock splits and stock dividends   [**]Includes extraordinary items

351

This company provides products and services to the commercial and military markets within the earth sciences, aerospace, and electronics industries. Whitehall participates in carefully selected segments of these markets through the application of advanced technology. The company has achieved substantial growth in net income since 1980, but gave some of it back in calendar 1984. It seems that the best Whitehall can expect for 1985 is a flat year.

However, the future brightened in October, 1985, when the Air Force awarded Aero Corporation, a Whitehall subsidiary, a $21.6 million contract to modify and maintain C-130 aircraft. More good news was announced on December 26, 1985 in the form of the Navy's fiscal 1986 budget, which includes a $20 million appropriation to lease underwater detection and surveillance systems from Whitehall.

BARRY WRIGHT CORPORATION

Corporate Headquarters: One Newton Executive Park
Newton Lower Falls, MA 02162

Telephone: (617) 965-5800
Incorporated in Massachusetts
New York Stock Exchange—BAR

Business: Operates two different lines of business. One involves products and systems for organizing data and the other involves controlling vibration.

Officers:

    Ralph Z. Sorenson, Chairman, President and Chief Executive Officer
    P. Norman Roy, Executive Vice President
    John F. Quinn, Vice President, President, Industrial and Aero Products Group
    Philip M. Croel, Vice President, President, Wright Line Inc.
    Milton E. Gilbert, Vice President, General Counsel and Secretary
    Jack L. Manes, Jr., Vice President, Human Resources
    Charles H. Sellman, Vice President, Controller and Treasurer
    Eustis Walcott, Jr., Vice President, Corporate Relations
    David M. Wright, Vice President, Wright Line Inc.
    Patricia A. Irwin, Assistant Treasurer and Assistant Secretary
    Edith C. McGuinness, Assistant Secretary
    William H. Gorham, Clerk

Statement of Income (Year ends 12/31—$ figures in 000's)

	1984	1983
Revenues		
Net Sales	$201,789	$162,171
Other Income	3,025	3,156
	204,814	165,327
Costs and Expenses		
Cost of Sales	111,875	84,981
Selling, General and Administrative Expenses	66,023	54,863
Interest Expense	300	338
	178,198	140,182
Earnings before Income Taxes	26,616	25,145
Provision for Income Taxes	11,590	11,487
Net Income	$ 15,026	$ 13,658

Stockholder's Equity, Jobs, and Labor Productivity ($ figures in 000's)

Year	Stockholder's Equity	Net Sales	Number of Employees	Index of Labor Productivity
1975	$17,454	$ 42,779	1,076	39.757
1976	19,163	47,745	1,138	41.955
1977	21,705	57,846	1,242	46.575
1978	25,960	70,442	1,429	49.295
1979	34,350	98,854	1,859	53.176
1980	42,555	124,489	2,022	61.567
1981	69,044	144,903	2,160	67.085
1982	77,510	140,849	1,885	74.721
1983	89,093	162,171	2,198	73.781
Change, 1983/1975	+410 %	+279 %	+104 %	+86 %

Capital Productivity ($ figures in 000's)

Year	Total Invested Capital	Net Income	Index of Capital Productivity
1975	$18,667	$ 1,899	.102
1976	20,185	2,320	.115
1977	23,077	3,300	.143
1978	27,396	5,022	.183
1979	36,025	7,684	.213
1980	49,667	10,007	.201
1981	71,732	12,768	.178
1982	79,974	10,907	.136
1983	91,265	13,658	.150
Change, 1983/1975	+389 %	+619 %	+47 %

Stock Prices and Earnings per Share[*]

Year	Stock Prices			Earnings[**] Per Share
	High	Low	Close	
1975	$ 1.875	$ 1.188	$ 1.406	$ .290
1976	2.813	1.406	2.719	.355
1977	4.219	2.500	4.125	.505
1978	7.906	3.594	7.781	.755
1979	12.500	7.000	12.438	1.020
1980	24.125	10.250	19.875	1.320
1981	23.375	13.750	18.250	1.550
1982	22.625	13.375	19.750	1.280
1983	33.000	18.000	30.000	1.570
1984	33.625	21.750	22.250	1.680

Change, 1975–84 +1,482%; change, S&P 500 Index, 1975–84 +82%

[*]Adjusted for stock splits and stock dividends   [**]Includes extraordinary items

354

The company is a diversified industrial company with two operating groups. Wright Line Inc. specializes in products, systems and services for organizing, filing, accessing, and protecting diversified information media. The Industrial and Aero Products Group provides engineered components and systems to control vibration and other dynamic forces and specialized products that improve the efficiency and productivity of industrial equipment and flexible automation systems. Other than the dip in net income during 1982, this company has compiled an excellent record of growth in its two widely different operating groups. While 1984 saw earnings in the Wright Line decrease, this was more than offset by results in the Industrial and Aero Products Group.

ZERO CORPORATION

Corporate Headquarters: 777 Front Street
                          Burbank, CA 91503

Telephone: (818) 846-4191
Incorporated in California
New York Stock Exchange—ZRO

Business: Manufactures and markets metal containers, cabinets, carrying cases, and thermoformed plastic parts, as well as custom products.

Officers:
  Wilford D. Godbold, Jr., President and Chief Executive Officer
  Howard W. Hill, Vice Chairman
  James F. Hermanson, Vice President
  James E. Osterman, Vice President and Secretary
  Ronald L. Hess, Vice President
  John B. Gilbert, Chairman
  Richard N. Holt, Treasurer

Statement of Income (Year ends 3/31—$ figures in 000's)

	1985	1984
Net Sales	$117,172	$93,726
Cost of Goods Sold	$ 72,199	$57,120
Gross Margin	$ 44,973	$36,606
Expenses (Income)		
Selling, General and Administrative	21,824	16,556
Depreciation and Amortization	3,357	2,698
Interest	1,546	1,465
Non-Operating Income	(3,052)	(2,750)
Income before Provision for Income Taxes	$ 21,298	$18,637
Income Taxes	9,836	8,788
Net Income	$ 11,462	$ 9,849

Stockholder's Equity, Jobs, and Labor Productivity ($ figures in 000's)

Year	Stockholder's Equity	Net Sales	Number of Employees	Index of Labor Productivity
1975	$11,443	$30,529	960	31.801
1976	13,498	42,309	1,240	34.120
1977	15,464	48,454	1,384	35.010
1978	18,843	56,558	1,509	37.480
1979	21,798	65,539	1,765	37.133
1980	27,348	79,266	1,478	53.631
1981	38,613	81,730	1,391	58.756
1982	44,228	79,699	1,208	65.976
1983	50,292	93,726	1,530	61.259
Change, 1983/1975	+340 %	+207 %	+59 %	+93 %

Capital Productivity ($ figures in 000's)

Year	Total Invested Capital	Net Income	Index of Capital Productivity
1975	$19,668	$1,967	.100
1976	21,208	2,387	.113
1977	25,363	2,883	.114
1978	28,878	3,824	.132
1979	35,998	4,740	.132
1980	40,901	5,883	.144
1981	53,279	7,431	.139
1982	58,247	8,087	.139
1983	65,279	9,849	.151
Change, 1983/1975	+232 %	+401 %	+51 %

Stock Prices and Earnings per Share*

Year	Stock Prices			Earnings** Per Share
	High	Low	Close	
1975	$ 1.101	$ .629	$ 1.049	$ .236
1976	1.485	1.027	1.464	.287
1977	2.294	1.485	2.294	.346
1978	3.714	1.993	2.458	.452
1979	5.325	2.731	5.086	.549
1980	8.021	4.480	7.211	.672
1981	10.720	6.880	10.720	.828
1982	13.867	7.200	12.667	.848
1983	20.800	11.900	20.800	1.016
1984	22.125	14.375	19.125	1.180

Change, 1975–84 +1,724%; change, S&P 500 Index, 1975–84 +82%

*Adjusted for stock splits and stock dividends   **Includes extraordinary items

Note: The fiscal year financial results in the tables above are shown in the year in which most of the results were achieved.

357

Zero has established itself as the leading producer of specialized enclosures, cooling equipment, and accessories for the electronics industry. Zero also markets a high-value line of luggage and camera cases under the Zero Halliburton® brand name. The Zero enclosures line include instrument housings, carrying cases for portable equipment, cabinets for electronic equipment, consoles for controls, and acoustical cabinets. To support the needs of customer systems, Zero also offers a wide range of complementary products, including blowers, cooling systems, PCB card files, chassis slides, and other accessories. These products are manufactured in one European and 14 U.S. locations, thus allowing Zero to fulfill its customers' needs for availability and service. The company has a stated objective of achieving an annual growth rate in earnings in excess of 15 percent. Acquisitions are expected to continue to play a role in aiding the company in meeting this objective.

4

AMERICA'S 101 BEST PERFORMING COMPANIES—BUT FOR HOW LONG?

The previous chapters of this book examined in detail a decade of outstanding performance by the 101 Best Performing Companies in America. At the same time, their most recent two-year Statement of Income comparisons presented in the company profiles indicate that 24 of these companies failed to increase their profit levels from one year to the next. In other words, their most recent available income statements show "down" years in profits after taxes.

Since these *down years* all occurred after the 1975-83 period that was used to establish the 101 Best Performing Companies, it is important to ask the question, "What guide is past performance to future performance?" It behooves us to examine very carefully William Shakespeare's advice that "past is prologue" to see if it holds true in this situation.

WHAT CAUSED THE "DOWN" YEARS?

While it is usually impossible to tell with 100 percent accuracy from outside an organization exactly what has transpired within, some reasonably informed analysis suggests that the causes of these "down" years fall into six or seven categories. One such category is the "one-time event." What happened in this category is that some one-time event drove the earlier period profits to exceptional heights. Then, even though current year profits are higher than *other* previous year results, they don't exceed the prior year that includes the one-time favorable event. Adams-Russell, Holly, Public Service of New Mexico, and Stewart Information seem to fit this category.

Another category is the "strong dollar effect," which can either reduce a firm's international competitiveness or drag down the value of its overseas earnings. Aydin, Gelman Sciences, Loctite, and Wang appear to have suffered from this condition.

A third category involves the demands of "expansion/growth/R & D financing." These companies seem to be investing current profits in future strength. Auxton Computer, D.O.C. Optics, Research Industries, and Whitehall probably fit this situation.

The largest category is simply "down markets." The 1985 winter was mild in Entex's market and, as a consequence, natural gas demand was down. New housing starts were down in 1984, and, therefore, so was Pulte's business. The Houston area's economy was depressed in 1985, and National Convenience Store's per store sales were off. There were significantly fewer stock issues floated in 1984, so there was less for Bowne & Co. to print. The number of satellites launched declined, and so did California Microwave's sales in 1985. Personal computer sales came to a screeching halt at yearend 1984, and Tandy ended up with a big inventory write-down.

In another situation, "fierce competition" drove prices and margins down. This happened to Heileman in beer and Texas Oil & Gas in both of its markets.

Two companies made errors in "newly deregulated businesses" and correcting the mistakes cost profits. Multimedia and Pacific Telecom paid this price.

Finally, there is a miscellaneous category. It includes Pacific Scientific, which "stayed too long at the party" and didn't replace its nuclear piping shock protection products before the nuclear reactor business took a dive. It also includes Alpha Industries, which "played too rough" and got involved in a messy, expensive bribery situation.

The first conclusion from this analysis is that there does not appear to be any widespread, symptomatic cause for the 24 companies' down years. That would be consistent with year-to-year changes during the median 30-year life spans that the 101 companies have been in business. Another observation is that many of these causes are transitory. Mild winters are followed by cold ones. One-time events don't usually reoccur. The strong U.S. dollar will have to come down sooner or later. The housing market has always been cyclical, and slowdowns in housing starts are followed frequently by record years. Presumably lessons were learned from the mistakes in newly deregulated markets. Admittedly, it is more difficult to be nonchalant about the companies

360

that had trouble meeting the fierce competition or stayed too long at the party. Those are two causes of corporate illness that could be symptomatic and nontransitory.

In concluding this examination of the causes of the recent down years experienced by some of the 101 companies, it should be remembered that 1985 was a particularly difficult year for a large number of U.S businesses.

Although the causes of the down years do not, for the most part, seem alarming in the long view, the point remains that 24 percent of America's 101 Best Performing Companies most recently reported a year of decreased profits. That raises the issue of what constitutes a "normal" pattern of year-to-year profitability.

A REMARKABLE "NEW" DEVELOPMENT IN AMERICAN BUSINESS

For some time now, conventional wisdom has held that American business managers are so intent on achieving short-term profit goals that they neglect long-term investments in productivity, and that is why American business is on the decline. Robert H. Hayes and William T. Abernathy present this argument forcefully in their widely read 1980 *Harvard Business Review* article. They said:

> We refuse to believe that this managerial failure is the result of a sudden psychological shift among American managers toward a "super-safe, no-risk" mind set. No profound sea changes in the character of thousands of individuals could have occurred in so organized a fashion or have produced so consistent a pattern of behavior. Instead we believe that during the past two decades American managers have increasingly relied on principles which prize analytical detachment and methodological elegance over insight, based on experience, into the subtleties and complexities of strategic decisions. *As a result, maximum short-term financial returns have become the overriding criteria for many companies.* [1]

Five years later, John Broder echoed exactly the same complaint in the *Los Angeles Times*, when he wrote:

[1] Robert T. Hayes and William J. Abernathy, "Managing our way to economic decline," *Harvard Business Review* (July–August 1980): 67-77. Emphasis added.

American business executives and economists, in a burst of soul searching brought on by U.S. industry's declining international competitiveness, have concluded that *American business performance has been hurt by an obsession with short-term profits over long-range planning and investment.*[2]

Now if this view is correct, American businesses should have demonstrated at least a consistent record of year-to-year profitability as a result of their short-term focus on managing profitability. Since the 101 companies display behavior that is in complete contrast with this piece of conventional wisdom because a substantial number of them have reported year-to-year profit declines, it would be incumbent upon us to explain this phenomenon.

Because this is such an important point in understanding the behavior of America's 101 Best Performing Companies, it is worth summarizing the problem. It goes like this: For whatever reasons, it is claimed that American managers concentrate almost exclusively on managing short-term profits, but the 101 companies, because of the surprisingly high number of recent down profit years, either cannot, or refuse to, behave in this manner.

To investigate this issue, we examined the year-to-year profit records of more than 6,000 publicly owned companies over a two-decade period. We asked a simple, straightforward question, "In *each* of the 20 years, what percentage of the companies increased *their* profits over the previous year?" The results appear in this table:

Year	Percentage of Companies with Profit Increases Over Previous Year
1965–66	96.1%
1966–67	95.8
1967–68	95.5
1968–69	93.4
1969–70	89.0
1970–71	88.2
1971–72	89.2
1972–73	90.9
1973–74	87.3
1974–75	84.2
1975–76	85.8
1976–77	87.1
1977–78	88.4
1978–79	87.6
1979–80	87.5
1980–81	85.2
1981–82	81.5
1982–83	81.9
1983–84	84.0

[2] John M. Broder, "U.S. Too Short Term, Minebea Says," *Los Angeles Times* (December 13, 1985), Part IV, p 3. Emphasis added.

362

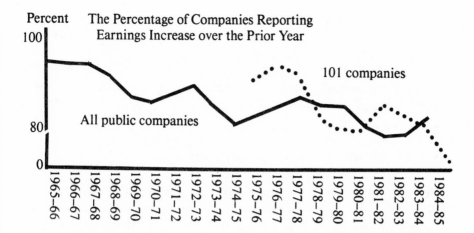

Percent   The Percentage of Companies Reporting
Earnings Increase over the Prior Year

The results are striking! They directly contradict the conventional wisdom! Rather than increased control over profitability, it seems there has been a 20 year trend toward *less control over profits*!

What is truly remarkable is that the trend has moved steadily through the good times of the late 1960s, through the turbulence of the early 1970s, through the raging inflation of the late 1970s, and through the recession of the early 1980s. This is a finding of enormous significance. If the trend continues, by the end of the century, a scant 14 years away, only 7 out of 10 U.S. businesses can expect to be able to increase earnings over the prior year. The graph shown here makes this point even more dramatically.

HOW DID AMERICA'S 101 BEST PERFORM?

Since the youngest member of the 101 companies was founded in 1974, we can't examine the performance of the group as a whole for the full two decades. However, the following table presents their results for the past 10 years:

Year	Profit Increases Over Previous Year
1975-76	92.1%
1976-77	94.1
1977-78	92.1
1978-79	84.2
1979-80	82.2
1980-81	82.2
1981-82	87.2
1982-83	84.4
1983-84	83.2
1984-85	76.3

These data are also plotted on the all companies graph. It is easy to see that trend for the 101 companies is exactly the same as it is for all publicly owned companies.

To confirm that the trends are the same statistically, we performed various mathematical analyses. Those tests indicate that the chances are 99 out of 100 that the all-company trendline and 101 company trendline are the same.

AN ALTERNATIVE EXPLANATION

To be complete in this investigation, we must point out that there is a possible explanation that is consistent with both the conventional wisdom *and* our data. It goes like this: Yes, American managers are increasingly concentrating on short-term profits, but they are becoming increasingly inept as managers and can't even manipulate short-term profits very well.

We don't accept this explanation for an instant! We have spent too much time examining the results of America's 101 Best Performing Companies to accept this explanation. The managers at the 101 companies are superior! They decide what they want to happen and then they make it happen!

ADDITIONAL EVIDENCE

The American Business Conference is an organization of mid-sized, fast growing companies from all segments of U.S. business. Member companies must have grown at least 15 percent annually for the past five years and have sales volumes between $25 million and $1 billion. The ABC contains some very good companies. Seven of the 101 companies are members of the ABC: Adams-Russell Company, Inc., Charter Medical Corporation, Chilton Corporation, Dynatech Corporation, Loctite Corporation, Herman Miller, Inc. and Teradyne, Inc. are ABC members.

In 1981, the ABC hired the management consultants, McKinsey & Company, to study their members. One finding from that study is particularly relevant to our purposes here:

> Among the seventy longer established, publicly owned ABC members, the facts reveal more than an occasional blip. . . . In the two decades between 1964 and 1983:
>
> - Fifty-one have suffered at least two years of profit downturn.

- Thirty-two have seen their profits decline in two consecutive years and at least one other time as well.
- Eighteen had earnings declines in at least five of the twenty years.

While the 101 companies cover a much broader span than do the ABC companies, and while Clifford and Cavanagh's research direction was somewhat different, the similarity of findings is interesting. Companies that perform well do not necessarily record unbroken strings of profit increases.[3]

STILL MORE EVIDENCE

Forbes magazine does an annual analysis of relatively smaller companies, those with sales less than $250-$300 million. The companies that Forbes studies also have to meet a minimum standard for return on stockholder's equity, they must have a record of earnings growth and consistency, and total debt cannot exceed total stockholders' equity. Forbes calls this group of companies, "America's Best Small Companies." Each year *Forbes* compares the current list with the previous year's list to identify the companies that repeat from year to year.

In 1983, Forbes found 277 smaller companies that met its minimum criteria. By 1984, only 166 could still meet the standards, 59 percent of the 1983 group. In 1984, *Forbes* indicated that 300 companies could meet their criteria. When the 1985 list was being prepared, *Forbes* found that fully 211 companies from the 1984 list were not able to qualify in 1985. Five of the 211 simply grew too large to continue to meet the small business criteria. Another 10 companies disappeared through merger and acquisition. Thus, between 1984 and 1985, 65 percent of Forbes Best Small Companies in America stopped being best.

It seems clear that smaller companies certainly face very volatile operating environments.

EVIDENCE FROM BIG COMPANIES

If *Forbes* keeps track of smaller firms, *Fortune* magazine has long made a tradition of tracking the fortunes of America's biggest companies through their annual Fortune 500 list of companies. Of the 100

[3] Donald K. Clifford, Jr. and Richard E. Cavanagh, *The Winning Performance—How America's High-Growth Midsize Companies Succeed* (New York: Bantam Books, Inc., 1985): 153–54.

biggest industrial firms in the United States in 1955, only 46 of the original 100 were still on Fortune's list in 1985, just 30 years later. Volatile environments exist for large companies as well as for smaller companies.

SUMMARY OF THE EVIDENCE

While there are certainly differences in the frameworks, the requirements, and the treatments of individual companies among the ABC group of mid-sized companies, *Forbes'* group of small companies and the *Fortune* list of very large companies, the common fact is that they all seem to have to face difficult and uncertain environments. Our findings suggest very strongly that this phenomena is only going to become more extensive and severe as the future unfolds.

We believe that the underlying cause of this phenomena is the long-range trend toward unpredictability that has been growing since the 1960s. There are some very fundamental structural changes occurring in countries around the world that are producing this unpredictability.[4] Three of the most important are:

> *The inability of governments to manage their economies.*
> For a very long time now, governments have thought they could manage the behavior of their economies. In olden days, the instrument that was most likely to have been used to make everything come out according to the government's wishes was the "divine right of kings." In more recent times, this technique seems to have been transmogrified into the "divine wisdom of economists." The new version doesn't work any better than the more ancient technique it replaces.
>
> As a consequence, governments around the world are attempting to remove many of the governmental control structures that have been erected in the past fifty years to control the economy. What is particularly instructive is that this movement is apparently without political ideology. Conservative governments in the United States, the United Kingdom and in Japan are all trying to loosen the government's

[4] Ronald N. Paul, Neil B. Donavan, and James W. Taylor, "The Realty Gap in Strategic Planning," *Harvard Business Review* (May–June 1978): 124–30.

grip on their economies. But, so are liberal governments in France, Australia and New Zealand.

The rapid communication of new developments in technology. A primary source of instability in markets is the appearance of new products that do old jobs better than existing products. Not very long ago, manufacturers of products that were going to face new competition from new products attempting to capture their markets had substantial time lags working in their favor. It took customers a long time to learn about these new alternatives, so there was sufficient time to assess the nature and seriousness of the threat presented by the new products and to develop a measured response.

The time lag is simply disappearing. More and more markets are becoming vulnerable to threats from outside suppliers from just about anywhere in the world. Another way of saying the same thing, is to observe that product life cycles are getting shorter and shorter. It is becoming more difficult to make profits from new products because they are being replaced so quickly.[5]

The internationalization of business. For a very long time, an accurate description of an international company (and only a minority of all U.S. businesses could be described as international) was a company that had a strong position in its domestic, or home, market and shipped some extra product overseas in order to keep the company's production facilities at full capacity. An international, or global, company nowadays is one that has a strong position in its home market, as well as equally strong positions in foreign markets, such as Japan and Europe. Its "off-shore" position may may be a solo one, or it may have been forged from an alliance with a local Japanese or European company.

This new "internationalized" company has considerable power to be an effective competitor in the two-thirds of the developed world that is *not its home market*. It also has the ability to take new products developed outside of its home markets and bring them "home" with its full economic

[5] James W. Taylor, *Planning Profitable New Product Strategies*, (Radnor, Penn. Chilton Book Company, 1984): 24.

367

might. Thus, competition is no longer just domestic, with some importing or exporting, it is truly becoming a global contest with substantially more "places" for new competitive developments to arise.[6]

FACING AN UNCERTAIN FUTURE

As the future environment grows increasingly unpredictable, management will have to develop new ways of dealing with the surprises that will appear in their markets. Forecasting the future to avoid surprises is, by now, a quite discredited technique. Companies that survive and prosper, companies that make real contributions to our society and well-being, will be those companies that accept surprises in their environments as inevitable and develop the internal mechanisms to spot them as early as possible and to formulate the most effective responses.

In turn, that means that the standards of performance that were useful in an earlier, more predictable era are becoming less and less useful. In particular, single measures of performance such as unbroken records of increasing sales or profits may hide more than they reveal.

We have proposed that a more useful way to evaluate performance is to identify the multiple criteria that superior performing companies should meet, and continue to meet over an extended period. Creating jobs to provide useful work for the next generation of workers, increasing the productivity of labor and capital to make U.S. businesses more competitive in the world market, and creating wealth for company owners appear to be such multiple criteria. We have identified over 500 U.S. companies that have met all four criteria simultaneously over a long and very difficult period of time. We have examined the performance of 101 of these companies in considerable detail in this book. Their performance, both individually and as a group, is extremely impressive. These companies are improving our standard of living. They are providing superior value for their stockholders, their employees, and for society at large. They truly are America's 101 Best Performing Companies.

[6] For a more comprehensive description of this trend toward international competition, see Kenichi Ohmae's book, *Triad Power—The Coming Shape of Global Competition* (New York: The Free Press, 1985). At least one of America's 101 Best Performing Companies, SmithKline Beckman Corporation, is organizing itself along just these lines to increase its ability to compete on a global basis.

AMERICA'S MOST IMPORTANT COMPANIES

All 500 companies listed below have increased labor and capital productivity, created jobs, and increased stockholder's wealth, beyond inflation levels, from 1975 through 1983.

Abbott Laboratories, Inc.
Acme General Corporation
Adams-Russell Company, Inc.
Advanced Micro Devices, Inc.
ARX, Inc. (formerly Aeroflex
   Laboratories, Inc.)
Affiliated Bankshares of Colorado
Airbourne Freight Corporation
Alaska Air Group, Inc.
Alatenn Research, Inc.
Alden Electronics, Inc.
Allegheny Power System, Inc.
Allen Organ Company
Allied Bancshares, Inc.
Alltel Corporation
Alpha Industries, Inc.
Amerada Hess Corporation
American Broadcasting Corporation
American Business Products, Inc.
American District Telegraph, Inc.
American Electric Power, Inc.
American Filtrona Corporation
American Home Products Corporation
American Hospital Supply, Inc.
American Medical International, Inc.
American Stores Company
American Water Works, Inc.

Ametek, Inc.
Amp, Inc.
Analogic Corporation
Anaren Microwave, Inc.
Apogee Enterprises, Inc.
Arizona Bancwest Corporation
Arrow Automotive Industries, Inc.
Associated Dry Goods Corporation
Astronics Corporation
Atlantic Bancorp
Atlantic City Electric Company
AtlanticRichfield Company
Auxton Computer Enterprises, Inc.
Avery International, Inc.
Aydin Corporation
Bacardi Corporation
Ball Corporation
Baltimore Gas & Electric Company
Banc One Corporation
Bangor Hydro-Electric Company
Bank of Boston Corporation
Banks of Mid-America, Inc.
Bank of New England Corporation
Bank of New York Company, Inc.
Basix Corporation
Bassett Furniture Industries, Inc.
Baxter Travenol Laboratories, Inc.

Baybanks, Inc.
Becton, Dickson & Co.
W. Bell & Company, Inc.
Best Lock Corporation
Betz Laboratories, Inc.
Black Hills Power & Light Company
Black Industries, Inc.
John Blair & Co.
Boeing Corporation
Boonton Electronics Corporation
Bowne & Co., Inc.
Bristol-Myers Company, Inc.
Brooklyn Union Gas Company
Brown Group, Inc.
BRT Reality, Inc.
Brush Wellman, Inc.
Burlington Northern, Inc.
Burroughs Corporation
CACI, Inc.
California Microwave, Inc.
Camco, Inc.
Canandaigua Wine Company
Care Corporation
Carlisle Corporation
CBT Corporation
Centel Corporation
Centex Corporation
Central Illinois Light Company
Central Illinois Public Service Company
Central Maine Power Company
Central & Southwest Corporation
Cerberonics, Inc.
Charlotte Motor Speedway, Inc.
Charter Medical Corporation
Chase Manhattan Corporation
Chemical New York Corporation
Chesebrough-Ponds, Inc.
Chilton Corporation
Cincinnati Gas & Electric Company
Citicorp
Citizens Utilities Company
J. L. Clark Manufacturing Company
Cleveland Electric Illuminating
    Company
Coast Manufacturing, Inc.
Coleman Company, Inc.
Coleman National Corporation
Collins & Aikman Corporation
Collins Food International, Inc.
Colorado National Bankshares

Columbus Mills, Inc.
Commerce Bankshares, Inc.
Commerce Clearing House, Inc.
Commonwealth Edison Company
Communications Industries, Inc.
Community Psychiatric Centers
Connecticut Water Service, Inc.
Consolidated Freightways, Inc.
Consolidated Papers, Inc.
Consumers Power Company
Continental Telcom, Inc.
Conwood Corporation
Cooper Laboratories, Inc.
Cooper Tire & Rubber Company
Coventry Care, Inc.
Cox Communications, Inc.
Crawford & Company
CRS Sirrine, Inc.
Data Packaging Corporation
Data Products Corporation
Dayton-Hudson Corporation
Delmarva Power & Light Company
De Luxe Check Printers, Inc.
Dennison Manufacturing Company
Deposit Guaranty Corporation
Detroit Edison Company
Diebold, Inc.
Digital Equipment Corporation
Dillard Department Stores
Diversified Energies, Inc.
D O C Optics Corporation
Dollar General Corporation
Donaldson, Lufkin & Jenrette, Inc.
R. R. Donnelley & Sons Company
Dover Corporation
Dow Jones & Company, Inc.
Doyle Dane Bernbach International, Inc.
Dranetz Technologies, Inc.
Dreyfuss Corporation
Dun & Bradstreet Corporation
Dunkin Donuts, Inc.
E. I. DuPont de Nemours & Company
Duquesne Light Company
Durr-Fillauer Medical, Inc.
Dynamics Research Corporation
Dynatech Corporation
Eaton Vance Corporation
Echlin, Inc.
E G & G, Inc.
Electro Catheter Corporation

370

Electrospace Systems, Inc.
Elizabethtown Water Company
El Paso Electric Company
Emerson Electric Company
Emhart Corporation
Empire District Electric Company
Engraph, Inc.
Entex, Inc.
Espey Mfg. & Electronics Corporation
E-Systems, Inc.
Evans, Inc.
Ex-Cell-O Corporation
Fairchild Industries, Inc.
Family Dollar Stores, Inc.
Faraday Laboratories, Inc.
Farmer's Group, Inc.
Federal Company
Federal-Mogul Corporation
Federal Signal Corporation
First Alabama Bancshares, Inc.
First Atlanta Corporation
First Florida Banks, Inc.
First Hawaiian, Inc.
First Interstate Bancorp
First National State Bancorp
First Union Corporation (North
  Carolina)
First Union Real Estate, Inc.
First Virginia Banks, Inc.
Flexsteel Industries, Inc.
Florida Progress Corporation
Florida Power & Light Company
Freeport McMoRan, Inc.
Frigitronics, Inc.
H. B. Fuller Company
Galaxy Carpet Mills, Inc.
Gannett Company
Garan, Inc.
Gelman Sciences, Inc.
General Cinema Corporation
General Foods Corporation
General Instrument Corporation
General Microwave Corporation
General Signal Corporation
Georgia-Pacific Corporation
Gerber Scientific, Inc.
Giant Foods, Inc.
C. R. Gibson Company
G & K Services, Inc.
P. H. Glatfelter Company

Glosser Brothers, Inc.
Gray Communications Systems, Inc.
Great Lakes International, Inc.
Green Mountain Power Corporation
Grey Advertising, Inc.
Groff Industries, Inc.
Gross Telecasting, Inc.
Grow Group, Inc.
Guardian Industries, Inc.
Guardsman Chemicals, Inc.
Gulf States Utilities Company
Hammermill Paper Company
John H. Harland Company
Harris Corporation
Harvey Hubbell, Inc.
Haverty Furniture Companys, Inc.
G. Heilman Brewing Company
H. J. Heinz Company
Hercules, Inc.
Heritage Bancorp
Hewlett-Packard Company
Holly Corporation
Honeywell, Inc.
Hook Drugs, Inc.
Hoover Universal, Inc.
Hospital Corporation of America, Inc.
Houghton Mifflin Company
Hughes Supply Company
Humana, Inc.
Huntington Bancshares
Hunt Manufacturing, Inc.
IBM, Inc.
Idaho Power Company
Illinois Power Company
Illinois Tool Works, Inc.
Indiana Gas Company
Intermark, Inc.
Internorth, Inc.
Interpublic Group of Companies, Inc.
Iowa Electric Light & Power Company
Iowa Resources, Inc.
Ipalco Enterprises, Inc.
Irving Bank Corporation
James River Corporation of Virginia
Johnson Controls, Inc.
Johnson & Johnson, Inc.
Josten's, Inc.
Kaman Corporation
Kansas City Power & Light Company
Kansas City Southern Industries, Inc.

Kansas Gas & Electric Company
Kansas Power & Light Company
Kellog Corporation
Kelly Services, Inc.
Kentucky Utilities Company
Key Corp. (formerly Key Banks, Inc.)
Key Pharmaceuticals, Inc.
Kimberly-Clark Corporation
K N Energy, Inc.
W. A. Krueger Company
Lamaur, Inc.
Lancaster Colony Corporation
Lane Company, Inc.
Larsen Company
LA-Z-BOY Chair Company
Lear Petroleum Corporation
Lear Siegler, Inc.
Leaseway Transportation, Inc.
Lehigh Press, Inc.
Lil'Champ Food Stores, Inc.
Eli Lilly & Company
Lilly Industrial Coating, Inc.
Limited, Inc.
Arthur D. Little, Inc.
Loctite Corporation
Logicon, Inc.
Long Island Lighting Company
Louisville Gas & Electric Company
Lowe's Companies
Luby's Cafeterias, Inc.
M/A Com, Inc.
R. H. Macy & Company
Madison Gas & Electric Company
Mankato Citizens Telephone Company
Manufacturers Hanover Corporation
Marine Corporation
Marine Midlands Banks, Inc.
Marriot Corporation
Marshall & Ilsley Corporation
Mary Kay Cosmetics, Inc.
Mass Merchandisers, Inc.
May Department Stores Company
Mayflower Corporation
Maytag Company
McCormick & Company
MCORP
McDonald's Corporation
McDonnell Douglas Corporation
McGraw-Hill, Inc.
Medtronics, Inc.

MEI Corporation
Melville Corporation
Merck & Company
Middle South Utilities
Midlantic Banks, Inc.
Midwest Energy Company
Mile High Kennel Club
Herman Miller, Inc.
Minnesota Mining & Manufacturing
   Company
Minnesota Power & Light Company
Mite Corporation
MDU Resources Group (formerly
   Montana-Dakota Utilities Company)
J. P. Morgan & Company
Motorola, Inc.
Multimedia, Inc.
Murray Ohio Manufacturing Company
Myers Industries, Inc.
National Convenience Stores, Inc.
National Gas & Oil Company
National Medical Care, Inc.
National Medical Enterprises, Inc.
NCNB Corporation
Neutrogena Corporation
Nevada Power Company
New Hampshire Ball Bearings, Inc.
New York State Electric & Gas
   Company
New York Times Corporation
New Yorker Magazine, Inc.
Niagra Mohawk Power Company
Nordson Corporation
Norfolk Southern Corporation
Northeast Utilities, Inc.
Northern Indiana Public Service
   Company
Northrop Corporation
Northwest Natural Gas Corporation
Northwestern Financial Corporation
Noxell Corporation
Nucor Corporation
Occidental Petroleum Corporation
Ocean Drilling & Exploration Company
Ogilvy & Mather International, Inc.
Ohio Edison Company
Oklahoma Gas & Electric Company
Old Kent Financial Corporation
Omark Industries, Inc.
Oshman's Sporting Goods, Inc.

O'Sullivan Corporation
Otter Tail Power Company
Overnite Transportation Company
Owens-Corning Fiberglass Corporation
PACCAR, Inc.
Pacesetter Corporation
Pacific Gas & Electric Company
Pacific Lighting Corporation
Pacific Scientific Company
Pacific Telecom, Inc.
Packaging Systems Corporation
Palm Beach, Inc.
Panhandle Eastern Corporation
Papercraft Corporation
Peerless Tube Company
Penn Engineering & Manufacturing
   Corporation
Pennsylvania Power & Light Company
Pfizer, Inc.
PHH Group, Inc.
Philadelphia Electric Company
Philip Morris, Inc.
Pic'n Save Corporation
Piedmont Aviation, Inc.
Piedmont Natural Gas Company
Piper, Jaffray, Inc.
Pitney-Bowes, Inc.
Plenum Publishing Company
Ply-Gem Industries, Inc.
PNC Financial Corporation
Ponderosa, Inc.
Porta Systems Corporation
Portland General Electric Company
PPG Industries, Inc.
Pratt & Lambert, Inc.
Premier Industrial Corporation
Prentice-Hall, Inc.
Prime Computer, Inc.
Public Service Company of Colorado
Public Service Company of Indiana
Public Service Company of New Mexico
Public Service Company of North
   Carolina
Puget Sound Power & Light Company
Pulte Corporation
Purolator Courier Corporation
Quaker Oats Company
Quebecor, Inc.
Questar Corporation
RAI Research Corporation

Ranier Bancorporation
Randy Group Ltd.
Raytheon Company
Republic New York Corporation
Research Industries Corporation
Revco D.S. Inc.
Revlon, Inc.
Reynolds & Reynolds, Inc.
Rochester Gas & Electric Company
Rockcor, Inc.
Roseville Telephone Company
Rubbermaid, Inc.
Ruddick Corporation
Russell Corporation
Ryan Homes, Inc.
Ryder Systems, Inc.
Ryland Group, Inc.
Saga Corporation
San Diego Gas & Electric Company
Santa Fe Southern Pacific Company
A. Schulman, Inc.
SCANA, Inc. (formerly South Carolina
   Electric & Gas Company)
SCI Systems, Inc.
Scripps Howard Broadcasting Company
Sealed Power, Inc.
Sears Roebuck & Company
Security Pacific Corporation
Servicemaster Industries, Inc.
Seton Company
Shawmut Corporation
Shell Oil Company
Shop & Go, Inc.
Sierra Pacific Resources
Sigma-Aldrich Corporation
Signal Companies
SimKar Lighting Fixtures Company
Simkins Industries, Inc.
Smithfield Foods, Inc.
SmithKline Beckman Corporation
Snap-on Tools Corporation
Society Corporation
Sonat, Inc.
Sonoco Products Company
South Carolina National Corporation
Southeast Banking Corporation
Southern California Edison Corporation
Southern Company
Southern Indiana Gas & Electric
   Company

Southern New England Telephone
Company
Southwest Gas Corporation
Southwestern Energy Company
Southwestern Public Service Company
Sovran Financial Corporation
Stanadyne, Inc.
Standard Motors Products, Inc.
Standard Oil Company of Indiana
Standard-Pacific Corporation
Standard Register Company
State o Maine Inc.
State Street Boston Corporation
Stepan Company
Stewart Information Services, Inc.
Sun Company, Inc.
Superior Surgical Manufacturing, Inc.
Supermarkets General Corporation
Syntex Corporation
Tab Products, Inc.
Tandy Corporation
Tektronix, Inc.
Telex Corporation
Teleflex, Inc.
Tenneco, Inc.
Teradyne, Inc.
Texas American Bancshares
Texas Commerce Bancshares
Texas Eastern Corporation
Texas Oil & Gas Corporation
Texas Utilities Company
Third National Corporation
Three D Departments, Inc.
Times Mirror Company
TNP Enterprises, Inc.
Toledo Edison Company
Transamerica Corporation
Transco Energy Company
Transtechnology Corporation
Trust Company of Georgia
TRW, Inc.
Tultex Corporation
Tyco Laboratories, Inc.
Union Electric Company
Union Pacific Corporation
United Aircraft Products, Inc.
United Banks of Colorado

United Energy Resources
United Illuminating Company
United Industrial Corporation
United Jersey Banks
United Missouri Bancshares
United Parcel Service, Inc.
United Technologies Corporation
United Virginia Bancshares
Unitrode Corporation
Universal Foods Corporation
Universal-Rundle Corporation
U. S. Leasing International, Inc.
U. S. Shoe Corporation
U. S. Tobacco Company
Utah Power & Light Company
Utilicorp (formerly Missouri Public
Service Company)
Valspar Corporation
Vari-Care, Inc.
Versa Technologies, Inc.
VF Corporation
Vishay Intertechnology, Inc.
Vulcan Materials Company
E. R. Wagner Manufacturing, Inc.
Walgreen Company
Wallace Computer Services, Inc.
Wang Laboratories, Inc.
Washington Gas Light Company
Washington Post Company
Washington Water Power Company
Waste Management, Inc.
Watkins-Johnson, Inc.
Waverly Press, Inc.
Wells Fargo & Company
West Co., Inc.
Whitehall Corporation
Whittaker Corporation
Wisconsin Electric Power Company
Wisconsin Finance Corporation
Wisconsin Power & Light Company
Wisconsin Public Service Company
Barry Wright Corporation
Woodward Governor Company
Woodward & Lothrop, Inc.
Zero Corporation
Zimmer Corporation
Zions Utah Bancorp

APPENDIX *B*

RESEARCHING AMERICA'S 101 BEST PERFORMING COMPANIES

Anticipating that a number of readers would be interested in how to use and expand their knowledge of the information presented in this book on the 101 Best Performing Companies, we turned to one of America's leading information specialists. We asked him to comment on how the 101 Companies can be monitored for investment purposes, competitive intelligence, employment research and so on. Here are Trey Taylor's ideas about information management and America's 101 Best Performing Companies.

HOW TO KEEP TRACK OF THE PERFORMANCE OF THE 101 COMPANIES

Trey Taylor
Manager, Marketing Services
ITT Dialcom, Inc.
1109 Spring Street
Silver Spring, Maryland, 20910

The key to monitoring the 101 companies is *speed*. These are fast-moving companies! Events that affect the performance or stock prices of these companies can develop fast and furiously. You cannot rely on other people to keep track of developments in these companies. You are going to have to take the initiative. Fortunately, in this electronic age, it is easy to keep on top of fast-moving news.

You will need just three things to bring the full power of electronic news to the task of tracking the 101 companies. One is a personal computer, a PC. I am assuming that most business people already have a PC that they are using for a wide variety of job- and home-related tasks. If you don't have one, now might be the time to get a PC and learn to use it.

The second thing that may be helpful, especially if you intend to invest in the 101 Companies, is a software package specifically designed to manage a stock portfolio. There are a number of good ones available. I like the "Dow Jones Market Manager Plus" software package. It is available from Dow Jones & Co. and Teleare, Parsippany, New Jersey.

The third, and perhaps most important tool that you will need is a "data base." A data base or electronic library is simply a large amount of accurate, up-to-date information organized in such a manner as to allow you to gain immediate access to just the information that you need. At ITT Dialcom, Inc., we manage a sophisticated, integrated electronic system that gives you access to many highly valuable information data bases, as well as a state-of-the-art message distribution system, an electronic bulletin board, an electronic publishing service, an electronic calendar/appointment scheduling service, plus text processing.

The first data base that will be of great interest is the Dow Jones News/Retrieval Service. The Dow Jones News/Retrieval Service is more than just stock quotes. Through many information sources, this service also provides general financial, economic, and investment news, and news on competitors, prospective employers, and the 101 companies. The service also covers federal regulations and regulatory decisions from more than a dozen government agencies.

Following is a brief summary of some of the information services available through Dow Jones News/Retrieval that would be particularly helpful for monitoring the 101 companies.

- Dow Jones News provides news as recent as 90 seconds and as far back as 90 days from *The Wall Street Journal, Barron's,* and the Dow Jones News Service. A review of the week's top economic events and a look at the month ahead are also offered.
- Dow Jones Quotes offers a 15-minute delay on common and preferred stocks and bonds, mutual funds, U.S. Treasury issues, and options. This service also offers daily historical stock quotes accessible by specific dates, as well as monthly stock quote summaries back to 1979.
- Disclosure II offers 10-K extracts, company profiles, and other detailed data on over 9,400 publicly held companies, as well as information filed with the U.S. Securities and Exchange Commission.

- Corporate Earnings Estimator provides earnings forecasts for 3,000 of the most widely followed companies.
- Detailed corporate financial information on 3,150 companies and 170 industries includes such categories as revenue, earnings dividends, stock trading volume, ratios, shareholdings, and price changes.
- Dow Jones also provides a weekly survey of the U.S. money market and foreign exchange trends.
- Japan Economic Daily offers same day coverage of major business, economic, and political news from Japan's Kyodo News International, Inc., in addition to a comprehensive daily wrap-up of activity in Japan's financial markets.
- Weekly highlights of investment research prepared by the Securities Research Division of Merrill Lynch are also offered.

The next important data base is UNISTOX. UNISTOX offers the latest UPI news reports on stock market and commodities exchange quotations. The financial newswire also provides historical summaries of selected stocks and commodities.

A third key database is ABI/INFORM, which provides abstracts covering the principal articles of more than 650 publications, comprising virtually all key management and business publications, many dating back to 1978. These publications cover such areas as accounting and auditing, data processing and information management, economics, finance and financial management, general management, human resources, law and taxation, management science, real estate, telecommunications and marketing, advertising, and sales.

The database is exhaustive, with more than 220,000 citations as of 1985. Abstracts are continually being added at the rate of approximately 700 per week. New publications are also periodically added to the list. Abstracts enter the database from two to five weeks after receipt of the source journals.

The 200-word abstracts are accessed through a controlled vocabulary that includes the following: the 500 largest U.S. and 500 largest non-U.S. industrial companies, 50 largest U.S. and 50 largest non-U.S. commercial banking organizations; and 50 largest U.S. life insurance companies, diversified financial companies, retailing companies, and utility companies. Searches can also be conducted through a controlled vocabulary of geographic areas, subject names, and organizations, the latter including professional and trade associations, nonprofit organizations, government agencies, and commissions and boards. The full text of most of the citations included on

ABI/INFORM is available by ordering online, by telephone, telex, mail, or facsimile transmissions.

Another source of articles that is available through Dialcom is UMI Article Clearinghouse. This online catalog and ordering service offers access to nearly 8,000 periodicals. Periodicals from the following indexes are included in the database: Applied Science and Technology Index; Biological and Agricultural Index; Business Periodicals Index; Current Index to Journals in Education; Index Medicus; Readers' Guide to Periodical Literature; Social Sciences Index; Engineering Index; and Cumulative Index to Nursing and Allied Health Literature.

While ABI/INFORM and UMI Article Clearinghouse cover the news in periodicals and journals, it is also important to examine breaking news stories. Dialcom Services offers access to several key news sources, including United Press International (national, regional, state, sports, and Washington Special Wire) and Associated Press Videotex, a headline service developed specially for the business community.

Newly available through Dialcom is USA TODAY Update, an online news service from The Gannett Company. The Newswire's Hotline service offers the top national and international news, business, finance, and weather, with hourly updates. Decisionline offers executive news summaries targeted specifically to the following industries and professions: technology, banking and economy, energy, telecommunications, legal, insurance, and travel. Bulletins and special reports are also featured with USA TODAY Update.

Another important source of business information is the federal government. Dialcom offers its FED-NEWS service, which offers access to news being released by the following U.S. government agencies: Food and Drug Administration, Department of Agriculture, the U.S. Reserves, National Aeronautics and Space Administration, Federal Emergency Management Agency, and the Department of the Interior. More agencies are expected to be added in the near future.

Dialcom is also the source of the White House News Services, which electronically transmits news releases, speeches, statements, personnel appointments, announcements of new legislation, and other White House news to subscribers. Information is provided by the White House Press Office, the Office of the Vice President, and the Office of Management and Budget.

The Bureau of National Affairs, Inc. is another important source of information on the government and its policies as they affect the business community. BNA AdvanceLine, also available through Dialcom Services, provides notification of legal, legislative, and regulatory developments in business, finance, taxation, labor and securities. BNA

AdvanceLine actually consists of seven different data bases. Those of special interest to readers monitoring specific companies are:

- Daily Washington Advance is a daily report of legal, regulatory, and economic developments that affect business planning and corporate decision making. Of particular interest to someone monitoring specific companies are securities regulation, energy developments, product liability, federal grants and contracts, antitrust and trade regulation, and environmental controls.
- Daily Tax Advance is a daily report covering matters of taxation. Of particular interest are regulatory proposals and rulings and federal court tax decisions.
- Daily Labor Advance is a daily report of nationwide labor activities, including the National Labor Relations Board and the courts.
- Daily SEC Advance includes summaries of SEC decisions, information on recently filed 13D, 14D, and 8K reports, and registration statements.
- Securities Law Advance is a weekly report covering securities and court decisions, plus developments in corporate governance, enforcement activities, and commodity futures regulation.

In addition to all of these information sources and databases described, Dialcom also provides links to other public databases. A user can tap into such databases as Lockheed's DIALOG, the Bibliographic Research Service, the New York Times InfoBank, and others.

One of the great advantages of electronic mail services is that any of the information drawn from the above sources can be mailed, filed, or incorporated into reports using other services available through Dialcom. One of the more commonly used of these services includes POST, an electronic bulletin board.

The filing features of Dialcom's electronic mail service also provide automatic storage of any communications and information, easily accessible by keyword, names, datas, subjects, and other convenient indices. File transfer also allows a user to disperse files to other workstations.

An important element of all the newswire services offered by Dialcom's NEWS-TAB, in essence, an electronic clipping service. This service scans the newswires and automatically delivers articles deemed relevant by subscriber, designated by key words (such as the stock symbols of the 101 companies) to the subscriber's electronic mailbox. The custom-designed news is then ready to read at the subscriber's convenience.

And lest computer anxiety scare anyone away from the incredible array of services just outlined, a new subscriber can begin his or her education very easily through an online instruction system known as LEARN. The typical user should be able to learn Dialcom's electronic mail service within 90 minutes.

I think that you will agree that the data bases and electronic information services I've described can provide you with all the help you could possibly need to keep on top of fast-moving events at the 101 companies (or any other company for that matter). From these services, you can select those that will support your informational goals most closely and organize the information to make it most valuable to you.

LIST OF COMPANY TABLES
AND PROFILES